ZION RISING

What others are saying about Zion Rising

Zion Rising is a great book, not just in that it reveals the lessons of Enoch, but that it also reveals the values discovered from deep spiritual wisdom from the challenges of life in family, personal, and business struggles. It is in itself a restoration not just of the story of Enoch, but also a restoration of beliefs that should be in every person.

—Nikky Kho, entrepreneur, educator

ZION RISING

YOUR PERSONAL RESTORATION AND AWAKENING IN CHRIST

Samuel D. Castor

CFI
An imprint of Cedar Fort, Inc.
Springville, Utah

ISBN 13: 978-1-4621-4253-8
(Updated edition, August 2022)

Published by CFI, an imprint of Cedar Fort, Inc.
2373 W. 700 S., Springville, UT 84663
Distributed by Cedar Fort, Inc., www.cedarfort.com

Library of Congress Control Number: 2022933516

Front cover design by Sam Castor, manifested by the talented Austin Simkins
Cover prepared for press by Shawnda T. Craig

Edited and typeset by Spencer Skeen

Printed in the United States of America

10 9 8 7 6 5 4 3 2 1

Printed on acid-free paper

For my grandfather George W. Pace, who, like a mountain peak pointing skyward, steadily pointed me (and many others) to Christ, Zion's Lord and King.

CONTENTS

AUTHOR'S INTRODUCTION

I HAVE HAD A PROFESSIONAL LIFE-COURSE IN WHAT ZION IS *NOT.* I have worked in every branch of the U.S. federal government, from the courts and the legislature to time under Republican and Democratic U.S. presidents. For over a decade as an in-house attorney and executive for a multi-billion-dollar tech company, I made my living off of dealing with conflicts that often boiled into contention. While I have been richly blessed and worked beside exceptional people, I have also seen many hearts harden, including my own, in pursuit of wealth, power, and prestige, without realizing we were often simply chasing the dust of Babylon.

I yearned for something more. I took courage in Moses's teaching that all men and women could become prophets and prophetesses and Joseph Smith's teaching that "even the least Saint" can know *all* things of Heaven as quickly as we are able to bear them.[1] These books became my "quarantine quest" during the global 2020 pandemic—to *receive* Zion within myself.

I felt called to Zion months before the global emergency. I had dreams of police and ambulance sirens surrounding our house and a sense of urgency to prepare for something. I would awaken—often as early as 4:37 AM, as if the clock itself were pointing me to Zion with the numeric symbolism I discovered while writing this book—and feel prompted to arise and study for answers to these burning questions: How do I create Zion—in myself, in my home, and in my family? And how do I do it now?

A few months later, COVID-19 hit, followed by a maelstrom of natural disasters. My questions echoed in the silence of global quarantine. My studying intensified, and it became clear to me that phrases like "taken up," "sealed up," "lifted up," and "carried up" throughout the scriptures are not only symbolic but also *literal*. Height is associated with divinity. Why else do prophets climb mountains to seek the Lord, and refer to Christ as the *Most High God*? I also kept coming back to prophetic teachings that during Christ's return, Zion would literally rise up from *below* to meet Zion descending from *above*.

The *Most High* God is a God of wonders, power and miraculous purpose. Of course, His triumphant return from Heaven will include something as earth shaking and undeniable as portions of purified earth literally lifting up to meet His Zion from above, as the skies themselves part to reveal Heaven and angelic armies. It will be the most momentous, celebrated, victorious moment in earth's history, a finale so grand and so brilliant that Heaven and earth will *sing*.

We are accelerating toward that promised Second Coming—the reunion of Zion and her Lord and King. The world is in upheaval: earthquakes in diverse places, grasshopper swarms of biblical proportions in Africa[2], murder hornets[3], fire tornadoes[4], raging cities, and unending global pandemics. Fear abounds. All things appear to be in commotion and men's hearts are failing them as they surrender to fear.[5] As prophesied, war has begun to flare up like a barbed weed spreading hate, pride, and apathy as people's hearts harden and "wax cold" and fail.[6] Babylon the great—the world—is self-consuming, self-imploding into darkness.

The rising generation is under attack by this looming, seeping, and pervasive darkness. For example, the suicide rate tripled between 2007 and 2017 for children aged ten to fourteen, after years of decline.[7] These numbers spiked in the wake of COVID-19, as many felt alone, isolated, or disconnected.[8] Many of the rising generation struggle to know which way is *up* as they yearn to emerge from the shadows that surround them. They lack *purpose.*

Zion is that missing purpose. This is my yearning attempt to point myself (and all of us) to our communal "why": finding Christ, and each other, in Zion. Zion is what we came to earth to build. And building Zion is how we awaken to who we really are, join hands, and return home to Heaven above. Zion is the pinnacle of restoration, for Christ is not only working to fully restore His kingdom on earth but also to restore each of us—*personally.* His love and truths restore us to who we really are and help us see that we were made for Heaven. Our uniqueness, race, gender, and history all play a part in Heaven's orchestration for peace, light and love. We *need* each other.

Christ is calling to us to remember our gifts and why we came to earth and to let our purpose replace our fear until we *awaken* "out of a deep sleep . . ., put on the armor of light," and join His kingdom here on earth.[9] He is calling to awaken us and restore us. I yearn for that *personal restorative awakening in Christ,* for myself and for each of us. That promised day when Christ will wipe away all tears as we sing His song of redeeming love in our hearts, in our families, in our communities, and throughout the world.

Zion has been calling in each of our hearts since Adam and Eve fell, inviting us to remember, receive light from Christ and create. So, I hope you hear the voice of the Lord in this book rather than mine. He is the author of all divine and elevating virtues—the Creator, the Lamb, the Lion, the source of living waters, the Prince of Peace, the Redeemer. He is the architect of Zion, and as we follow Him, *so . . . are . . . we.* As we join hands in Christ, we will begin to shine—and Zion, in her glory . . . will *rise.*

INTRODUCTION ENDNOTES

1 *History of the Church*, 3:380; see also D&C 1:20; D&C 111:11; Numbers 11:29; Moses 6:5.

2 Revelation 9:2–3.

3 "'Murder Hornets' in the U.S.: The Rush to Stop the Asian Giant Hornet," *New York Times*, May 2, 2020; *compare* Revelation 9:3–10 describing flying scorpions similar to the murder hornets.

4 "California Is on Fire: What are Fire Whirls, Fire Tornadoes, Fire Clouds and Dry Lightning?" *USA Today*, August 20, 2020.

5 D&C 88:91; see also D&C 45:26 and Moses 7:66; emphasis added.

6 D&C 45:27.

7 "NCHS Data Brief," No. 352, October 2019, PDF on CDC website, https://www.cdc.gov/nchs/data/databriefs/db352-h.pdf.

8 "Surge of Student Suicides Pushes Las Vegas Schools to Reopen" *New York Times*, January 24, 2021, https://www.nytimes.com/2021/01/24/us/politics/student-suicides-nevada-coronavirus.html.

9 Romans 13:11–12; D&C 76:94; 1 Cor 13:12; Obadiah 1:21; see also https://www.churchofjesuschrist.org/blog/my-2020-invitation-to-you-share-the-message-of-the-restoration-of-the-saviors-gospel?lang=eng.

BOOK ONE:
ZION ANCIENTLY

CHAPTER 1

ZION: IN THE BEGINNING...

"My kingdom is not of this world."
—Jesus Christ, John 18:36

All of humanity has been influenced by the Heavens above. Religions throughout time teach of a heightened existence of elevation and illumination, where peace and joy abound: a holy place that is glorious, peaceful, and bright, our collective next destination—a haven from the noise of the earth—calling to us from above. Most obvious are the Abrahamic religions of Islam, Christianity, and Judaism, pointing to Heavens above the earth, filled with brightness, glory, and holiness. But this tradition is not just Abrahamic.

The tradition also shines in the Greek and the Roman religions, where a family of gods and goddesses ruled from Mount Olympus, a celestial city that floated above the earth and radiated golden light. These "deus" or shining ones descended Olympus to influence events on earth and inspire invention, art, and love.[1] Buddhism also has roots above, inviting us to a layered universe with various "planes," where earth is only one "realm" where we can progress in refinement through a stepped continuum crowned with Heavens.[2] Hinduism similarly reverences radiant beings in the sky: female "devi" and male "deva"—the "heavenly or shining ones"[3]—like the divine couple of Shiva and Shakti with their sons who dwell on Mount Kailasa in the

Himalayas.[4] Likewise across the globe the ancient American Mayan described brilliant gods who framed Heaven above, *then* earth beneath for glory.[5] Since the dawn of time, there has been a pervasive belief in our collective origin in Heaven above.

Consequently, elevation and light have universally symbolized majesty, authority and power. Hopeful to harness this, leaders claimed they were chosen by Heaven before birth—foreordained—to lead the people below. Examples of this heavenly right to rule abound: kings, monarchs, tzars, and emperors throughout time physically elevated themselves above their subjects on thrones and pointed to the Heavens, claiming they were invested with a divine authority because Heaven had chosen them and their bloodline to rule below.

Egypt coroneted its rulers as "sons of Ra"—a celestial god who rode his solar ark across the sky to raise the sun.[6] Kings and queens in England, France, Spain, Russia, Austria, and Germany were referred to as "Highness" to show they were higher than their subjects and closer to Heaven. Throughout China's and Japan's dynasties, over 550 emperors were titled "Son of Heaven," who could speak for God if they followed Heaven's "mandate" and ruled righteously.[7]

Nature itself directs us up. From the trees reaching for the sun, to the mountain peaks pointing skyward, to the clouds and birds soaring above us, the earth seems to direct us to a place above our realm, stirring our inner senses to never forget something just beyond our reach. This collective yearning for higher and brighter existence left its mark on our world's history. It has inspired colossal pyramids, temples, churches, and even soaring skyscrapers that point to the skies. Artists reaching for Heaven have depicted heavenly ascents to the clouds. But even our most glorious creations here on earth—in all their majesty—only remind us earth is not Heaven. At least not *yet*. Heaven above holds something greater for us, something familiar but also brighter, broader, and more magnificent. This *something* we feel calling to our hearts is the song of Zion.

God's servants have heard the song and echoed it. Moses, Isaiah, Nephi, Mosiah, Alma, Mormon, Mahonri, Ether, and others all pointed skyward, with references to "lifted up," "sealed up," "raised up," "laid up," "hid up," and "called up" throughout the scriptures, promising the Lord will "take up" the righteous at the last day.[8] It is our choice whether we rise with Zion or remain in the decaying darkness below. Zion is our glorious, communal purpose: to *rise* back home to Heaven—together.

Isaiah taught that just as the Heavens are *above* the earth, so are God's thoughts *above* our thoughts and His ways *above* our ways.[9] He pled for the time when the Heavens will drop down from *above*, as the earth opens and the righteous spring up to Heaven—together.[10] This springing, elevating, lifting glory comes as quickly as we accept Christ.

Achieving and ascending as Zion is such a central pillar of Christ's plan of redemption that Joseph Smith, taught "we ought to have the building up of Zion as our greatest object."[11] Likewise, Brigham Young taught that Zion should be our *sole purpose*, so we are prepared to meet and abide the brightness and glory of Christ as He descends with Zion at His Second Coming.[12] We prepare *for* Zion above as we prepare ourselves *as* Zion beneath. This preparation starts as we answer the call of Zion in our own hearts until the peace and unity that emanates from our hearts fills the earth. Zion is our individual, familial, and global purpose.

Christ is calling to us to frame and create what God intended all along—Heaven on earth. I hope the following doctrinal foundation stones help us answer the call to "awake and arise" together. To receive Heaven here on earth, we must awaken to the truths we knew before. We can remember this life is simply a place to "become" something more, a stage set for a glorious finale, where we join hearts and rise together back home to Christ—as Zion.

OUR COLLECTIVE BEFORE

Isaiah taught that peace comes as we learn doctrine.[13] I think this is because doctrine is correct perspective—seeing things as they really are. It is easy to believe that this life is our only reality and become lost in the hum of existence: the world with its cultures, people, movements, and momentum that vibrate and collide, buzzing about us. We may feel alive, but we are in a deep sleep and all is not as it seems.

When we look at the sky and feel the majesty of the sun, moon, stars, and all the galaxies that surround us, it is natural to feel we are not only witnesses but *part* of something grand, noble, . . . *eternal.* God Himself tells us that the majestic and powerful movements of the Heavens are evidence of His glory, and that He knew us there in the beginning before we entered our mothers' wombs.[14] We are more than our fallen, broken, darkened state. We are a composite of our glorious past, our fallen present, and our bright potential, our eternal future.

Our past was with Heavenly Parents, who were and remain our home.[15] As children of the divine, we inherited the potential to become like them. Our inherited divinity defines us far more than *any* experiences we might endure here below. The only boundary to the glory of eternity is *our* willingness to receive it.[16]

HEAVEN'S WAR

Before coming to earth, we looked upon our Heavenly Parents and their exalted state with admiration, hope, and longing. The blinding contrast between our glory and that of our Heavenly Parents was undeniable. They have mastered their spirits, physical bodies, time, light, and all creative power. They have ascended higher and higher as Elohim—the Gods—male and female.[17] As such, they burn brighter than the noonday sun.[18]

We wanted to rise to their level, to create like them, to be full of light and happiness—*like them*. But we needed more experience than the peace of Heaven could provide. They had a "great plan" for us—a way for all of us to ascend and receive everything they have.[19] The plan would allow us to join our spiritual matter with physical matter, to amplify and extend our senses, test ourselves, grow, make mistakes, and learn by personal experience.[20] But before we could ascend, we would need to descend.

To prove the purity of our hearts and minds, we would be "blindfolded"—with a veil of forgetfulness drawn over our heavenly senses—to see if we would truly choose to accept the divinity within us. I have wondered if this spiritual blindfold was also a gift, to ease the pain of our homesickness for Heaven. This veil would shut out the brilliant and pure light, peace and joy of Heaven. But it would allow us to tune our hearts to feel, our ears to hear, and our spiritual eyes to see Christ in each experience. He could help us feel, hear, and eventually see our Heavenly Parents, our friends, family, and loved ones calling to us from beyond the veil, pleading with us to remember who we are and that we are loved and that we can choose to return, urging us to remember that blindfold is temporary and nothing compared to the expansive eternities of Heaven. The test of the veil could help us become like our Heavenly Parents.

This test struck many with dread. In this blinded state we would make mistakes and experience pain, exhaustion, violence, and horrors unknown in Heaven. We would be hurt and we would hurt each other. We were warned earth life could stain and damage us in ways that could prevent us from returning, for "no unclean thing can enter the kingdom of God."[21] Worst yet, some of us might settle for the temporary dust of this earth rather than rise back up for the eternal gold of Heaven.

Debate about the wisdom of our Heavenly Parents' plan flared into spiritual warfare. There were those who looked at our Heavenly Parents' glory and status as something to be taken, rather than achieved through experience, sacrifice, and grace. Lucifer objected. He believed he could "ascend into heaven" and place his throne above God's without obedience to the laws of Heaven.[22] He insisted all could rise above God without trial, experience, or risk *if* we followed and surrendered our hearts to him, and he openly rebelled and sought to "destroy the agency of man."[23] His insurrection led him down dark paths until he became Satan: the devil, the dragon, the serpent, the father of lies.[24] The Heavens wept over Lucifer's rebellion.[25]

Imagine, for a moment, how difficult this choice must have been for all of us, itself a test of our faith. Many abandoned the potential glory. A "third part" of the hosts of Heaven chose to reject that plan.[26] The rest chose to descend to earth.

We chose to trust that, because of Christ, what Satan depicted as a tortuous descent of damnation could be turned into a glorious ascent of fulfillment. We trusted that even if we were not "good enough" on our own, we could be good enough in Christ. We also believed He would help us unite our hearts and minds in love and weave our gifts and talents together as families and communities to create a tapestry of salvation that could lift us back home to Heaven.

THE FALL AND THE NEED TO RISE

After the war in Heaven, Satan was cast down to the earth and immediately sought "to destroy the world" and tear at that tapestry of salvation we planned to create together with Christ.[27] His first step was to "beguile" (deceive) Adam and Eve.[28] Apocryphal books describing the Fall note that before Adam and Eve ate the forbidden fruit, they had divine light—a "bright nature"—radiating within them. This light lifted up their hearts and with it they could see and hear angels singing praises in Heaven above the Garden of Eden. Upon eating the fruit, "all creation became hidden," and their bright nature was withdrawn so they could not "see things afar off." Adam and Eve wept bitterly after learning they had lost their "brightness within" and could no longer see each other, Heaven's angels, or hear Heaven's songs.[29]

After Adam and Eve ate the fruit of the tree of knowledge of good and evil, our Heavenly Father asked Adam, "Where art thou?" or in Hebrew "*ayekah?*" meaning literally "where is your light?"[30] This was not God asking where Adam was physically. Rather, He was inviting Adam to recognize that Adam had *chosen* to fall and in doing so was now separated from God and without Heaven's light.[31]

This loss of light still affects us today. After the Fall, our ability to see our role in creation became hidden. We do not radiate or see light as we did before. We are now caught in a deep sleep, living as if in a dream, blind and deaf to Heaven's harmonic burning.[32] But we can still feel that something is now lost. This may be one reason we often yearn to feel *seen* and *heard* in relationships. As luminous beings now caught in darkness—bruised and stumbling with limited sight—we ache for the ability to *feel* and *hear* but especially *see* the brilliance of home.

The light we *can* see is only a sliver of God's power that radiates in the universe. Like when faint light from a sunrise first pierces the canvas of a dark tent without revealing the full glory of the sun, we are currently blind to the full spectrum of brilliance that Christ, the

Father of Lights, has placed around us.[33] Even with our most powerful scientific instruments that track individual photons and sense ultra-violet and infrared light, our senses are veiled to the true nature of the endless space that surrounds us.

Einstein's theory of gravity suggested we perceive less than five percent of the energy, light, and matter in the universe.[34] Unable to prove this, he later considered this theory his greatest failure. But the theory of gravity was later confirmed when, for unknown reasons, our first interstellar satellites were drawn to mass and gravity undetectable by our most sophisticated tools. Scientists had painstakingly measured the thrust and rocket fuel necessary to help these satellites escape our solar system. Yet, as they reached the edge of the galaxy, Pioneer 10, and months later Pioneer 11 slowed faster than anticipated.

This happened the same for both satellites even though they were launched from the earth at different times from different angles. Still unable to see or calculate these effects from earth, the scientists dubbed the unknown gravitational forces "dark matter" and "dark energy," not because they radiate no light, but because we cannot see them, even with our most advanced scientific instruments.

Not only are we blinded by the Fall, but we are also separated from God's presence, not only spiritually but *physically*. Joseph Smith taught when Adam and Eve fell, the earth itself also fell as a scroll from Heaven.[35] This separation from our Heavenly Parents was so traumatic it is described as spiritual death and removal from God. But the earth's current location in the universe is not our final destination. When we are redeemed from the Fall, the earth will "be rolled back into the presence of God and crowned with celestial glory."[36]

Some scientific theories support this notion that we fell planetarily and that our sun is like a comet with the planets caught in its wake, as if ejected from *somewhere*—still falling.[37] It is as if the earth and the entire solar system were launched from their original celestial orbit—like a boat leaving port—to explore the universe and return home enriched with experience. NASA has reinforced this and shows the earth light years away from God's creative bar at the center of the universe, giving new meaning to the prophets' reminder that one day we will all be raised in the air to be judged at the "pleasing bar of God."[38]

Image 1 *Courtesy of NASA/JPL-Caltech/R. Hurt (SSC/Caltech)*

The gaping galactic chasm between fallen earth below and Heaven above left us craving to return home to regain our light and our full senses. Overcoming this separation and spiritual blindness is our collective aching, to become more than we are now. Rising from the Fall is humanity's universal pilgrimage. It is the objective of every hero's quest, the golden thread of every protagonist. It pulls at each of our hearts to journey through life until we awake and arise.

In fact, the Hebrew word for pilgrimage (עֲלִיָּה) pronounced "aliya" means to "ascend" or "go up." My friend and Isaiah scholar Avraham Gileadi notes, the pilgrimage tradition "expresses our inborn desire to reach a higher, transcendent state."[39] We all desire to rise back home from the Fall.

Just as we consciously chose to go down to earth below, Christ consciously exercised His agency to descend and *stand under* our fallen, darkened state. In doing so, Christ *understands* each of us. By standing under us, He can declare He knows us, can perfectly heal us, and help us join together to rise up from the Fall and return home filled with His light.[40]

GIFTS TO HELP US RISE

We have always been free to choose who we become. Joseph Smith declared, "free independence of mind" is one of Heaven's "choicest gifts."[41] To foster that divine independence, our Heavenly Parents struck the perfect balance between their parental responsibility and our freedom. They did not force or coerce us—to do so would have crushed the seeds of divinity they had placed in each of us. Instead, they gave us space to act for ourselves—with boundless potential to grow—and taught us the laws we could follow to become like them.

As we come to earth, some of us show this pre-development more than others. Many have an aptitude or even genius-level talent for music, art, literature, science, math, or engineering. These "gifted," "talented," "prodigies" are said to be "born to do" this or that, because such pre-existing talents are undeniable. Mozart created his first musical compositions at age five. Pablo Picasso painted his first masterpiece at age nine. Blaise Pascal revolutionized math and pioneered modern computer science at age eleven. Each reveal a prior existence beyond their short years on earth.

In 1950, my wife's grandmother, then fourteen years old, attended the Mid-Century White House Conference for American Youth with U.S. President Harry Truman. She heard speakers from across the country, including physicist Albert Einstein. She recalls him saying, "There had to have been a life before this, because I have not lived here long enough to understand the dimensions of mathematics that I do. *I came here knowing.*"[42] How could we not have a knowledge of something more as children of the divine?

You may be saying to yourself, "*Okay*, but what does this have to do with me? I am not Einstein." Whether we sense it now or not, all of us came knowing, at some level, like Einstein. And more importantly we came with gifts, spiritual gifts that are powerful and essential, designed to help us feel God within us, recognize truth, build Zion, and return home enriched by experience rather than damaged by it. Our gifts include power to transcend our mortal state and connect with each other and with the divine. These gifts include faith, hope, charity, healing, miracles, prophecy, discerning spirits, speaking tongues, and many, many, many more.[43]

We are urged to not forget the gifts that are in us, as all gifts "come from above."[44] The Apostle Paul assures us that every one of us has *at least one* spiritual gift from God[45] and that we have the potential to obtain *all* divine gifts.[46] This is true for each of us and everyone around us. And Christ's invitation to come and partake of His heavenly gift—to receive "all that He hath"—still rings out in the universe. It calls to us to belong, build, and become Zion—*together*.

This is true especially now as society begins to fracture. Our Heavenly Parents orchestrated a grand collection of their most gifted children in these last days. Equipped with heavenly power, we are destined to burn brightly against the darkness; work miracles in Christ's name; and gather, purify, and lift Zion here and now. Our Heavenly Parents showed us how to weave our gifts and talents together into families and communities, in a grand tapestry of salvation, to interconnect our hearts and minds in Christ, and rise back home to Heaven.

A PHYSICAL BODY—A TEMPLE FOR OUR SPIRITS

When we are born into this world, we continue to progress.[47] We join our spirits with matter and are commanded to fulfill the "measure of our creation," magnify our gifts and talents here on earth and build Zion like communities in joy.[48] Our physical bodies are one of those divine gifts.[49] Ancient scriptures teach that after Adam and Eve's spirits were first clothed in the flesh, before they fell, the angels trembled at their presence and light.[50]

Satan is insatiably jealous of Adam and Eve's bodies. Because he and his followers lack physical bodies, they are damned, forever stopped in their progression. They are unhappy, miserable, and self-consumed, and they rage in their own darkness. Without a body, they will never know what it is like to eat a cheeseburger and fries and top it off with a cool milkshake. They will never feel the warmth of a hug or of holding someone's hand or the thrill of a first kiss. They will never feel the joy of holding a little one in their arms.

Because they lack the ability to permanently possess and enjoy physical matter, Satan and his followers seek to cover us in darkness to suppress our divine gifts. Without our consent, Satan has *no* power. Thus he works overtime to obtain our consent by enticing us to sin and violate the alignment between our bodies and our spirits so the spirits that follow him can have greater influence over us and "possess" us to destroy us.[51]

An example of this Satanic manipulated *consent* occurred in 1929, when it was culturally considered "unladylike" to smoke. Cigarette companies, eager to sell more cigarettes, hired one of America's most influential men of the time, Edward Bernays, to remove the stigma of smoking. Mr. Bernays and his wife Doris, hired fashionable and attractive women to light their "torches of freedom" and smoke in the Easter Day Parade in New York.

The national press shared photos of these women smoking, smiling, and parading. Overnight the stigma of smoking was erased and women across America began to smoke. Years later, Mr. Bernays lamented the unknown ill-health effects of smoking but noted his stunt worked because in a democratic society, where consent is necessary to effectuate change, his actions were the "engineering of consent."[52]

Satan, like a spiritual virus seeking a physical body for a host, is the master of engineering consent. Unable to generate any lasting light of his own, he persuades us to surrender our light to his evil ways. God's commandments center on helping us stay in control of our bodies so we can enjoy them to the fullest and radiate light—forever. Our battle is with an invisible enemy. As Apostle Paul declares, "we wrestle not against flesh and blood, but . . . against the rulers of the darkness of this world."[53] Without Christ's enmity and commandments, Satan and his followers could overpower us to give up our agency and take control. With them, we "have right to the tree of life" and can "enter in through the gates into the city" of Zion.[54]

At times, I have heard friends justify sin by saying "I was born this way" or "God made me this way." But this tension between our physical bodies and our spirits is a test of this earth. We're here to learn to let our spirits and bodies learn to dance, sing, and work together—to reconcile them in Christ.[55] This is why prophets declare the "natural man is an enemy to God, and has been since the Fall of Adam," and we will remain enemies to God until we yield to Christ and our foreordained paths.[56] Christ's invitation to "lose our life to find it" is abandoning our *own* paths, appetites, and natural desires and letting the Lord fill our vision with heavenly perspective, trusting that our life can be full of what we created before with Christ if we are willing to receive it. We yield to Christ, purify our fallen natures, and fill ourselves with light by obeying His laws and ordinances.

LAWS AND ORDINANCES TO RISE TOGETHER

Every blessing of Heaven has an associated law.[57] Following divine laws brings elevation and illumination—height and light. This was true before we came earth, and it remains true now. Every gift, blessing, power, talent, skill, or opportunity we obtained up above and strive to have here below requires obedience to divine law and rules of godhood.[58] Joseph Smith taught, just as we are rewarded when we follow man's good laws, following Heaven's laws are more perfect, and if obeyed they will give us eternal life and "inheritance at God's own right hand."[59] Agency was key to our growth before and remains key now. It is up to us to obey the laws of Heaven to receive it here on earth.

That may sound like a painful oversimplification. There are a lot of factors that go into our ability to choose, including our environments, opportunities, and how others treat us. Having been manipulated by others and admittedly done my own share of manipulation as a husband, father, and lawyer, I have asked myself if we really are free.

Doing what is right has such obvious blessings and doing what is wrong leads to such obvious misery that I have often asked myself if life is just a manipulation game without real choice. Are our lives manipulated by a God who controls us like a puppet jostled about by its master—punished if we sin until we repent and only rewarded when we obey? After pondering this for decades, I now ask, "is it manipulation if we willingly chose to be manipulated, knowing that by allowing God to work in us, He would make us into what we wanted to become?"

In the law we refer to this type of arrangement as "informed consent," meaning we were fully informed of the risks, and consequences and rewards of a decision before consenting—even though we might forget later. Similar to performing surgery, even if we are not awake while he operates. Or when we watch a heart-breaking movie, expecting the emotions to which we are about to expose ourselves. We know what we are getting into in these events and still pay for admission, buy popcorn, or bring tissue.

Given the fact that we fought a war over agency, is it reasonable to conclude that we chose our lives, all the good and the bad, like choosing what movies we watch? That Christ showed us exactly what we were getting into before we descended, like watching a movie before being born as a character in that film? Following this same logic, did we also get to choose the lessons we wanted to learn, similar to how our Heavenly Parents let us choose what gifts and talents we developed in Heaven before coming to earth?

We know Christ creates everything spiritually before He creates it physically.[60] We are also taught "we saw the end from the beginning" before coming to earth and many of us made covenants with each other.[61] Is it possible we not only saw but helped draft the equivalent of "spiritual blueprints" for our life paths with Christ, including our family-ties and relationships to help us here below? Did we get to plan out our lives like spiritual architects, carefully measuring out time, space, and relationships to frame the experiences and trials we would face with whom, where, when and how, to have the best chance to return home with the divine virtues we sought? Did we look at earth life as a place we could physically manifest our spiritual blueprints and practice being cocreators of our own Heaven here on earth, with Christ?

Looking at it this way, following Christ in our lives on earth here below can be viewed as receiving lessons in *celestial physics*, designed to teach us to soften, then purify and ultimately unite our hearts, to enrich us and lift us home to our Heavenly Parents. As we keep His commandments, take His name upon us, and love God and others, I believe we align our physical and spiritual selves to physically manifest what was spiritually created before we came to earth. We can live the life we *feel* we should, because we already chose the path spiritually to grow as we overcome the Fall. In time, Christ helps us progress from crawling, to walking, to running until at last we jump heavenward in joyful flight, sailing homeward, filled again with Heaven's radiating light. This process of allowing Christ to help us manifest what we created spiritually and obtaining light and lift as eternal families starts in our hearts.

HEARTS OF CREATION

As children of the Creators, we have inherited the divine ability to create and we get to practice our abilities here below. The power of creation exists in our hearts. Our hearts are the creative seats of our souls—beating as connection points between Heaven and earth. Christ taught there is nothing He takes into His heart to do, save "he will do it."[62] This truth governs us as well, for that which we take into our hearts becomes.[63] Our hearts can create light as well as darkness.

Christ knows the thoughts and intents of our hearts and calls to us to have tender, pure hearts that create light, rather than hard, corrupt hearts that create darkness.[64] Just as angels declare "fear not" when ministering, Christ taught us that fear in our hearts prevents us from receiving the bounty of Heaven on earth, and leads us to sin and sorrow.[65]

The world's first *sin* came after Cain feared and *set his heart* upon the things of the world and blackened it in sin until he killed his brother Abel.[66] Ancient records suggest Cain was not only fearful and jealous of Abel's righteousness and ability to obtain favor with God, but Cain also lusted after Abel's wife.[67] Cain was so wounded and angry that Satan took control of him until Cain's heart created death and darkness as the first murderer.

Our hearts create our reality—and we are here to learn to guard them well—for what we take into them *becomes*. This is especially true for our appearance and countenances. Just as a mirror reveals our outward appearance, our hearts eventually reveal our inner ugliness or beauty.[68] Similarly, our hearts not only lead us to our treasure, but create it.[69] This is why it is so important to let the Lord hold, soften, heal, and cleanse our hearts. He works to turn our creative seats into blazing creative thrones of light and love.[70]

This is universal truth. The Quran notes that the Lord, as the possessor and creator of "the heavens and earth," has power such that "whenever he decrees a thing, he says to it, 'Be' and it becomes."[71] Likewise, the Quran teaches that wickedness is heart sickness.[72] It makes us blind, deaf, and beyond feeling, as darkness covers our hearts. Because of our agency, *we control* whether our hearts grow soft and receptive to Christ and His miracles or hard, allowing Satan to have "great hold upon" our hearts unto death.[73]

Lacking a heart or creative seat, Satan desires to reign over us and sit on the throne of our hearts.[74] He tries to entice us to create darkness, and spoil God's plans for earth. I have learned by painful experience that when I depart from my foreordained life path, violate others' agency, or commit evil, my heart sinks and my spirit aches. In those moments, I have found I can either repent or seek to justify myself by creating even *more* evil and darkness around me.

I find it more than coincidence that the English word "heart" contains the word "hear." We control whether our hearts *hear*. We choose whether our hearts listen in softness and tenderness or whether they are past feeling, suffocated in the evil that turned Satan from a glorious "son of the morning"[75] into the "prince of darkness" and hate.[76] His own heart self-consumed into a black hole of swollen darkness that now endlessly wars against the light.

Recognizing this, Satan often attacks our hearts with thoughts of shame or reproach, as he did right after Adam and Eve first ate the fruit in the Garden of Eden. Satan first convinced Adam and Eve to transgress God's law, and then injected shame into them by declaring that Adam and Eve were "naked" and needed to "hide."[77] When Adam admitted to Father that after eating the fruit in the garden, he hid himself because he was naked, our Father asked him, "Who told thee that thou wast naked?"[78] It was not the Lord.

Satan is a poisonous storyteller who seeks to keep us from Heaven. He does all he can to persuade us to fail and then ridicules us when we do. He rages with a desire to get us to forget our divine heritage, celestial potential, and relationship with God. He shames us with the lie that our difficult experiences in life *mean* God doesn't love us, that we are worthless, alone and that we should further separate ourselves from Heaven, even when the joy, light and connection of Heaven is within our reach!

Shame is not from Heaven. Christ does not try to keep us away but calls to us to awaken, arise and return home. His love and atoning sacrifice were designed to cut through the shame, darkness and lies, and open our hearts until we create Heaven here on earth with love.

ENMITY TO PROTECT OR DESTROY

Recognizing that Satan would use fear, shame and sin to try to control our hearts, the Lord placed enmity as a barrier of defense between us and Satan. As with most tools, enmity can be used righteously or unrighteously. We are taught, although Satan would have power to wield enmity—with contention, shame, and bloodshed—to bruise Christ's heel, Christ would use enmity to crush Satan's head.[79]

An example of unrighteous enmity occurred after Jesus began to teach the apostles of His pending death and suffering. Concerned about this Peter, "rebuked" Christ, and insisted it would not happen. What happened next is a powerful visual of righteous enmity. Christ turned to Peter and declared, "Get thee behind me, Satan: for thou art an offence unto me: for thou savourest not the things that be of God, but those that be of men."[80]

Christ's enmity was not directed at Peter *but at Satan*, as Christ rebuked Satan's influence over Peter's heart.[81] Once Satan was removed, Christ taught Peter some of the most beautiful truths of His ministry: that we are to lose our lives to find them, and that even gaining the whole earth and all its wealth means nothing if we lose our own souls. This is Christlike enmity, a barrier with an open gate. Christ used enmity to defend and lift, not to offend and condemn.

Satan is an expert at using this wall of *defense* as a wall of *offense*, to cause enmity to block healing connections with each other and with Christ. Satan seeks to turn our walls against us and uses the opposition to poison our hearts. He convinces us that the walls meant to protect us from his lies and controlling influence should be used to protect us from *each other*—and to separate us from the love of the Lord. When we sin and refuse to repent, we place walls between us and God and give room for Satan to wield shame and enmity to harden our hearts.

My wife and I have felt the destructive walls of misplaced enmity in our own marriage and in the marriages of others. I have seen Satan convince spouses they are enemies until they rage against each other. In my own failings, when Satan has convinced me to choose offense and anger—often in a late-night argument—I have felt like I was miles away from my wife, separated by a dark expanse, even though I was lying next to her. At such times, it was as if I were experiencing a marital version of the gap created by the Fall, which is only removed as our hearts soften and reconnect in love.

When any of us refuse to let the Lord heal and soften our heart, our Heavenly Father's gift of enmity becomes a barrier to connection with each other and with the Lord. Instead of enmity serving as a wall of protection to surround and unify our hearts, Satan wields enmity to divide us. The result? Marriages fracture, brothers and sisters war, and hearts that ache to be close and belong, turn inward, pained—wounded—and drive us to push each other away in defensive anger. But the Lord continues to call to us, for "our walls are continually before Him."[82] If we allow Him, He will help us build bridges of hope and break down the walls created by wounds and injury.

A FOREORDAINED PATH HOME

Before sending us to earth, our loving Heavenly Parents considered our unique talents, strengths, and weaknesses and how we might fit together in purposeful harmony. Together, we modeled our lives like blueprints made of ribbons of light. With our permission and love, they orchestrated relationships, families, trials, hardships, and life paths into a multi-dimensional tapestry of these ribbons to help us grow and return home. At the center of their plan was Christ. He perfectly embodies all gifts, talents, and celestial traits and loves us as much as they do.

Led by Christ, our gifts and talents can bring us home, despite the blindfold of the veil and Lucifer's war. Together with Christ, we can continue to develop, grow, learn, become, and, most importantly, be forgiven when we sin. Though fallen, we can be lifted back up—on the shoulders of our Savior who lovingly carries us home to our Heavenly Parents.[83]

Christ awakens us to what we were before and helps us see our God-given spiritual foreordinations. He helps us fulfill the measure of our creation. In Hebrew, the word "fulfill" (םישְׁגהֲלְ) means to carry out, materialize, realize, or implement. The command to "fulfill" the measure of our creation is to bring into existence, materialize, realize or implement our pre-created spiritual reality—if we choose to receive.

To perfectly preserve our agency, our Heavenly Parents showed us their plan, beginning to end, to redeem us in Christ.[84] We joined hands and promised each other we would do everything we could to help each other come home—as brothers and sisters. We knew that even if Satan worked to destroy our agency, Christ would repair the damage, turn any bitterness into sweetness and ensure adversity and affliction in this life would become bread and water to our souls.[85]

Realizing these truths, it makes sense why the first and great commandment is to *love God with all our heart*, the second like unto it: to love our neighbors as ourselves.[86] Love helps us rise. It unlocks our gifts, talents, and prior relationships.

We *chose* to come to earth to be saved by Christ and to save each other. We covenanted to use our gifts to point each other to Christ, help each other accept His atoning love, and become perfected in Him. Divinely infused with gifts and love, we charged into this existence trusting that Christ would help us to eventually return home. He was our answer then, and He is still our answer now. If we choose Him again, He will fulfill His promise to help us fly home to Heaven.[87]

PROPHETS, REPENTANCE, AND PERSONAL RESTORATION

Even though we are fallen and have forgotten who we are, we remain fully free to choose who we will be and what we will do. This is the perfect setting for us to prove ourselves and show God and ourselves what we treasure and that we are fit for the creative keys of the universe. It is also the perfect setting for Satan to attack.

He and his angels continue to tirelessly subvert the agency of man, twist our perceptions and expectations. Satan wants us to define ourselves by our pain, not our potential. Each day, he entices us to forget our divine purpose and that it is possible for us to return home, together with our brothers and sisters.

But Christ's word's will not return void, and He will "accomplish all his works among the children of men."[88] He sends angels, prophets, and prophetesses to awaken us. These "noble and great ones"[89] were "called and prepared from the foundation of the world according to the foreknowledge of God, on account of their exceeding faith and good works" to participate with Christ in a "preparatory redemption,"[90] a preestablished plan for us to work together toward salvation.

Adam and Eve, Abraham and Sarah, Miriam and Aaron, Moses and Zipporah, Joseph and Emma[91] and many others were foreordained to point us to Christ. They did so in the spirit world and continue to do so here on earth. The Lord reveals His secrets—those plans for redemption, foreordained before the world was—to holy men and women, so that they might help *Him* fill the measure of creation and help *us* uncover our true selves.[92]

In Hebrew the word "reveal" or "galah" (הלֶגֶ) means to uncover, discover, or show *oneself*.[93] Isaiah notes this type of self-revelation occurs as Christ invites the prisoners in darkness to awaken and show themselves to join the Lord and Zion above.[94] We are all fallen prisoners that sit hidden in darkness, and hunger to return to our home on high. Through Christ's Atonement our true selves can be revealed.

Prophets, endowed with authority, serve as an extension of Christ's power on earth. They are often called to serve the earth when life does not proceed as divinely planned, or when men use their agency to attempt to frustrate God's plan. In such times of distress, they engage the powers of Heaven to course correct, realign the temporal reality with the spiritual foreordination, and use nature and its forces to call His children to repentance.

Joseph Smith taught prophets have "the celestial and divinely purposed power by faith, to break mountains, to divide the seas, to dry up waters, to turn them out of their course, to put at defiance the armies of nations, to divide the earth" and all things according to Christ's will.[95] Prophets use their foreordained heavenly powers and the spirit of revelation to point to the plan of salvation and teach faith and repentance in Christ. They remind us that Christ is working "a marvelous work and a wonder" among all nations, kindreds, tongues, and people, "to *restore* his people from their lost and fallen state" and "bring about the *restoration of his people* upon the earth."[96] One such prophet, called to awaken and restore the Lord's people and help them be "taken up into heaven," was Enoch—the first founder of Zion.[97]

CHAPTER 1 ENDNOTES

1 *See* https://www.etymonline.com/search?q=deva.
2 Jan Chozen Bays "Jizo: Guardian of Children, Travelers, and Other Voyagers," http://www.many-lives.com/lives/paradise.html.
3 Monier Monier-Williams, *English Sanskrit Dictionary* (Delhi: Motilal Banarsidass, 2001 [first published 1872]).
4 *See* https://www.britannica.com/topic/Shiva.
5 Popol Vuh, sacred book of the Quiche Maya people, translation and commentary by Allen J. Christenson, 2007, p. 61; available at www.mesoweb.com/publications/Christenson/PupulVuh.pdf. Likewise, the Navajo believe in Father Heaven and Mother Earth.
6 The Editors of Encyclopedia Britannica, May 6, 2019, https://www.britannica.com/topic/Re.
7 Boscaro, Adriana; Gatti, Franco; Raveri, Massimo, eds. (2003). *Rethinking Japan: Social Sciences, Ideology and Thought* II, Japan Library, p. 300.
8 1 Nephi 13:37, Mosiah 23:22, Alma 26:7, Alma 36:28, Alma 40:20, Mormon 2:19, Ether 4:19.
9 Isiah 55:9.
10 Isaiah 45:8.
11 History of the Church, 3:390–391.
12 Brigham Young, *Discourses of Brigham Young,* (abbreviated as DBY), 443.
13 Isaiah 29:24.
14 D&C 88:47; Romans 11:2, Jeremiah 1:5, D&C 93:29.
15 William Wordsworth, Arthur Quiller-Couch, ed., "Ode Intimations of Immortality from Recollections of Early Childhood," *The Oxford Book of English Verse*: *1250–1900* (1919), p. 536.
16 *Doctrines of Salvation*, comp. Bruce R. McConkie [1954], 1:59. *See also* Abraham 3:18–23; *Teachings of Presidents of the Church: Joseph Smith* [2007], 210.
17 In Hebrew *Elohim* is plural for "the Gods" and includes both male and female genders.
18 Joseph Smith—History 1:16.
19 Dallin H. Oaks, "The Great Plan," April 2020 general conference.
20 1 John 4:6.
21 D&C 109:20; Deuteronomy 23:4.
22 Isaiah 14:13; 2 Ne. 23:13.
23 Moses 4:3–4.
24 Revelation 20:2; Joseph Smith Translation, Revelation 12:8.
25 D&C 76:26.
26 D&C 29:36; the term "third part" does not necessarily mean equal portions but suggests there were three unequal parts or groups: perhaps, first, the covenant people of the Lord; second, those who refused to make covenants;

and third, those who chose to stay behind as followers of Lucifer.

27 Moses 4:3–4; Joseph Smith Translation, John 14:30.

28 Moses 4:6.

29 *The First Book of Adam and Eve*, CHAP. VIII, in *The Forgotten Books of Eden*, translated by Rutherford H. Platt Jr., 1926.

30 Rabbi Shimon Apisdorf, online series: *God in a Nutshell*, "Part 14: Adam and the Hidden Light"; *see also* https://www.chabad.org/kabbalah/article_cdo/aid/379633/jewish/Hide-and-Seek.htm, noting God was asking, where is your *shekinah* or *holy fire.*

31 Isaiah 6:10; Jeremiah 5:21; Ezekiel 12:2; Matthew 13:15; Acts 28:27; Romans 11:8.

32 1 Corinthians 13:12; Romans 13:11; Jacob 7:26.

33 D&C 84:45; *see also* Orson Pratt, in *Journal of Discourses* 3:97.

34 Available at https://science.nasa.gov/astrophysics/focus-areas/what-is-dark-energy#:~:text=It%20turns%20out%20that%20roughly,than%205%25%20of%20the%20universe.

35 Brigham Young, in *Journal of Discourses*, Vol. 17, p. 144; Mormon 9:2, D&C 88:95.

36 *Teachings: Joseph Smith,* 258.

37 *See* https://www.forbes.com/sites/startswithabang/2018/08/30/our-motion-through-space-isnt-a-vortex-but-something-far-more-interesting/#1b8494697ec2.

38 *See* https://www.nbcnews.com/id/wbna8972222; *see* Jacob 6:13; Alma 10:34.

39 *Isaiah Decoded: Ascending Jacob's Ladder*, Avraham Gileadi, 2012, Loc 1707.

40 D&C 121:8; D&C 88:6.

41 *Teachings of the Prophet Joseph Smith*, p. 49.

42 Interview with Anna Peterson on June 12, 2020, at 4:30 PM.

43 1 Cor. 12:8–12.

44 1 Timothy 4:14; D&C 6:10.

45 1 Cor. 7:7.

46 1 Cor. 12:31.

47 *The Mortal Messiah*, 1:23, 25, Bruce R. McConkie, 1979.

48 2 Nephi 8:11.

49 D&C 77:12; Moroni 9:6; 1 Corinthians 3:16; D&C 131:7–8.

50 *The First Book of Adam and Eve*, CHAP. XXXVI, v. 5. in *The Forgotten Books of Eden* trans. Rutherford H. Platt Jr., 1926.

51 Matthew 8:16; Matthew 9:32–33; Acts 8:7; Alma 30:42; Alma 48:17.

52 Edward L. Bernays, Howard Walden Cutler, *The Engineering of Consent* (January 1, 1955).

53 Ephesians 6:12.

54 Revelation 22:14.

55 Galatians 6.

56 Mosiah 3:19.
57 D&C 130: 20–21.
58 D&C 82:10.
59 *Teachings of the Prophet Joseph Smith*, p. 49.
60 Moses 3:7; D&C 29:32.
61 Dallin H. Oaks, "The Great Plan," April 2020 general conference.
62 Abraham 3:17.
63 Luke 6:45.
64 1 Samuel 16:7; Hebrews 4:12; Genesis 4:8.
65 D&C 67:2–3.
66 Genesis 4:8.
67 "Cain becomes jealous of Abel because of his sisters." *The First Book of Adam and Eve*, CHAP. LXXVI, in *The Forgotten Books of Eden*, translated by Rutherford H. Platt Jr., 1926.
68 Proverbs 27:19.
69 Proverbs 23:7; Matthew 6:21.
70 D&C 137:2–4.
71 Noble Quran 2:116 available at www.islamcity.org.
72 Quran 2:7.
73 D&C 10:20, Alma 8:9; Alma 10:25; Alma 27:12; Helaman 6:31; Helaman 7:15; Helaman 6:23.
74 D&C 86:3.
75 Isaiah 14:12–14; D&C 76:25–29; 2 Nephi 24:12.
76 Joseph Smith Translation, John 14:30.
77 Genesis 3:7.
78 Genesis 3:11–15.
79 Moses 4:21.
80 Mark 8:32–33; Matt 16:22–23.
81 Christ's command to "get thee behind me Satan" was the same he made to Satan after fasting for forty days and nights in Luke 4:8.
82 Isaiah 49:16; 1 Ne 21:16.
83 Dieter F. Uchtdorf, "He Will Place You on His Shoulders and Carry You Home," April 2016 general conference.
84 Dallin H. Oaks, "The Great Plan," April 2020 general conference: "*We saw the end from the beginning.* All of the myriads of mortals who have been born on this earth chose the Father's plan and fought for it in the heavenly contest that followed. *Many also made covenants with the Father concerning what they would do in mortality.* In ways that have not been revealed, our actions in the spirit world have influenced our circumstances in mortality."
85 Isaiah 30:20.
86 Matthew 22:37–38.
87 Isaiah 46:4.
88 1 Nephi 9:6.

89 Abraham 3:22–23.

90 Alma 13:3.

91 Emma was an essential companion for Joseph, like Sarah for Abraham. She was promised her heart would rejoice in Christ, see her redeemer, and that no one could rob her of her joy. "Blessing from Joseph Smith Sr., 9 December 1834," Patriarchal Blessing Book 1, 4–5, josephsmithpapers.org.

92 Amos 3:7.

93 *See* https://biblehub.com/hebrew/1540.htm.

94 Isaiah 49:8–9.

95 Joseph Smith Translation, Genesis 14:25–40.

96 2 Nephi 25:17; 2 Nephi 30:8.

97 Moses 7:21.

CHAPTER 2

ZION'S FIRST RISE WITH ENOCH

"And Enoch walked with God: and he was not; for God took him." —Genesis 5:24

We have very little written about our first parents, Adam and Eve, and even less about their fourth-great-grandson Enoch. He is introduced in the book of Genesis as the "seventh son of Adam" but has otherwise been erased from King James's Bible.[1] We know more about Noah, Enoch's own great-grandson, than the original founder of Zion. It is as if Enoch's song of Zion has been hidden from those who would look beyond the mark, saved for only the most earnest seekers of light and truth.[2]

This hiding of Enoch continues today. Books once considered central scripture by Judaism and Christianity that speak of Enoch rising to the Heavens, are regularly discounted as apocryphal and mythical, too fantastic to believe. Christ instructed Joseph Smith that these apocryphal books—although filled with improper influences of men—do contain many things that are true, which can be discerned with the spirit of truth.[3]

These apocryphal books include teachings that Enoch was lifted up to Heaven or "raised aloft to that Son of Man and to the Lord of Spirits." They note Enoch was "raised aloft on chariots of the spirit" and "his name vanished."[4] Even though Enoch's name *has* mostly vanished from accepted scripture, reference to his Zion has not.[5] Zion glitters at times in the King James Bible, like unmined gold peeking through a mountainside, awaiting our questions. And once uncovered, Zion radiates as a central guiding star in the constellation of our celestial potential.

The word *Zion* is not Hebrew. It predates the Hebrew spellings of *tsion*, or *slyon*, *tslyyon* (צִיוֹן or צייון). It also predates ancient Sanskrit, without a clear etymology or discernible root word.

Some suggest Zion means "castle" or dry land, referring to a Jeshubite fortress King David conquered near Jerusalem.[6] But the word and meaning of Zion is much more than these concepts. Zion's true meaning is its *purpose*.

Zion is the destiny of this planet and of God's people. Zion is restoration, unity, and joy in Christ and will be our own fullness of joy if we accept it. Joseph Smith taught the "building of Zion . . . has interested the people of God in *every* age." Zion's cause has inspired prophets, priests and kings, and "they have looked forward with joyful anticipation to the day in which we live . . . fired with heavenly and joyful anticipations they have sung and written and prophesied of this our day, but they died without the sight."[7]

Building Zion will "bring about the destruction of the powers of darkness, the renovation of the earth, the glory of God, and the salvation of the human family." Just as Christ is the why, Zion is the how. Christ uses Zion to "unite the heavenly priesthood with the earthly" and bring about His great purposes and establish eternal peace.[8]

The patriarch Benjamin prophesied of this rejoining of Heaven and earth, when the Lord would reveal salvation to all, a day when we would see Enoch, Noah, Shem, Abraham, Isaac, and Jacob, "rising on the right hand in gladness," and when as many as believe on Christ will rejoice and "all men shall rise, some unto glory, . . . some unto shame."[9]

Rising from the Fall and following Christ upward into Zion is our celestial target. *It always has been.* But the upward flight to Heaven as Zion must be made *together*. Only together can we be fully empowered by Christ, vanquish darkness, liberate the captives, and, as divine children, fulfill the measure of our creation.[10]

Christ tells us we are not His unless we are one.[11] Unity is a law of Zion. Unity brings lift and light, and Zion's ascent is meant to be communal—not just individual. Zion is a place where we reverence the divinity in each other as we strive to be like Christ. We need each other to be our best selves, and Enoch needed Zion as much as Zion needed Enoch. But before Enoch could build Zion, Christ built Zion *in* Enoch.

Christ purified Enoch and then led Enoch to gather and purify His chosen people before He helped Enoch build Zion. After Enoch walked with God, he was able to teach his people to walk with God. Only after he gathered his brothers and sisters do the angels record, God "took him."[12]

Enoch's path can be our path too.

Enoch—like all prophets—was called to awaken us. He pointed to Christ's ability to bridge the gap of death and sin that separates us from our foreordained potential and where we actually stand here on earth. While much of this gap between us and Heaven is due to our lack of earthly experience, some of it is our failing to be our true selves and receive God's plan for us.

This failure—when we make choices that violate our premortal plan—is sin. Sin creates disharmony or dissonance between our spiritual selves and our physical selves. Such dissonance is self-betrayal and causes physical and spiritual pain.

God invites each of us to be true to ourselves, follow our foreordained paths, and celebrate His gifts on this journey of coming to ourselves. He invites us to rejoice in our potential and the potential of those around us. This is a journey where Christ changes our hearts and helps rouse us "out of a deep sleep," and delivers us from the "midst of darkness," the "bands of death," and the "chains of hell" to illuminate our souls "by the light of the everlasting word."[13] This awakening allows us to spread our heart's wings and hear Christ's songs of redeeming love to sing that celestial melody to those around us, when we know others as we are known and see others as we are seen—by Christ.[14]

In Enoch's day, there was great need to bring peace to the hearts of men. Even before Enoch was born, "Satan had great dominion among men, and raged in their hearts." The devil and his angels of darkness caused wars and bloodshed as "a man's hand was against his own brother, in administering death, because of secret works, seeking for power."[15]

God called Enoch to help others remember and be true to who they really were. But first, Enoch had to remember who he was himself. Enoch had to let go of the lies of man about himself that ran contrary to his divine heritage and premortal purpose. He had to undergo his own *personal restorative awakening in Christ.*

THE LORD PURIFIES AND RESTORES ENOCH

It is unclear when the Lord called Enoch—but we do know Enoch did not feel ready or qualified. Enoch describes himself as slow of speech and hated by all men.[16] This was true even though (or possibly because) Enoch's life was surrounded by the miraculous and prophetic experiences of Adam and Eve and their righteous children.

As the seventh-generation grandson of Adam and Eve, it is likely much was expected of him. Enoch was ordained to the priesthood at the young age of twenty-five.[17] His father Jared taught him "in all the ways of God."[18] Enoch clearly felt the truth of Christ's word and strove to preach faith and repentance in Christ like his great-grandparents.[19]

Enoch is also referred to as the scribe of righteousness. He recorded Adam's final blessings, prophecies, and counsel for three years while Adam and Eve spent their last days in the valley of Adam-ondi-Ahman in modern-day Missouri.[20] There, Adam and Eve met with their righteous prosperity, as an aged Adam, full of the Holy Ghost, prophesied of the full future of the earth.[21]

This prophetic record was preserved in the lost books of Enoch.[22] Some records suggest Enoch himself wrote 366 books regarding the Heavens and the earth.[23] Joseph Smith prophesied the book of Enoch would be one of the means by which God will fulfill the prophecy of Isaiah. Namely, that "the knowledge of God will cover the earth, as the waters cover the great deep" to gather all believers home[24] until the earth is finally fully awakened and restored.

But before Enoch could awaken and restore others, he needed to be awakened himself. Christ himself declares that *knowing* Him and

God the Father *is* eternal life.[25] What is knowing? And how do we know Christ and the Father in a way that creates eternal life?

This type of knowing involves more than just awareness. It is even more than declaring we trust Him, or believe in Him. This type of knowing involves *understanding* Christ like He understands us, feeling the weight He carries for us and our true relationship with Him. This type of knowing is realizing we are defined by Christ, His love for us, His claim on us, His sacrifice for us.

This knowing only occurs if we accept it. It often starts with a *feeling*, a burning inside, a yearning to remember who we really are. When we choose to act in ways consistent with those feelings, we learn divine law—that while certain acts and thoughts lead to light and fulfillment, others lead to darkness and emptiness. As we obey divine law, we answer His call to our hearts and reawaken to the divinity within us.

As we trust in Christ and accept His cleansing power in our lives, we progress from *feeling* to *hearing* Him. When we start *hearing* His voice calling to us, guiding us on the right and on the left, leading us in the path home, we begin to hear His word calling to us to care for those around us. We can also hear Him in the voices of those seeking relief, comfort, and those rejoicing in Christ. As we show we are receptive to His call, and love others as ourselves, our hearts progress from *feeling* and *hearing* Him to eventually *seeing* Him as He is. Thus, we rise.

Enoch's own journey to the Lord started first with *feeling*, then *hearing*, then *seeing* Christ. Enoch acted on his *feelings* and preached despite being hated. He sacrificed his own comfort to help awaken his brothers and sisters until he *heard* the voice of the Lord.

The Lord visited Enoch as he journeyed "among the people" to preach faith and repentance in Christ. Enoch related "the Spirit of God *descended out of heaven* and abode upon him."[26] The Lord's voice called to him from Heaven, directing Enoch to help open others ears, awaken their eyes, and soften their hearts. For "their *hearts have waxed hard, and their ears are dull of hearing, and their eyes cannot see afar off.*"[27]

Christ warned Enoch that because men refused to pray and instead "sought their own counsels in the dark,"[28] they were allowing Satan to "rage in their hearts" and destroy God's plan.[29] They were defying our Heavenly Parents' foreordained path—violating their own divine purpose.

The apocryphal books of Enoch record that fallen angels (at times interpreted as sons of Adam) defied the plan of Heaven for their lusts of the flesh and secret combinations for power. Given this wickedness, the Lord warned these men were bringing upon themselves death and hell reserved for the most corrupt of God's children.[30] The apocryphal book of Jasher captures one glimpse into how Satan raged in men's hearts. It records wicked sons of Adam caused their wives to consume a contraceptive plant or tea to make them barren. They sought to prevent the creative power in the women "that they might retain their figures and whereby their beautiful appearance might not fade" in child birth.[31]

The test of divinity is how we treat people. Gods do not selfishly consume, they selflessly create. These evil men treated women as *objects*. They prized the temporary lust of consuming an image over the eternal power of creation in intimacy. They chose pleasure over purpose.

Christ's love is selfless creation, growth, and joy. His compassion and love are so transformative, so powerful, they are the energy by which our sun radiates.[32] Defying the creative power of human intimacy with permanent contraception was the same as denying Christ. It was such a violation of God's plan, such a destructive self-deception, it led men to war in their hearts and to hate and murder their own blood.

Enoch was sent to call out the evil, destruction, and war these wicked men were creating with their hearts. To do this, Enoch first had to face his own fears—fear of man, fear of rejection, fear of failure, and fear of judgment. When Enoch had heard Christ's call, he bowed to the earth and asked Christ "Why is it that I have found favor in thy sight, and am but a lad, and all the people hate me; for I am slow of speech; wherefore am I thy servant?" Even in the influence of the Lord, Enoch was afraid of men's judgment.[33] Enoch is not alone in such fear.

On this fallen earth, behind the veil of forgetfulness and the silence of no longer living in our Heavenly Parents' loving presence, it is easy for us to believe the raucous voices that surround us rather than the still small voice of Heaven that calls to us.[34] But what happens next is a powerful example of how Christ can awaken each of us despite the noise around us.

After the Lord heard Enoch's doubts, He had compassion on him, spoke truth to him, and then invited Enoch to act. In doing so, the Lord replaced Enoch's fear with purpose. Christ assured Enoch that if he followed Him, no man would pierce him.[35] It was as if the Lord was saying, others may hate you, call you names, and attack you, but I will keep your heart safe. As you listen to me, you will know who you really are, and you will *know* that *you are mine.*

Christ then told Enoch to anoint his eyes with clay and wash to *see.*[36] As he washed his eyes, Enoch not only saw the Lord, he saw himself as the Lord saw him—foreordained to cry repentance, command lions, mountains, and rivers to gather Zion—but Enoch was also given power to behold the "spirits that God had created" and things "not visible to the natural eye."[37]

This is a pattern of undergoing a personal restorative awakening in Christ. Enoch felt Christ's love, then was taught Christ's truths, was invited to act and wash his eyes, and then he saw what Christ saw. Through Christ, Enoch was "born again into the kingdom of heaven."[38] From this restored and awakened position, Enoch saw and walked with the Lord, and was "before his face continually."[39] He knew truth—things as they really were, are, and will be.[40]

In other words, Enoch was redeemed from the Fall and returned to the truth and light of his prior position and presence with Christ. Enoch saw truths about himself and all those around him. He saw who people were before they came to earth, what their life could be here on earth if they followed Christ, and how Satan was working to damn them. He became a seer, fully empowered to do God's work in truth and love. He was given the ability to become like God and have all things (past, present, and future) continually before Him.[41] He could see.

The apocryphal books of Enoch shed even more light on how Christ transformed Enoch. They relate that as Enoch awoke, he was carried up to higher and higher degrees of the Heavens by his future grandson Gabriel (Noah) and the past great-grandfather Michael

(Adam) until he saw God's throne surrounded by cherubim and seraphim singing endless glory to His name.[42] Upon seeing Christ, Enoch sank to his knees in worship, overwhelmed by the greatness of Christ's brightness and beauty, and fearful of his unworthiness before God.

In gentle assurance, Christ invited Enoch to fear not, arise, and stand before His face for eternity. He then commanded Michael to remove Enoch's earthly garments, and clothe Enoch in garments of glory. Upon wearing these radiant garments, Enoch's appearance shone like the sun, transfigured into one of Christ's "glorious ones" with wings of light at his back, and the terror of friendly lions at his feet.[43] It is little wonder angels since have been depicted with wings.

I feel an exhilarating chill when envisioning Enoch radiating light, vested with these superhero-like powers.[44] The first warrior prophet, he was given heavenly power to defy man's propensity for self-destruction and to invite all to Christ. Consistent with Enoch's title as the "Scribe of Righteousness," Christ then gave Enoch access to His "choice and comforting books" and a "reed of quick writing"[45]

After Enoch's eyes were opened, he could speak with the tongue of angels.[46] At his word mountains moved, lions roared, rivers turned, and men's hearts burned. Empowered to wield the elements and armed with the first set of scripture—the book of remembrance—Enoch went forth upon the hills and the high places, crying with a loud voice—with heart-piercing accuracy, truth, and power.

Enoch reminded people of Heaven and earth, their relationship as brothers and sisters, and of the gap between their foreordained path and current state. His words rang so clear and with such electrifying power that "the people trembled and could not stand in his presence" and all men were offended.[47] Word spread quickly. The Lord had raised up a *seer*.[48]

ENOCH PURIFIES AND RESTORES A PEOPLE

Enoch was not called to save himself alone, but to save all who would receive. To do this, he used the Lord's prophetic priesthood power to awaken and gather the righteous. Enoch's message to his brothers and sisters was clear: choice.

At the Lord's command, Enoch warned the people to "Choose ye this day, to serve the Lord God who made you."[49] Joshua later gave this same charge to the Israelites in the Old Testament, when he declared "choose ye this day whom ye will serve . . . as for me and my house, we will serve the Lord."[50] Enoch's message was a reminder that we choose whether we *feel* and *hear*, *see* and *know* Christ.[51]

Without his message we might never have been born. Death, darkness and distortion were suffocating and threatening the peace and purpose of all mankind. Satan was stirring men's hearts to war with*in* to create war with*out*. Adam and Eve's children had begun to "love Satan more than God" and were "carnal, sensual, and devilish," unrepentant, without respect, and "damned."[52]

Enoch pointed them to "the book of remembrance," written by the finger of the Lord in the Adamic language,[53] and asked them why they sought counsel in the dark rather than in God's word—why they chose to "deny the God of heaven" and remain blind.[54] This message must have been chilling given Enoch's gift of seership that allowed him to simultaneously see past, present, and future. With his gift, Enoch could look at someone and see the person's true identity, not only understanding him and his thoughts and intents in the moment but also who he was premortally. I have wondered if this is similar to how parents can hold an adult child's face in their hands and see the infant they knew at birth.

This gift was more powerful. Like prophets to come, Enoch's spiritual sight allowed him to look not only on the outward appearance but directly into a person's heart, and comprehend their gifts, potential, and purpose as well as who they were destined to become *eternally*.[55] This must be similar to how bishops can discern their congregations' spiritual gifts and how those gifts can be orchestrated to strengthen the community.[56]

His ability to see also made him a skillful spiritual healer perfectly capable of discerning what was hardening someone's heart. With his spiritual senses restored, he could discern what separated them from Christ and their true selves. He could see the faintest shadows in their countenances and hear the disharmony in their voices evidencing how and why they were abandoning Christ and their missions on earth.

So, Enoch cried repentance. He spoke of things as they really are and called others to Christ with such faith and power that he "offended all men."[57] Like prophets to come, others could *not* disbelieve him—which only enraged them more.[58] But Enoch's message was one of invitation, not damnation. His heart yearned for the hearts of those around him.

He knew the sweetness of Heaven's love and invited all who would listen to be "reconciled unto Christ."[59] We can find the same peace today by *choosing* and accepting Christ's cleansing and awakening ordinances. Just as we were born by water, spirit, and blood as infants, Enoch taught we need to be "born again into the kingdom of heaven" by the water, spirit, and blood of Christ.[60] In other words, the Spirit justifies us and lifts us to Christ, who in turn sanctifies us and lifts us to our Heavenly Parents.[61] Once our spiritual eyes are fully open, we too can see things as they are, were, and will be.

SEPARATING RIGHTEOUS FROM WICKED

The Lord repeatedly tells us His word is quick and powerful, sharper than a two-edge sword, that cuts with such precision it divides even the tough joints and marrow.[62] In Enoch's case, the word of the Lord was so sharp, it cut out the righteous from the wicked.

Many answered Enoch's calls to faith and repentance and joined their hearts to find Christ. As Zion began to shine, the wicked raged even more. They came to battle to prevent the light of Zion from reminding them they were living in darkness and self-deception.

When the wicked came to attack, Enoch "*spake* the word of the Lord, and the earth trembled, and the mountains fled . . . the drivers of water were turned out of their course; and the *roar of the lions* was heard out of the wilderness." Enoch's speech was so powerful that "all nations feared greatly."[63] When faced with their wicked army, Enoch spoke and by the power of God's word raised a new barren land from the ocean floor. Shrinking in their own darkness, the enemies of Zion and the "giants of the land" were so afraid of Enoch they fled to the desolate place Enoch had raised from the ocean, and abandoned their attack.[64]

While the wicked descended to barren land once below the ocean, Enoch and his followers ascended to the mountains and high places where they "flourished."[65] So great was their righteousness and willingness to do their part to build Heaven on earth that Christ visited and then dwelt among them. He taught them the laws of Heaven, and helped them join hearts and minds as one. He led them to raise each other to mountains, to heights, to *Him*.[66] They blossomed as Zion until the Lord lifted Enoch, the community *and* the entire city itself by its foundations "up into heaven" until they were "high and lifted up even into the bosom of the Father and of the Son of Man."[67]

In Zion, Christ fulfills His promise made at the foundation of the world—to perfect and redeem His people from the Fall so they can literally rise back home to Heaven by teaching them how to make Heaven on earth. He uses the premortal and mortal gifts of every individual in the community to knit the hearts of His people together like the simple Quaker saying: "Thee lift me and I'll lift thee, and we'll ascend together." They cared for each other with such common purpose that there were no poor among them, and each person was able to manifest their gifts and talents to purify each other in love and the earth around them, as they had planned to do with Christ before coming to earth.[68]

The contrast between Zion's blossoming in the mountains—as the unified kingdom of God—and the warring of the fallen in the valleys—as divided nations of Satan—was like the contrast between the sun and a black hole. On one hand, the Lord's people increased in unity, righteousness, and shared their light with each other in love, until "in the process of time" they were "taken up into heaven."[69] They were one in Christ, possessions, compassion, and joy.

On the other hand, after the righteous removed from among them, Satan's control over the wicked steadily grew. They continued to violate their foreordained paths, worship Satan, and defile the gifts of the Lord: their bodies; their time; and their eyes, ears, and hearts. They remained divided, preying upon, murdering, and consuming each other with war and bloodshed.

This contrast reinforces the simplicity of God's great commandments—to love God and to love our neighbors as ourselves.[70] Without this love, we implode and sink into selfish darkness, unable to unite our hearts and our minds. With this love, Christ restores Zion and her people and helps them awake and arise—not only emotionally, socially, and spiritually but also literally and physically.

ZION'S FIRST RISE

Enoch's people began to purify their hearts, and allowed Christ to teach them how to love each other more perfectly. They loved each other so perfectly with heart and mind that there were "no poor among them."[71] Eventually, their united hearts and minds purified the city so thoroughly, it rose up from the fallen telestial state to the terrestrial Heavens.[72] This elevation change was not just symbolic but literal. Christ carried the city and its people through the air to the Heavens by its foundation stones.[73]

For those who doubt this miraculous event of an entire city rising to Heaven, I would point you to Jacob who asked "if God being able to speak and the world was, and to speak and man was created, O then, why not able to command the earth, or the workmanship of his hands upon the face of it, according to his will and pleasure?"[74] Here, the Lord *literally* moved Heaven and earth to accomplish His work, and gathered hearts and minds into a community fit to be caught up, restored from the Fall. Orson Pratt taught this raising of Zion to the Heavens is the grand method for gathering and redeeming all of the righteous across all fallen worlds throughout the galaxy.[75]

The same is true for us, whether it happens to us while we are alive, or after we pass away. The prophet Joseph Smith declared:

> [T]he nearer man approaches perfection, the clearer are his views, and the greater his enjoyments, till he has overcome the evils of his life and lost every desire for sin; *and like the ancients, arrives at that point of faith where he is wrapped in the power and glory of his Maker and is caught up to dwell with Him.*[76]

Even though the community was translated to a terrestrial state, it was not yet able to fully return to Heaven. They had to master additional virtues and divine law necessary to become what the Apostle Paul later referred to in Hebrews, as the city of the Living God, the heavenly Jerusalem surrounded by angels.[77] So the community—city and all—hovered in "an aerial position with the limits of our solar system" with "a large piece of earth immediately connected with the foundations and the city."[78] From this aerial perch, aloft in the Heavens, the people continued their work of sanctification and ministered to the righteous below still seeking Heaven, who the Lord refers to as the "remnant."

Like the three groups in Heaven, it is helpful to distinguish between the following three groups on earth (1) the *redeemed* lifted to Heaven with Enoch in Zion, (2) the covenant *remnant* below who continued to seek Zion, and (3) the *residue* that was left behind in chains of darkness and destroyed.[79] The redeemed, the remnant, and the residue.

Enoch and his people were *redeemed*. The *residue* are those who seek their own wealth, their own love and their own paths. The *residue* are so dark hearted they are purged from the earth by fire, floods, and wars because they consciously reject Zion, and use their dark hearts to create evil continually, rather than pursue our Heavenly Parents' foreordained paths.[80]

The *remnant* are the salt of the earth, those who covenanted premortally to stay below (after the redeemed rise to Heaven) to help the Lord course correct that which Satan has been working to derail.[81] They point themselves and others to Christ to make the Lord's paths straight.[82] As the righteous children of the prophets and prophetesses they pave the way for Abraham and Sarah, Israel, and Christ as the Messiah and Redeemer of the world.[83]

THE PROCESS OF TIME

You might ask, how long did it take to build Zion? Enoch was called to be a prophet at 65, after he and his wife Edna (or Aadanah) had Methuselah.[84] But Zion was not translated to a celestial level immediately. It occurred "in the process of time" as the people fully purified their hearts, over 365 years.[85] It takes 365 days for the earth to circle the Sun and the Lord himself associates His majesty with the movement of the planets and stars in the Heavens.[86] So, this number might be symbolic of celestial rotations, and literal in that the turning of the Heavens are meant to remind us that it takes time to become like Christ.

Some debate whether these years were lunar or solar.[87] But a focus on the technical workings of the stars alone will not bring us any closer to Heaven than wishing on a star. We unlock Heaven here on earth as we soften, then purify, then knit our hearts together as one.

Christ's compassion and truth unite things that otherwise naturally rage against each other. He creates oneness despite dichotomy, as warring elements are "reconciled to God"[88] and made one in Christ.[89] His power unifies hearts and minds, bodies and spirits, men and women, individuals and communities, Heaven and earth, like aligning us as threads of color in a tapestry of salvation and glory.

The need for this "process of time" to achieve oneness in heart and mind—and to fully enter Heaven—is consistent with what the Prophet Joseph Smith and others have declared about the city of Enoch. It took hundreds of years before it was fully translated from a terrestrial to celestial state, when the residue finally declared, "Zion is fled" as if claiming victory over Zion, despite their obvious loss.[90]

Time is necessary for us to learn to obey the laws of our Heavenly Parents and subdue the flesh. This life is an opportunity for us to learn to consciously turn time into growth. Arriving at a celestial state in our own hearts until we are wrapped in light and love and caught up to dwell with Him like Enoch and Zion takes time. Joseph Smith declared Zion "is a station to which no man ever arrived in a moment" and only comes as we learn Heaven's laws and obey the same.[91] But it can happen! Zion, like a bud is just waiting for the sun to blossom, and we choose how quickly that occurs by where we look, what we think on, and how we act.

The premortal plan that Christ created spiritually before the world, will not be frustrated. This is true for our role in that plan—if we choose to accept it. Whatever darkness exists in our history, or in our life today, we can still repent and accept as much of our foreordained path as we are willing to receive. We can rise up from the pain around us, re-awaken to who we really are, and be restored to who we are meant to be—through Christ.

ZION ALOFT IN THE HEAVENS

I first learned of Enoch's righteousness and Zion's ascent in Apostle Neil A. Maxwell's fictional story entitled The Enoch Letters. My father asked me what would happen if a few less-than-righteous saints skipped church the Sunday that the city of Enoch finally lifted up into the skies. Imagine those kids—ditching church on Sunday—only to return after their home had vanished. Fortunately, the Lord is forgiving and always inviting. In His tireless grace, He did not forsake His people, or the yearning righteous who had yet to gather to Zion before Enoch raised it skyward. The Lord continued to call to all who would listen. Christ sent angels, "bearing testimony of the Father and Son; and the Holy Ghost fell on many, and they were also caught up by the powers of heaven into Zion."[92] Thus did the Lord gather a harvest of souls unto Himself, of those who believed and obeyed the gospel and worked righteousness."[93]

Enoch's community remained poised between the Heavens and earth as a watchful satellite sending down angelic ministers for at least 365 years. As Zion soared among the clouds, generation after generation, its mere presence invited the righteous and the wicked below to look to Heaven for redemption from the Fall. At that height—ascended in the Heavens—Enoch had a celestial vantage point to see earth below. He counseled with the Lord about his brothers and sisters and their wars, wickedness, and bloodshed.

From Enoch's position, he watched the ongoing battle for the souls of men on both sides of the veil. He mourned with Christ over the Satanic bondage, destruction and waste that ravaged the earth, as Satan held "*a great chain in his hand, and it veiled the whole face of the earth with darkness*; and he looked up and laughed, and his angels rejoiced."[94] Enoch saw the spirit of the earth groan and weep under the weight of wickedness and Satan's enslavement of hearts, deafening of ears, and darkening of eyes. As Satan poisoned men's hearts, men—invited to create Heaven on earth—instead created hell, intoxicated with their own lustful imaginations.[95]

Enoch himself mourned as he watched the Lord weep, and the earth ache and sorrow. Now fully aware of Christ's glory, Enoch asked, "how is it *thou*" and "*the heavens weep, and shed forth their tears as the rain upon the mountains?*"[96] Imagine this exchange. Enoch knew Christ's power and authority over Heaven and earth, His unquestioned role as Creator and Savior, but also knew the Lord as a personal friend and felt the endless reach of His love. In this setting, he witnessed the Lord—the Great Giver—weeping over His creations. I think we would all be painfully amazed at seeing Christ's glory clouded in sorrow.

Christ explained, the wicked of Enoch's day were *the most wicked* among all Christ's creations. They hated their own blood, worshiped Satan, and were destroying Heaven's plan of happiness and exaltation.[97] He sorrowed as His cherished children warred and heartlessly consumed each other when all He desired was that they would love each other and choose to love Him also.

Without love, coexistence is impossible. The strong crush the weak, the wealthy suppress the poor, and we self-consume—hating our own blood. Thus, Christ sorrows when our hearts grow cold and lack tenderness, love, or affection. He sorrows when we refuse to hear His song of creative love and how amazing life can be when we join our hearts together.[98]

The behavior of the wicked of Enoch's day, and throughout history, is a chilling demonstration of an existence without divine light, compassion, and love. Without love, existence becomes a dark, wilting, sorrowing damnation. The only solution was to cleanse the earth with the Flood.[99] At this point in history, we might ask if Lord decided His foreordained plan for His children's joy on this earth had been stopped. We might wonder if God took Zion up in an effort to salvage what He could of His creation—before destroying it. But Christ's plan cannot and will not be frustrated. He himself fills the gap to ensure His redemption is available to all who seek it.

He is the "great I AM" who creates light despite the darkness.[100] No matter how dark our world might be, our Savior has the power to ignite it. He can restore and reveal that which is already created spiritually within us. He can turn any hell into Heaven if we let Him, and invites us to join Him in His work of gathering and lifting up to Zion (through salvation and exaltation). And He invited Enoch to join him as a "Savior on Mount Zion"[101]

After He was raised to Heaven, Enoch wrestled with the awful gap that stands between Heaven and earth. As he contemplated the wickedness of men, he "wept and stretched forth his arms, and *his heart swelled wide as eternity;* and his bowels yearned; and all eternity shook."[102] God continued to refine Enoch's heart, breaking and stretching it even after raising him to Heaven. He turned Enoch's creative seat—his heart—into a creative throne.

Enoch watched for his great-grandson Noah and his wife Naamah who were about to face the cleansing power of the Flood designed to swallow the wicked.[103] As Enoch saw the first rains descend, he wept over his brethren, and in bitterness of soul He refused to be comforted—even by the Heavens—until the Lord invited him to lift up his heart. Christ pointed Enoch to the salvation that would come in the "day of the Lord," when Christ would descend to the earth, and save the world.[104]

To symbolize this promised salvation, Christ gave Enoch a heavenly sign. It was a sign that the Flood was not the end of Noah or of the earth. A sign that Christ would continue to point others to Zion above, and raise them to the Heavens as they purified themselves in His truths and love. That sign of divine purpose was the rainbow.[105]

RAINBOWS, GOD'S COVENANT SYMBOL FOR ZION

We often associate the rainbow with Noah, but Christ first placed the rainbow in the Heavens as a covenant with Enoch, a promise that the Lord would preserve the remnant and that He Himself would descend to earth as an eternal sacrifice to atone for our sins.[106] What a perfect symbol for the promise of Zion! Rainbows display the full spectrum of light we can see on this earth. They represent oneness and diversity in a unified yet individual array of colors. Just like the individual colors by themselves are not a rainbow, we need each other to be our true colors.

The rainbow stands to this day as a symbol of love, forgiveness, covenants, unity and integrity. It reminds us of the promised return of the city of Enoch, as Zion. My eight-year-old son once commented, upon seeing a rainbow, that he felt when he saw rainbows that it was

Image 2 *Chinese Temple of Heaven*

as if Christ was peeling back a small corner of the veil to show the beauty that awaits us in Heaven.

Is it any wonder the Irish have a tradition that a pot of gold resides at the end of a rainbow, suggesting that if you get close to the rainbow, it will bring you magical wealth? There is no greater magic or wealth than finding eternal life in Jesus Christ.[107]

God set this ribbon of light—His rainbow—in the Heavens as a reminder of His invitation for us to rise and join Him. Rainbows arch as bridges from earth to Heaven then back to earth as if showing us Heaven is within reach as we follow God's path. What's even more remarkable is that from above, rainbows appear as a circle, reinforcing this symbol of how Christ helps us descend from above, gain experience, and rise back to the Heavens in "one eternal round."[108]

This rainbow is a symbol from Heaven itself. Our Heavenly Parents sit on a glorious rainbow throne.[109] They radiate with "everlasting burnings" behind circling gates of fire.[110] From the light that burns, celestial rainbows emanate to reveal God's presence, a heavenly invitation to unite all in Zion. This also symbolizes how in Zion, our unique talents and gifts radiate separately *and* jointly, like how a rainbow is an arrayed unification of light but also unique colors.[111]

Satan and his forces have corrupted the Lord's ancient symbol of Zion. The world's new "pride symbol" is an incomplete counterfeit, containing only six colors (it omits indigo), not the full seven (violet, indigo, blue, green, yellow, orange, and red).

Satan strives to blind us to the covenants and symbols of Zion. He works to deceive us that the individuality and unity symbolized by God's rainbow justifies embracing independence in individuality *without* responsibility to others. Many of our brothers and sisters have picked up this counterfeit of the heavenly banner to champion individuality and freedom. Those virtues are powerful and essential to Zion. And, in addition to these truths, the true rainbow reminds us that obedience to the laws of Heaven is necessary to achieve physical and spiritual harmony.

My heart breaks for all of us who struggle with appetites of the flesh. We all yearn for the completeness we felt in Heaven before coming to earth. At times, it may seem that sensual pleasure will fill the aching we have in our hearts for the peace, light and joy of home above. But lasting peace and joy only come as we surrender and channel our appetites to Christ—to create with Him.

In our fallen state, it is natural for us to feel defined by our experiences and our feelings. But the temporary life we live here below cannot erase the eons we spent in Heaven nurtured by Heavenly Parents. We are not defined by our experiences or our yearnings, and as children of the divine, we always remain free to choose what we do with them.

Our Heavenly Parents are working to redeem each of us from our fallen state. We need everyone—especially those who are struggling through the darkness of sexual pain, abuse, or appetite that threaten to define them. Each of us yearns to be our *true selves*, full of light, love, *and* truth. Regardless of the form of our earthly stains, as we awaken in Christ, cleanse ourselves in His atoning sacrifice, and put off the lies of the world, each of us can rise to Heaven wrapped in God's rainbow of light.[112]

In my experience, it is often the attacked that have the most to offer to the kingdom. Heaven cheers for the underdogs and Satan is terrified by them: Enoch against the Giants, Moses against all of mighty Pharaoh and Egypt, David against Goliath, Elijah against the Ammonites, the faithful two thousand stripling warriors against the massive army of Lamanites. Satan, knowing us from before, sees the noble and great ones who were prepared to create Zion and rallies his attacks against them. Little does he realize, his war against those underdogs gives them power to rise up as conquerors in Christ, like eagles rising on the wind.

Anciently, and into eternity, full *seven* colored rainbows in the skies—caused by light radiating through cleansing rain—have been and will *always* be a symbol of Zion. They remind us of God's invitation to be cleansed in Christ's Atonement and rise home, bridging the gap as Heaven and earth achieving oneness in Zion. To this day, the rainbow stands as a bridge of light between Heaven and earth, reminding those who seek Zion below of our foreordained destiny to rise back to the Heavens from the Fall cleansed, healed, and whole in Christ.[113]

This covenant was particularly fitting given the destructive cleanse of the Flood.

RAIN, A GIFT FROM HEAVEN

Several scriptures suggest before the Flood, mists, not rain watered the earth.[114] This may explain why although rainbows in the mist might be common, the appearance of a full rainbow in the Heavens would be miraculous. It also explains why those with hard hearts disbelieved Noah's prophecies and scoffed at the need for a boat.

Good symbols have almost endless layers. Water is the perfect symbol of fluid unity and is used throughout the Lord's interactions with men to point their hearts and eyes heavenward. From faithful farmers and fishermen, to the forgetful and fearful, here are just a few examples:

Rain is a restoration cycle. Rain falls from the Heavens to earth, is gathered to the oceans with other water, and rises to Heaven again by the light of the sun, a symbol of how we fall from Heaven, and, as we gather, rise again to the Heavens by the light of the Son. Water then returns again as a gift from Heaven—pure, cleansing, life-giving—just as angels descend from Heaven and minister, seeking those yet to rise.[115] Isaiah also compares God's words to rain that does not return empty but blesses and makes the earth bud up with life and bounty.[116]

Water gives life and rebirth. As Christ taught Nicodemus, water is life. We are born of it in the womb. When we are baptized in water, we descend into a watery grave and born again from the water unto Christ.[117]

Water is a symbol of the Godhead. Molecularly, water is symbolic of the Father, Son and Holy Ghost. It is two hydrogen atoms and one oxygen atom. These individual atoms, each unique can be fluid and forceful when united as one.

Tears are symbols of compassion. Our own water in the form of tears is a sign of love, yearning, and emotion. We cry when moved emotionally. Enoch witnessed Christ's love for us: "the God of Heaven looked upon the residue of the people, and he wept, and Enoch bore record of it, saying: How is it that the heavens weep, and shed forth their tears as the rain upon the mountains?"[118] Tears are evidence of yearning love, as shown by an unnamed woman who washed Christ's feet with her tears to be forgiven of her many sins, which tradition suggests she had collected in a tear bottle to mourn the death of someone she loved, as if mourning the death of her old self to find her true self in Christ.[119]

Christ conquers the waters. Christ's children are often confronted with the obstacle of water as a test to finding Him or His promised land. The Brother of Jared crossed the "great deep" in his barges; Moses divided the waters[120] and walked on dry ground—surrounded by water on the right hand, and on the left. Likewise, Christ walked on and called Peter out onto the water.[121]

Christ is the Living Water. Water flowed out of the Tree of Life in the Garden of Eden;[122] by Moses, Christ caused water to gush from stone for the Israelites when they thirsted;[123] Christ turned water into wine as his first miracle;[124] and Christ offered the woman at the well living water of truth, to never thirst again.[125] We are promised crystal clear water will issue from Christ's throne Temple in Jerusalem and heal the Dead Sea with Christ's Second Coming.[126] All these symbolize Christ as the Living Waters that nourished the Garden of Eden and will nourish future gardens in Zion, with water that will purify, heal, and bring eternal life.

In addition to the multi-layered symbolism of water noted above, the Flood came with a new and everlasting covenant that Christ Himself would restore the earth to its foreordained glory and deliver it from the filthiness and weariness caused by the wickedness of men.

THE TOWER OF BABEL

Noah's three sons, Shem, Japheth, and Ham, flourished after the Flood, founding cities and nations including Ham's founding of Egypt. Shem's descendant Nimrod—the king of the residue—eventually founded the kingdom of Babel, later known as Babylon.[127] At that time, all spoke the same language and united to "build a city and a tower, whose top may reach unto heaven."[128] Seeing the city of Babel and men's wicked plans, the Lord confounded their language and scattered the people, causing them to babble.[129]

Some believe the common language was confounded not simply because they were wicked but because they refused to spread out and raise seed. Rather than multiplying and replenishing the earth as they had covenanted to do before coming to earth, and like Adam and Eve were commanded, they choose to cling to the landing site of Noah's ark. Thus, the Lord confounded their speech to "scatter them abroad" and disperse the wicked city.[130]

I wonder if Satan invented cities. Cain is recorded as the first city builder.[131] And cities often become a mass of disconnected humans, where people are more concerned with themselves than their neighbors. On the contrary, *communities*—like Zion—even if referred to as a city—obey higher law, speak truth, reinforce righteousness with compassion, and support their neighbors as themselves. These communities thrive, while heartless cities decay.

I saw this during my mission in Bucharești, Romania. The name, "Bucharești" means "city of joy." At one time it was a city of joy and faith, but communism robbed Romania of its soul. The most common saying when I was in Bucharești was "ce sa fac?" or "what can I do?" It was their way of expressing they had given up, as if communism had crushed any notion of choice and responsibility.

I remember walking the streets of Bucharești one evening and feeling their hopeless defeat. The massive Communist "house of the people"—the largest building in the world built by communist dictator Ceaușescu—loomed in the distance like a grotesque modern Tower of Babel. A man brazenly reached out to try to molest a woman on the street. She flinched and fled. He laughed unafraid of consequence. For many, the *city of joy* had decayed into a *city of terror.*

Like in Bucharești, in downtown areas throughout the United States, cold concrete threatens to interrupt the warmth of human connection. This disconnected congestion echoes of Isaiah's woeful warning against those in the last days that "join house to house . . . till *there be* no place, that they may be placed alone in the midst of the earth!"[132]

This tendency to decay is particularly true of big cities like New York City, Chicago, Los Angeles, and capital cities in otherwise more rural states like Denver in Colorado. While they have wonderful people, the size creates a sense of disconnection, a lack of responsibility from the neighbors. Psychologists refer to this as the bystander effect: someone's belief that they are not responsible because someone else will take care of a child being abused, help the wounded beggar on the corner, or care for the intoxicated.

I saw this in Denver, as a child. In the 1980s and 1990s, Denver was revered as a beautiful city with kind people. I visited in 2018, about a year after marijuana had been legalized, and found the downtown city in rotting decay and apathy. I stayed in a gorgeous, restored hotel with marbled, historic styles. I walked into the public restroom available in the hotel and found it destroyed. Stall doors were off the hinges, feces and human waste were smeared all over the floor and walls, and toilet paper was everywhere.

To my shock, everyone acted like it was normal—surrendered to the "legalization" of recreational marijuana use. When I asked about the mess, a hotel employee responded with a wince, a shrug, and one word: marijuana. I grabbed lunch at a café down the street and overheard two students talking about how they were trying to write a research paper about the ill effects of marijuana and couldn't find any scholastic evidence that it was detrimental. They were blind to their own hell. Denver is not alone.

The Lord declares, man's ways are not my ways.[133] Wicked men's act of declaring marijuana "legal" recreation did not make the drug of distraction "good." On the contrary, it endorsed the destructive distraction of drugging oneself rather than living with purpose. Legalization of sin furthered Satan's lie that choice is individual—and has no societal effect.

In downtown cities across the United States, many are lost in a daze, soil the streets, self-medicate sorrows with nicotine, alcohol, marijuana, and sex, and waste and wear their souls away without purpose. These wicked thorns infest even beautiful cities like Salt Lake City.

I visited Salt Lake months before coronavirus caused a global pandemic. Even this glorious city in the mountains has seen its share of human apathy and abuse that comes when people choose to act more like animals than divine children of God, and become lost in their own ways. The key to community is sharing compassion for those suffering with the death of the Fall but inviting them to find peace, light, and connection in Christ's ways and truths.

His principles of peace, community, and Zion were true before the Flood, and they were still true after the cleanse of the Flood. It was not long before wicked men chose to follow their own crooked paths. Rather than seeking the Lord's path, these souls sought to build their own. Thus the Tower of Babel, a counterfeit temple raised to Satan, was designed and built to further corrupt and control the souls of men.

Historians Lee Donaldson, V. Dan Rogers, and David Rolph Seely add color to this theory that the Tower was a counterfeit temple.[134] They note it was built by Nimrod as a pagan temple, designed to control and sacrifice others, with the false path of building a tower after man's design to contact Heaven. Among the Jews, Nimrod's name has always been a "symbol of rebellion against God and of usurped authority," for he "established false priesthood and false kingship in the earth in imitation of God's rule and 'made all men to sin.'"[135]

Joseph Smith shed the most profound light on the true purpose of the tower. He is recorded as teaching that Nimrod built the tower of Babel to get to *Zion* after the city of Enoch was lifted up in the air and remained there as it was translated. In other words, the Tower of Babel was man's effort to reach the city of Enoch. Likely sensing the electricity that fills the air when a prophet speaks, George Laub captured Joseph Smith's words in hurried shorthand, hereafter edited:

> Now I will tell the story of the designs of building the Tower of Babel. It was designed to go to the city of Enoch, for the veil was not yet so great that it hid it from their sight. So, they concluded to go to the city of Enoch, for God gave him place above the impure air, for above he could breathe a pure air. And Enoch and his city were taken up, for God provided a better place for them. For they were pure in heart.[136]

Seeing others translated to the kingdom of Zion above, Nimrod sought to build his own way to Heaven. He coveted the wealth and light of Enoch's people. He rallied the wicked residue to build their tower to reach the glory of Zion in the skies.

According to the apocryphal book of Jasher, Nimrod's mission became more important than his people, and the bricks he baked to build the tower of Babel more precious than human souls. If a brick fell and broke, "all would weep over it." But if while struggling up the tower a man fell to his death, he was treated as nothing and "none of them would look at him."[137] Imagine this! The people were so caught up in their work that lifeless stone became more precious than a living soul.

By persuading others to build him up with the Tower, and treat bricks as more important that people, the Tower appears as the first literal pyramid scheme, founded on selfishness and defiance, built by placing the poor beneath to raise the few up in pride. Inspired by the Satan's desire to compel and control, Nimrod attempted to counterfeit the principle of celestial elevation—by manipulation rather than obedience to God.

Orson F. Whitney reinforced this truth when he revealed that the Tower of Babel was built to get to the city of Zion suspended in the air, while it patiently pursued the work of its translation through the process of time:

> It has been taught that it was the object of the people who built the Tower of Babel to reach heaven, to attain to one of the starry planets, one of the heavenly bodies. This sounds, indeed, like a fairy tale . . . that they could actually reach the sun, moon, or one of the stars, simply by piling brick upon brick and stone upon stone. But the Prophet Joseph Smith, whose mission it was to shed light upon the darkness of this generation, is said to have declared that *it was not their intention to reach heaven, but to reach Zion, which was then suspended in mid-air, between heaven and earth,* or at such a height as to render the project feasible. This certainly is more reasonable.[138]

The world has not changed its twisted motive or approach since the time of the Tower of Babel. It continues to defy the Lord's fore-ordained path and seeks peace and comfort through the arm of flesh by building towers and great and spacious buildings. Even today the disciples of Babylon push others down in an attempt to elevate themselves in the eyes of others. Fueled by fear and pride, they attempt to reach Heaven on their own terms. Zion is not reached with the arm of flesh; it is reached by the pure in heart who follow Christ's steps up to Heaven.

Ponder on the permanence of this sight. The city of Enoch, Zion, brilliant and glorious, floated above the earth for around 365 years.[139] It stood "with a large piece of earth immediately connected with the foundations and the city . . . [in] an aerial position with the limits of our solar system," as a fixed reminder of earth's destiny to rise from its fallen state.[140] It also stood as a heavenly symbol of God's power over the elements, and the truth that man was made for more than his fallen and lowly state.

Zion was our original manifest destiny. It was a physical calling to rise up from the Fall. Is it any wonder that steeples point heavenward? Or that we—all of mankind—subconsciously believe that holiness is high up, lofty, above us? And that hell is beneath us? Or that the prophets hereafter refer to Christ as the God of the Most High, Lord of Heaven and earth?

This island of majesty stood out in the Heavens and in the traditions of men. In time it became distorted as a thing of legend. Like a pot of gold at the end of a rainbow, guarded by leprechauns that vanish when you approach or the floating kingdom in Jack and the Beanstalk with a golden goose guarded by giants, (reminiscent of the giants that walked the earth in Enoch's day) only accessible with magic beans and a beanstalk. But these legends remove the creator from the story.

The city of Enoch was undeniable proof that God *was* God—the master architect and designer of our earthly experience. Not only did Zion inspire Nimrod's wicked designs to assail it with unrighteousness, it also inspired the righteous remnant for thousands of years in hope of a better world. After Zion first ascended, the remnant began to gather the righteous wherever they could find them, calling to their brothers and sisters to hear Christ, be reawakened in Him, and rise and radiate. Even now the Lord invites all to "arise and shine forth"—*together*.[141]

THE BROTHER OF JARED

One prophet who sought this pathway to Heaven was Mahonri Moriancumer, known as the brother of Jared.[142] There were a few righteous remnant souls living nearby as the Babylonians built their tower to reach the "crystallized heavens" of the "city of Enoch caught up a little ways from the earth . . . within the first sphere above the earth."[143] Mahonri and his brother, Jared, led those righteous few, and sought blessings from the Lord to protect their families and friends from God's curses.

It would be reasonable to conclude that Enoch's descendants, Mahonri and Jared, had special faith in and ties to the Prophets Noah, as well as Enoch, and his father Jared. John Taylor taught they believed in Zion and looked to the Heavens, and at times rose up:

> The principle of translation was a principle that at that time existed in the Church, and is one of the principles of the gospel, and which will exist in the last days. Many of these that were left, continued to bear testimony to the truths taught by their

> predecessors; and they themselves were caught up from time to time.[144]

Jared and Mahonri saw the Lord was about to curse the people of Babel, and they pled with Christ to preserve their speech. Mahonri then asked the Lord to preserve the speech of his friends. Their willingness to seek the Lord preserved their ability to speak Adam's language. They then asked if the Lord would *carry* them forth "to a land choice *above* all others."[145] If the Babylonians saw Zion floating above the earth, it is easy to conclude that Jared and Mahonri hoped the Lord would carry them up to Zion above.

As the righteous remnant of Noah's seed, the Lord *did* carry them, not directly through the skies to Enoch's Zion above, but across the ocean, to Ancient America.[146] This land was a middle step on their path home, a place choice above the earth. Christ promised if they remained faithful, they would eventually be "*lifted up* to dwell in the kingdom prepared . . . from the foundation of the world."[147]

As they left the Tower of Babel, Jared and Mahonri brought many seeds with them and kept birds, fish, bees, and flocks.[148] Their method of life was very different from Nimrod the "mighty hunter," who rebelled against the Lord and used violence and murder to force his followers, consuming, conquering, and reaping where they did not sow.[149] They lived in harmony with the earth, sustaining, growing, and creating.

Although we have only a portion of the record of Mahonri and his people, there are evidences that many other visions, appearances of Christ, and more translations occurred. Through the generations, Mahonri and Jared's people—the Jaredites—went through cycles of righteousness and at times readopted the works of darkness brought with them from the Tower of Babel, treating others as objects.

This cycle of wars and destruction perpetuated, even as the last prophet of the Jaredites, Ether, attempted to reawaken the people to their potential translation as Zion. He saw and yearned for the days of Christ in vision.[150] And he prophesied that a New Jerusalem would return to America *from above*—heralding the return of Enoch's people—and Zion.[151]

Joseph Smith also noted that "the city of Enoch would again take its place in the *identical* spot from which it had been detached, now forming that chasm of the earth, filled with water, called the Gulf of Mexico."[152] He declared that "the people, and the city, and the foundations of the earth on which it stood, had partaken of so much of the immortal elements, bestowed upon them by God through the teachings of Enoch, that it became *philosophically impossible* for them to remain any longer on the earth."[153]

There is a crater known as the "Chicxulub Crater" in the Gulf of Mexico that could match Joseph Smith's vision and prophecy. It has rings stretching over 110 miles wide, and has been widely theorized by scientists to be the impact site of the meteor that caused an extermination level impact and wiped out the dinosaurs.[154]

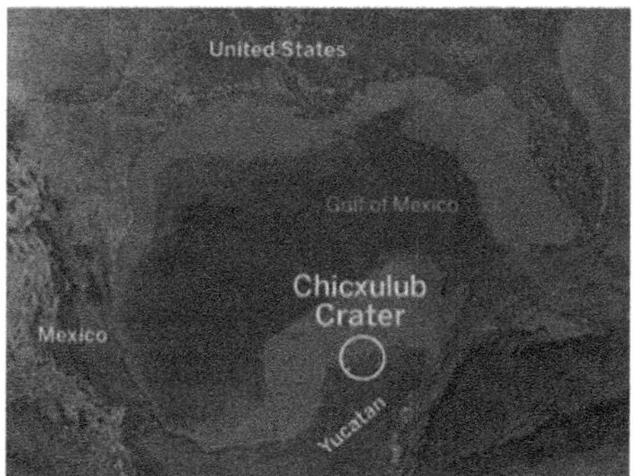

Image 3 Map of the Chicxulub Crater in the Gulf of Mexico
110 Miles Wide—No evidence of Meteor Impact

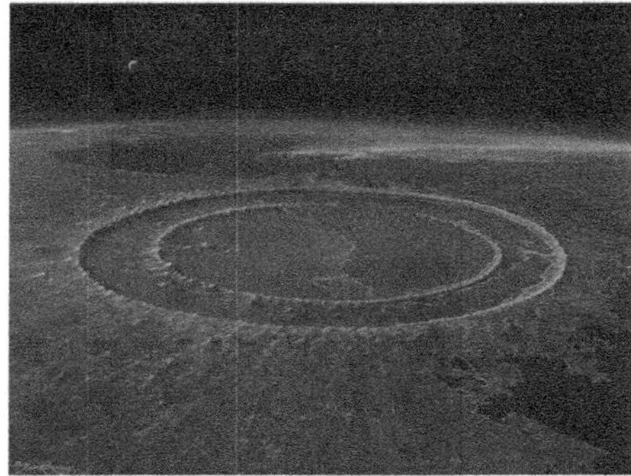

Image 4 Chicxulub Crater in the Gulf of Mexico
Courtesy of the National Academy of Sciences: "News Feature: Life after the asteroid apocalypse, National Academy of Sciences,"available at https://www.pnas.org/content/115/23/5820

Many scientists dispute this theory. There is no evidence of a meteor at the center, not even trace amounts of iridium which is common in meteoric impact sites.[155] This suggests the hole could be the site of something else, like an earthly gap left behind after Zion's foundation rising from the ocean to the Heavens.

Regardless of whether the Chicxulub Crater is the rising point of the city of Enoch, Joseph Smith's statement that Zion will return from above to the Gulf of Mexico gives us a sense of the sheer size of Enoch's celestial home floating in the skies. The impression of Zion hovering above and the reality of translation had such a significant impact on Jaredite teachings, that the last words of their final prophet were, "Whether the Lord *will that I be translated*, or that I suffer the will of the Lord in the flesh, it mattereth not, if it so be that I am saved in the kingdom of God. Amen."[156]

The kingdom of God that Ether trusted in, sought, and hoped for, either through translation or death, was Zion above. When I look at the scriptures through this lens—seeing Zion above as the next destination of the righteous—I can see the call to Zion woven throughout all ancient scripture. It is the destination hoped for by the righteous and the glorious end of the earth—the shared vision of the Lord's servants—our communal purpose. It has been so for thousands of years since Enoch and the Lord's people first rose to the Heavens above.

CHAPTER 2 ENDNOTES

1 Seven is symbolically significant. In numerology and Jewish tradition "seven" stands for completion or perfection and is referred to as the number that holds the universe together. The symbols appear throughout the book of Enoch and throughout the world. There are seven days in the week, seven colors in the rainbow, seven continents, and seven other planets in our solar system, and seven major, unique notes before an octave. Similarly, the number 7 itself is a right angle, or evidence of the symbol of a corner of a square of earth rising.

2 Jacob 4:14.

3 D&C 91:1–5.

4 *The Book of Enoch*, R.H. Charles, p. 92 LXX. *The Final Translation of Enoch* LXX I.-3 (1921). As for the name Enoch, curiously, it appears Lucifer, the great mimicker, ensured Cain named a son "Enoch," which is the only other reference to the name Enoch in the Old Testament (Gen. 4:17). Likewise, although Enoch wrote a "celebrated book" ancient records note "his wonders may not be told in this place" providing one reason why his name and acts would be lost." *Book of Adam and Eve* CHAP. XXII v. 2, *The Book of the Secrets of Enoch*, XXII v. 1; *The Forgotten Books of Eden*, Rutherford H. Platt Jr., 1926.

5 The word "Zion" appears 153 times in the Old Testament, 42 times in the Book of Mormon, and 216 times in the Doctrine and Covenants and Pearl of Great Price. Zion is referenced as "Sion" *three* times in the Old Testament and *seven* times in the New Testament whispering of the symbolism of the number three and number seven: the Epistle Dedicatory; Psalm 65:1; Deuteronomy 4:48; New Testament references to Sion: John 12:15; Romans 9:33; Hebrews 12:22; Matthew 21:5; Romans 11:26; Revelation 14:1; and 1 Peter 2:6.

6 Longman, Tremper; Enns, Peter, *Dictionary of the Old Testament: Wisdom, Poetry & Writings: A Compendium of Contemporary Biblical Scholarship* (InterVarsity Press: 2008), p. 936.

7 *Teachings of the Prophet Joseph Smith* p. 186 (emphasis added).

8 *Teachings of the Prophet Joseph Smith* p. 514–515.

9 *The Forgotten Books of Eden, the Testament of Benjamin*, CHAP. II, v. 16–20, Rutherford H. Platt Jr., 1926.

10 Henry B. Eyring, "Our Hearts Knit as One," October 2008 general conference.

11 D&C 38:27.

12 Genesis 5:24.

13 Alma 5:7.

14 1 Cor. 13:12; D&C 76:94.

15 Moses 6:15.

16 Moses 6:31.

17 D&C 107:48.

18 Moses 6:21 and 6:41.

19 Moses 6:23.

20 D&C 107:56–57. According to Joseph Smith, *Adam-ondi-Ahman* in Adam and Eve's original language (Adamic) means "The Valley of God where Adam Dwelt" and has be prophesied as the location where Adam will return all the priesthood keys to Christ upon His triumphant return and reign. Joseph Smith taught it is in Jackson County Missouri (D&C 116). *See* Journal of Discourses 18:343. *See also* Journal of Discourses 16:47, OP The valley of *Adam-ondi-Ahman* in Missouri is the place where Adam shall come to visit his people, or the Ancient of Days shall sit, as spoken of by Daniel the prophet"; *see also* D&C 116.

21 D&C 107:55.

22 D&C 107:48.

23 *The Book of the Secrets of Enoch*, XXII v. 1; *The First Book of Adam and Eve*, CHAP. VIII, in *The Forgotten Books of Eden*, Rutherford H. Platt Jr., 1926.

24 Orson Pratt, in *Journal of Discourses* 16:47; citing Isaiah 11:9.

25 John 17:3.

26 Moses 6:23.

27 Moses 6:26.

28 Moses 6:28.

29 Moses 6:15.

30 Moses 6:28–29.

31 Book of Jasher 2:20; 2 Samuel 1:18; Joshua 10:13 which refer to the book of Jasher.

32 D&C 88:6—*See also* Quran 24:35: "God is the Light of the heavens and the earth."

33 Moses 6:31.

34 1 Kings 19:12.

35 Moses 6:32.

36 Moses 6:35.

37 Moses 6:36.

38 Moses 6:59.

39 D&C 107:49.

40 D&C 93:24; Jacob 4:13.

41 D&C 130:7.

42 *The Book of the Secrets of Enoch*, Chapter 22, v. 1–10, in *The Books of Enoch, Complete Edition* translated by Paul C. Schnieders. *See also* Chapter 21, v. 1–4, pgs. 128–129.

43 *Ibid.* Enoch's ascent to Christ with the assistance of his great grandfather Michael (Adam) and his grandson Gabriel (Noah) is a clear reminder of how the Lord turns the hearts of the fathers to the children and the hearts of the children to the fathers to elevate and illuminate us. Adam and Noah literally helped Enoch rise to Christ and radiate.

44 D&C 93:17 noting Enoch "received all power, both in heaven and on earth, and the glory of the Father was with him, for he dwelt in him."

45 1 Enoch 12:4, 15:11; *The Book of the Secrets of Enoch*, Chapter 22, v. 1–10, in *The Books of Enoch, Complete Edition* translated by Paul C. Schnieders, Chapter 21, v. 10, pgs. 128–129.

46 2 Nephi 32:2.

47 Moses 6:5, 43.
48 Moses 6:36, 47.
49 Moses 6:33.
50 Joshua 24:15.
51 John 17:3.
52 Moses 5:13–15.
53 Moses 6:46.
54 Moses 6:43.
55 1 Samuel 16:7; Alma 18:18.
56 D&C 46:27.
57 Moses 6:37.
58 Compare 3 Nephi 7:17–18.
59 Jacob 4:11–12; 2 Ne: 33:9.
60 Moses 6:59.
61 Moses 6:61. Baptism by water is the first step of this rebirth. We enter the gate of God's kingdom by taking Christ's name upon us in baptism and accepting the gift of the Holy Ghost which enlivens our hearts so we can feel the light of Heaven. This first step is like starting to climb at the base of a mountain that points to Heaven. As we climb and follow Christ skyward, He changes us. Ascending higher, we begin to hear His voice. It pierces us, cleanses our hearts with holy fire, purifies our natures, and fills us with light. As we feel, hear and follow His promptings, we begin to be reborn of His spirit. In time we begin to see the others climbing Mount Zion heavenward. As we serve and love others, we become justified in His kingdom and are quickened by the Spirit. As we progress up Mount Zion and become one in Christ's purpose of loving God and others as ourselves, we become sanctified by Christ's blood. We continue following Him until at last, we meet our Redeemer at the peak where Heaven and earth meet; our very natures having become restored from the Fall, elevated for eternity.
62 D&C 6:2, 11:2, 12:2, 14:2, 33:1; Hebrews 4:12.
63 Moses 7:13.
64 Moses 7:14.
65 Moses 7:17.
66 Moses 7:20; book of Jubilees 4:20.
67 Moses 7:23–24.
68 Moses 7:17–18.
69 Moses 7:21.
70 Matthew 22:38–39.
71 Moses 7:18.
72 Moses 7:21, 23.
73 *Joseph Smith—Discourse,* 12 May 1844, as reported by George Laub, p. 25.
74 Jacob 4:9; This would not be the last time the Lord would lift or move mountains to bless the righteous or bury the wicked, like in 3 Nephi 8:10 where the Lord lifted earth to bury the wicked city of Moronihah.
75 *Journal of Discourses* 17:322, Orson Pratt, "Man is the Offspring of God, Etc." *See also* Orson Pratt, "God is Light, Etc.," in *Journal of Discourses,* 19:280.
76 *Teachings of the Prophet Joseph Smith,* 51, emphasis added.

77 Hebrews 12:22.
78 Joseph Young, "Enoch and His City," p. 10–11, Sen. Salt Lake City Utah, Deseret News Steam Printing Establishment, 1878 at 11.
79 D&C 38:5; note this may be similar to the three parts referred to in D&C 29:36 when a "third part" fell away.
80 Moses 8:22; D&C 38:5.
81 Matt 5:13.
82 Alma 7:19.
83 Moses 6:52–53.
84 Moses 6:25; *see also The Book of Enoch*, R.H. Charles, p. 114 LXXXV:3 (1921) where Enoch himself says his wife's name was Edna.
85 Moses 7:68; The book of Moses gives us timeline clues that reinforce the conclusion that the "process of time" for Zion to fully be taken into Heaven was 365 years. "And Enoch lived sixty-five years, and begat Methuselah" (Moses 8:1); And all the days of Zion, in the days of Enoch, were three hundred and sixty-five years (Moses 7:68); And all the days of Enoch were four hundred and thirty years (Moses 8:1). The math in Moses lines up: 65 years (before Enoch was called as prophet) plus 365 years with Zion equals 430 years—Enoch's known time on the earth (Moses 8:1). As later discussed, the numbers 4 and 3 are also symbols of earth and Heaven.
86 D&C 88:46–47.
87 Much debate has occurred over whether the 365 years were lunar (terrestrial) years or solar (celestial) years. *See* https://www.genealogieonline.nl/en/stamboom-homs/I6000000006376093098.php. It seems men anxious to achieve Zion and the prophetic power of Enoch became more focused on the astronomically technical rather than the spiritual. Their fixation on astronomy "missed the mark," along with the elegant accessibility of Christ's atoning process; receptiveness to His gift is worthiness.
88 Romans 5:10–11; 2 Nephi 33:9.
89 Ephesians 1:10.
90 Moses 7:69.
91 *Teachings of the Prophet Joseph Smith*, 51.
92 Moses 7:25.
93 Brigham Young, in *Journal of Discourses*, Vol.26, p. 215; *see also* Jacob 5, where Christ compares the world to a vineyard, and His people to fruit on trees.
94 Moses 7:26.
95 Moses 8:22.
96 Moses 7:28.
97 Moses 7:32–36.
98 Gratitude is key to hearing the Lord. See D&C 59:21.
99 Moses 7:37–38.
100 Exodus 3:14.
101 Obadiah 1:21.
102 Moses 7:41.
103 Noah married Naamah, per the book of Jasher 5:15.
104 Moses 7:44–45.

105 Joseph Smith Translation, Genesis 9:21.
106 Joseph Smith Translation, Genesis 9:21.
107 John 17:3.
108 1 Nephi 10:19; Alma 7:19–20; Alma 37:12; D&C 3:2; D&C 35:1.
109 Ezekiel 1:28, Revelation 4:3, Revelation 10:1, *see also* 3 Enoch 22:C4 in Odeberg, 3 Enoch part 2, 80; and Old Testament Pseudepigrapha, 1:306 (*as cited in* The Blessings of Abraham, Becoming a Zion People, E. Douglas Clark, p. 76).
110 Isaiah 33:14; *see also* D&C 137:2–3 which describes God and Christ reigning on a "blazing throne" of fire, after passing a gate like unto "circling flames of fire"; *see also* Joseph Smith Journal, January 21, 1836.
111 Joseph Smith Translation, Genesis 9:21–25.
112 *Teachings of the Prophet Joseph Smith,* p. 51.
113 Joseph Smith Translation, Genesis 9:21–25; Genesis 9:16–17; John Taylor, "Object of Gathering, Etc.," *Journal of Discourses* 26:30: "Will Zion be built up? I tell you it will. Will the Zion that Enoch built up, descend? It most assuredly will, and this that we are building up will ascend, and the two will meet and the peoples thereof will fall on each other's necks, an embrace each other." (*citing* Joseph Smith Translation, Gen 9:21–23, D&C 84:98–100; Moses 7:62–64).
114 Genesis 2:5–6; Moses 3:5–6; Abraham 5:5–6.
115 Moses 7:27.
116 Isaiah 55:10–11.
117 John 3:1–21.
118 Moses 7:28, suggests rain may have fallen in the mountains where Enoch and the righteous dwelt, but not in the valleys where the wicked.
119 Luke 7:36–50.
120 Exodus 4:21–22.
121 Matthew 14:25.
122 Genesis 2:8–10.
123 Exodus 17:5–6.
124 John 2:1–11.
125 John 4:4–42.
126 Ezekiel 47:8–9; Revelation 22:1–3.
127 Gen. 10:9–10.
128 Gen. 11:1, 4.
129 Gen. 11:5–9.
130 Genesis 11:8–9.
131 Genesis 4:17.
132 Isaiah 5:8.
133 Isaiah 55:8–9.
134 Josephus, the ancient Jewish historian, also noted that Nimrod had tried to gain power over the people and designed this counterfeit temple to further his control. *See Antiquities of the Jews,* Book 1, Chapter 4, Paragraph 2—original citation: https://www.churchofjesuschrist.org/study/liahona/1998/03/i-have-a-question/the-tower-of-babel?lang=eng.
135 Hugh Nibley, *Lehi in the Desert and The World of the Jaredites,* volume 5

of *The Collected Works of Hugh Nibley* (1980), 156.

136 "Discourse, 12 May 1844, as Reported by George Laub," p. 25, The Joseph Smith Papers, https://www.josephsmithpapers.org/paper-summary/discourse-12-may-1844-as-reported-by-george-laub/4.

137 Jasher 9:28.

138 Orson F. Whitney, *Collected Discourses*, Vol. 1, p. 359.

139 Joseph Young, "Enoch and His City," p. 10–11, Sen. Salt Lake City Utah, Printed at the Deseret News Steam Printing Establishment, 1878.

140 *Ibid.* at 11; compare 3 Nephi 8:10 where the Lord lifted earth to bury the wicked city of Moronihah.

141 D&C 115:5.

142 We know the name of the Brother of Jared by revelation, when Joseph was asked to give a baby boy a name and a blessing and named him "Mahonri Moriancumer. When he had finished the blessing, he laid the child on the bed, and turning . . . said, the name I have given your son is the name of the brother of Jared; the Lord has just shown or revealed it to me." ("The Jaredites," The Juvenile Instructor, 1 May 1892, p 282). *See also* https://www.findagrave.com/memorial/131108/mahonri-moriancumer-cahoon.

143 Orson Pratt, *Meeting of Adam with His Posterity* Journal of Discourses, 16:50a (parenthesis and emphasis added); see also Mosiah 28:17 which notes the Jaredites kept records—yet to be revealed—that contain even more detail about the Tower.

144 Journal of Discourses 26:90b – John Taylor – Hostility of the World, Citing Moses 7:27.

145 Ether 1:33–38.

146 Ether 1:33–42.

147 Ether 4:19.

148 Ether 2:1–3.

149 *See* Adam Clarke, *The Holy Bible* 6 vols. [n.d.], 1:84.

150 Ether 13:4.

151 Ether 13:2–3.

152 Joseph Young, "Enoch and His City," p. 12, Sen. Salt Lake City Utah, Printed at the Deseret News Steam Printing Establishment, 1878.

153 *Ibid.* at p. 11 (emphasis added).

154 *See* https://www.nationalgeographic.com/news/2017/11/dinosaurs-extinction-asteroid-chicxulub-soot-earth-science/ *see also* https://www.esri.com/about/newsroom/arcnews/gis-reveals-basis-for-ancient-settlement-location/.

155 *See* "The Dinosaur Extinction Debate," *The Atlantic*, available at https://www.theatlantic.com/magazine/archive/2018/09/dinosaur-extinction-debate/565769/.
See also Ron Clutz, "Chicxulub asteroid Apocalypse? Not so fast. August Update," rclutz.com, August 17, 2018, https://rclutz.wordpress.com/2018/08/17/chicxulub-asteroid-apocalypse-not-so-fast-august-update/.

156 Ether 15:34.

CHAPTER 3

ALL THE ANCIENTS SOUGHT ZION

"He looked for a city which hath foundations, whose builder and maker is God."
—Hebrews 11:10

SINCE ENOCH'S GLORIOUS ASCENT, GATHERING, RESTORING, AND raising Zion became the governing theme of prophets, priests, and kings.[1] For "all holy men" sought the community reserved by Christ and received unto Him.[2] Zion remained a universal invitation back home to Heaven, a pattern we are all invited to follow to unite our hearts until we are "wrapped in the power and glory of [our] Maker, . . . caught up to dwell with Him."[3]

The Lord invited all men to create the peace of Zion below, first in their hearts, then in their families, then their communities, until they were fit to join Zion above. Christ continues to labor in both this earthly kingdom and His Heavenly kingdom to harvest souls on earth by carrying them up to Zion; His "secret place of the Most High."[4]

The Lord's original invitation through Enoch to rise up to Him as Zion through righteousness and purity of heart was accepted by many. We are taught all "having this faith, coming up unto this order of God, were translated and taken up into heaven."[5] As such, *multiple* portions of this earth have risen up to meet Zion:

> The Lord, who created the earth, certainly controls it. Why try to deny him this power? Moreover, we are taught that *portions of this earth have been taken from it*, such as the city of Enoch, which included the land surface as well as the people.[6]

These multiple portions of earth lifted to Heaven were gatherings of saints, led by prophets and prophetesses, who turned their cities into communities, worthy of Heaven, until they were purified and lifted up to be "reserved unto the Lord."[7] They recognized earth was a place to unite, grow, become like Christ, and to return home together. In other words, Zion is not a city but a *community*.

ZION THROUGH COMMUNAL ASCENT

Ancient Jewish and Christian texts are influenced by the theme of Enoch's communal ascent and "groups or communities raised up to the celestial realm." This "Community Rule" sought to inspire entire communities to help each other on the path of love and purification until raised to the Heavens. Early saints would sing hymns, including a hymn of ascent, to unite the community within "the heavenly temple and its angelic priesthood" and to rise together and obtain "eternal possession" of Heaven.[8]

Throughout religious scripture, a pattern of exaltation (aka being lifted up) emerges.[9] A prophet communes with the Lord on high, returns edified and empowered by priesthood and purpose, prepares a people to enter the presence of the Lord, and takes them back with him to a higher plane. This is what Enoch and Melchizedek did and is the very thing Moses was trying to do. He wanted to lead his people up Mount Sinai to see the face of Christ. Likewise the Lord's prophets and prophetesses are inviting us to rise up, join Christ, and sing the songs of Zion above.

The ancients practiced rising through song. Early saints *sang* the book of Hebrews to purify the singers to enter the presence of the Lord, like a temple endowment. Larsen notes, "in Hebrews, *all of the patriarchs* were seeking to reach [Zion], and Jesus made it possible for all Christians to make it there."[10] In other words, they were seeking their personal and communal return to a place like the "Garden of Eden."[11]

The Dead Sea Scrolls maintained traditions and "tales about heavenly ascents of ancient heroes of the Israelite tradition" with the "angelic priesthood."[12] Specifically, they tell of six "ascents," including those of Enoch, Melchizedek (referred to as an "angelic commander in chief of heavenly armies"), Methuselah, Levi, Noah, and Moses. In my mind, the fact that we do not have these scriptures reinforces the likelihood that these translations occurred. These stories vanished, like Enoch's name.

There are other places throughout the earth that look as if an entire community was lifted to the Heavens, leaving an empty bowl of earth below. One such place is the Richat Structure in the African Sahara of Mauritania. Known as the "Eye of Africa," large rings of earth are visible from space and stretch twenty five miles in diameter, consistent with the size needed for an agricultural community.

The rings do not appear to be made of man or meteor and are treated by the locals as sacred. It lacks any evidence of an asteroid impact and shows human interaction for thousands of years around

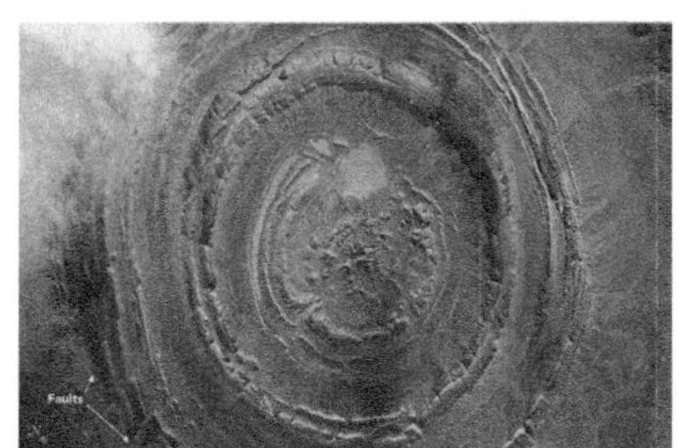

Images 5 and 6

Aerial photographs of the Richat Structure in Mauritania Africa courtesy of NASA

the periphery but not at the center, suggesting it was not a mine. Some have speculated it is evidence of a lost city, like Atlantis (possibly another name for Zion).

Traditions of heavenly ascent consistent with these craters are preserved in Aramaic, Ethiopic, Greek, and Slavonic, as well as Hebrew texts. These texts refer to hymns and songs for Heaven, sung to purify the singers: the Hymn of the Garden, the songs of the Sabbath Sacrifice and songs of the Sage, as well as the Self-Glorification Hymn. The example of Enoch, Melchizedek, Noah, Moses, Levi, Methuselah, and others show that if we live pure in heart, in communal righteousness and unity, we can rise up and join Christ and others in song who have also ascended to Heaven in a translated state.[13]

The Quran maintains the tradition of translation. The prophets Ishmael, Enoch, and Ezekiel were steadfast and so righteous they were admitted into God's mercy.[14] Enoch specifically, was "a man of truth, a prophet . . . *raised to a high position*."[15]

The Book of Mormon also refers to the translations of Alma, who was "*taken up* by the spirit and buried by the hand of the Lord, even as Moses," for "the scriptures sayeth the Lord took Moses unto himself."[16] Alma himself taught that the priesthood of Christ was created from before the foundations of the earth to purify people so they could be lifted up and redeemed from the Fall from Heaven. Like Enoch, he also taught his people to live the laws of love and give liberally "to every needy, naked soul" so that there would be no poor among them.[17] He encouraged his people to be humble like the people of Melchizedek, who because of faith and repentance were restored until an "exceedingly great many . . . were made pure and entered into the rest of the Lord their God."[18]

These records make it clear, *all* ancient patriarchs and matriarchs sought Zion. They taught their people to be harmonious, full of charity, and unified in godliness and to join their gifts together that "all might be edified with all."[19] These righteous men and women not only built Zion but defended its peace as the wicked railed against it. There are many examples of prophets and prophetesses who served as warriors for the Lord and entered the final stage of rising by first descending into the valley of death to climb back to the Heavens on the mountain of life. The following are just a *few* examples of the righteous remnants' communal ascent to Zion above.

MELCHIZEDEK—THE KING OF SALEM

Melchizedek was a priest of El Elyon or "the most high God."[20] He was first known as the "Prince of Salem," the word "Salem" being similar to the Hebrew word shalom or "peace." Salem was considered "the celestial Jerusalem" after it was also raised to the Heavens, like the city of Enoch, by Melchizedek as the "Prince of Shalom" or "Prince of Peace."[21]

Who was Melchizedek? The Hebrew words "*malki tzedik*," together mean "my king righteous," demonstrating the name was a title evidencing a desire to emulate and point all who heard it to Christ.[22] Many believe the first recipient of the title was Shem, the son of Noah and the great-great-grandson of Enoch.[23] This was taught anciently and to the early latter-day saints.[24] Shem's name change to Melchizedek is consistent with new names given other righteous men and women as they became more like God but also reflects how Shem desired to be like Christ because Melchizedek is *Christ's* title.[25] The title of Melchizedek itself highlights Shem's pure focus on Christ, a dedication that became so steady and pure that the emulation eventually replaced Shem's birth name.[26] But Shem's focus wasn't in name only. Shem *became* like Christ as he purified and united the hearts of his people to return the earth around them to the skies.

Similar to how Enoch's name vanished, the Old Testament only faintly references the ancient patriarch Melchizedek. First, when prophesying of a time when "the rod of the strength of Zion" (interpreted as Christ) will rule over all the earth after the order of Melchizedek.[27] Second, when Abram (later Abraham) pays tithing to Melchizedek, who served the "most high God of heaven and earth"—hinting of Zion above.[28] It is not until the book of Hebrews in the New Testament that we hear how the ancients "Melchisedec" and Abraham sought a heavenly city founded by God.[29]

As Noah's son, Shem, would have witnessed Zion's ascent to the heights of Heaven, and seen it hovering there even after the Flood. Thus it is likely that references to "the Most High" are Melchizedek's reverence for Christ's reign from Zion *above*. Melchizedek surely pointed his people to the Heavens above as their communal destination to purify and unify his people's hearts and minds. Rising to Zion was their common and visible goal.

Alma in the Book of Mormon speaks more openly about Melchizedek. He urged his people to study Melchizedek, who was amply taught in Ancient American scriptures. For as Alma notes, "of him they have more particularly made mention" and that of all the *many* others before and after Melchizedek appointed to the "high priesthood . . . none were greater."[30]

High Priests like Melchizedek were foreordained or called to that office before the world began.[31] Melchizedek was foreordained to be a symbol of Christ. He was given the power of prophecy and seership so that "men might look forward" to and rejoice in Christ's coming and redemption. He came, like Enoch, to cry repentance to a people "full of all manner of wickedness," who had "gone astray" from the Lord.[32]

Melchizedek and his people "*sought for the city of Enoch which God had before taken*, separating it from the earth, having reserved it unto the latter days, or the end of the world, [when] *the heavens and the earth should come together*."[33] To reach the Heavens, they honored the laws of the "*high* priesthood" which is "without beginning of days or end of years" and taught them of love, truth, light, and lift.[34]

Just like his forefather Enoch, Melchizedek used this "High Priesthood" or the "Holy Priesthood after the Son of God" to control the elements and the mouths of lions, to conquer armies, break mountains and seas, and defend Zion from wicked attacks.[35] Melchizedek had obtained and honed this power and authority in the premortal realm under the instruction of our Heavenly Parents long before he was born. *All who are given this priesthood* have this heavenly power to further God's work and glory—to bring to pass the immortality and eternal life of man—and bring to pass "the will of the Son of God which was before the foundation of the world."[36]

It is the power by which Christ created the universe, fully capable and empowered to do all things possible to save His children, if we accept His grace. Because of the power of the atoning sacrifice of Christ, agency remains intact through the eternities and God gives us allowance to fulfill or reject our premortal plans here on earth. When life does not proceed as divinely planned, the Lord in His infinite mercy gives His righteous children authority to engage the powers of Heaven to course-correct, to realign the temporal reality with the spiritual foreordination, and to do wonders in His name.

Thus Enoch, Melchizedek, and Abraham were given power, and *any*one ordained after this order will be given celestial and divinely purposed power to wield the elements in defense of Zion.[37] They possess the power to "break mountains, to divide the seas, to dry up waters, to turn them out of their course; to put at defiance the armies of nations, to divide the earth, to break every band, to stand in the presence of God." This power opens the Heavens to descending ministering angels and "lifts up" the prophets and all those who are willing to follow Christ back home until they are "translated and taken up into heaven."[38] In other words, *the priesthood is here to help us develop, improve, enhance, and lift each other, and lift the very earth back to Heaven.*

Even the offices in the priesthood point to Heaven. Why would the priesthood be referred to as "high" (with "high" priests) except to point us skyward? The very names reinforce that the authority comes from the Lord on High—Christ—who reins from Zion in the Heavens *above.*

Melchizedek's prophetic power and use of this priesthood to purify his people to be "lifted up" was commonly referred to in ancient scriptures that we do not have.[39] We only have a fraction of the miracles recorded. I have counted more than one hundred references to additional, lost, or hidden books alluded to in scriptures.[40]

It makes sense there would be many more records than the few we have now. Moses declared, *anyone* who calls upon God and hears His word may write in the book of remembrance, "by the spirit of inspiration."[41] Yet these inspired records have a habit of vanishing after their authors rise to the skies, as if to allow for those who will follow to exercise their own faith. But any interaction with Heaven leaves its elevating mark on the world, even if only symbolically. Melchizedek's name and greatness have inspired murals, art, mosaics, and even modern fiction and fantasy alike.

One of the clearest references to Melchizedek's transformative power is Paulo Coelho's fictional story, *The Alchemist.* Melchizedek appears briefly to the main character, Santiago, and refers to himself as the King of Salem. He possesses a *Urim and Thummim* and can see past, present, and future, hinting of the key concepts repeated throughout *The Alchemist*. Melchizedek's inspirational purpose is to help Santiago pursue his "personal legend," listen to his heart, and find his treasure.

Later, Santiago learns from an alchemist or follower of Melchizedek that "the world is only the visible aspect of God," and that alchemy brings "spiritual perfection into contact with the material plane."[42] An alchemist, a follower of Melchizedek's truth, then helps Santiago learn the language of the soul of the world. On the cusp of this discovery, Santiago testifies that "alchemy exists . . . so that everyone will search for his treasure, find it, and then want to be better than he was in his former life. Lead will play its role until the world has no further need for lead; and then lead will have to turn itself into gold."

The Alchemist has been widely read, printed millions of times, and translated into over fifty-six languages. Perhaps one reason this artistic work has resonated with so many is because it whispers of premortal truth and purpose; "alchemists" remind us of the Lord's prophets and prophetesses; and the truth that we can reach for something higher and become something more.

Like Santiago, we are each pursuing our personal legend, learning to listen to our hearts and commune with the soul of the world, so we can find our treasure and fill the measure of our creation. As we turn to God, hearts of lead become hearts of gold, and men become gods.

These works of art and fiction are inspired by bits of celestial truth—truth buried deep in our spiritual subconscious. Such art reminds us that we are made for celestial gold, not terrestrial brass. They sing of Zion. Even if the world forgets the purpose of priesthood is elevation, our spirits do not. This is why artistic works like *The Alchemist* echo with foreordained purpose and truth, and remind us that "when something evolves, everything around that thing evolves as well."[43] Similarly, when we start to obey one law, we naturally begin to follow more of His laws. Obedience brings light and lift into a cascading array of brilliance and glory that creates Heaven on earth.

This was true for Melchizedek. As he evolved into his true self—a righteous prophet, leader, and king—he assumed powers and even names originally only given to Christ, including the "Prince of Peace." Melchizedek did this by turning outwards, using his gifts to bless all those around him. He built a community of saints as Enoch had done—an entire community of believers. He and his people repented, worked righteousness together, and "*sought for the city of Enoch*" until they themselves "*obtained heaven*" and rose to meet Enoch above.[44]

For his righteousness, Melchizedek was crowned a king of Heaven, reigning under Christ, who is King of kings over all nations and Lord of lords over all religions. In celebration of their own awakening, his people named him "king of heaven" or "King of peace."[45] Like Enoch, Melchizedek would not forget the remnant left below. Enoch had passed the High Priesthood calling onto his great-grandson Noah, who passed this authority onto Shem as Melchizedek. In turn, Melchizedek passed the power to rise up with Christ into the Heavens, through the priesthood of God, on to *Abram* to awaken him as Abraham.

ABRAHAM AND SARAH

Scripture and tradition hold that around the time Melchizedek and ancient Salem rose in bright glory to the Heavens, the Lord called a couple to nourish the remnant souls in the Lord's vineyard. That couple was Abram and Sarai.[46] They eventually had their names changed by Christ to Abraham and Sarah and became the line of Christ, parents of all of Israel, and Zion to come.[47]

Abraham and Sarah described themselves as "followers of righteousness."[48] Following righteousness meant forsaking the wealth and power of the world around them, including the mighty power of Egypt. Rabbinic tradition suggests that in the shadow of Egypt's might, Abraham longed to have "wings like a dove" so he might "fly away and have rest" and join his fathers, in the Heavens.[49] The Islamic Quran also records a prayer by Abraham, yearning for Heaven, asking Christ to join him with the righteous, and "the heirs of the paradise of bliss."[50]

As with the ancient patriarchs before, Abraham and Sarah were called at a time of great wickedness, when the people refused to hear the Lord and hardened their hearts in war, rejecting peace. They were engaging in ritualistic sacrifice of women and children, including three virgins sacrificed after the manner of the Egyptians because they refused to "bow down to worship gods of wood or of stone."[51] Abraham's own father, his heart having failed him, even attempted to sacrifice young Abram on an altar to Egyptian idols.[52]

Historian E. Douglas Clark has compiled an exceptional history of how Abram became Abraham, and his and Sarah's constant pursuit of Zion. He notes that as Abram was on the altar about to be slain by Egyptian priests, the angel of power who rescued him was none other than *Enoch.*[53] Abram's miraculous rescue was part of his journey to know Christ. The journey was as much for Sarah as it was for Abraham and was impossible without her.

Enoch taught Abram and showed him the records of Zion—ancient prophecies, histories, and truths handed down by Adam, Seth, Enoch, and the Lord himself, written in Adamic, the "original language of creation."[54] They were given authority and the power of the word to *soften the hearts* of the people and point them to remembrance of who they were, why they were here, and how they could re-awaken and be restored to their true foreordained potential in Christ.

The name *Abraham* itself means "the father is *high*" or "the father who lifts himself on *high*" while Sarah means "woman of *high* rank" or "princess" in Hebrew and "joy" and "delight" in Arabic. These names referring to height or elevation are fitting as Abraham and Sarah pointed others to Enoch's "high and lifted up" terrestrial kingdom as the next step back home.[55]

Like their forefathers, Abraham and Sarah used the power of the word to call the righteous remnant to the Lord and join Zion. Abraham was shown a vision of the premortal realm and what was to come. He saw how the Lord had organized the spirits and intelligences before the world was, and how Christ had built His great plan of salvation around those that were "good," "noble," and "great" to be guardians of His children below.[56]

Abraham reminds us we were chosen before we were born to arrive on earth *at this time*—to serve, love, and use *our* unique gifts to point people to Christ, creating a vibrant, diverse tapestry of human and family connections to build Zion. We, too, can obtain the promised greatness of God and rise to Enoch's and the Lord's heights, if we so choose. Our willingness to receive in gratitude is a key to our ability to become what God foreordained us to be.

Christ's commandment to be perfect even as He is, is not a chastisement but an invitation. For although we "cannot bear all things now," Christ has reassured us that He will lead us along. He has promised us His kingdom, the blessing thereof, and the "riches of eternity." He assures us that if we "receive *all* things with thankfulness," then "we shall be made glorious." When we choose to see all experiences as gifts, Christ rewards us with "the things of this earth . . . even an hundred fold, *yea more*." Gratitude allows Christ to lead us until we ourselves become the gold of Zion and are lifted "up in a cloud" to Heaven.[57]

This power of elevation through thanksgiving was true for Abraham. He gave thanks in *everything*—the good, the bad, and the

Image 7 *Mosaic. Ravenna. Basilica of Sant'Apollinare in Classe, apse, right side—520 A.D.*

difficult—trusting that the Lord was refining him and would deliver. And Abraham *was* repeatedly delivered. Abraham risked his life and battled an army of kings led by Chedorlaomer in the valley of Shaveh to save brother-in-law Lot. Abraham conquered in the battle and, *miraculously,* not one of his men was lost.[58]

After the victory, Abraham praised the Lord, saying, "Sovereign of all the worlds! Not by the power of my hand, nor by the power of my right hand have I done all these things, but by the power of Thy right hand with which Thou dost shield me in this world and in the world to come." He gave thanks, declaring, "Had Your glory not fought alongside me and aided me, how could one man have prevailed against such an overwhelming force. They fell into my hands only because You helped me."[59]Abraham offered tithing of the spoils to God through Melchizedek, who rejoiced in Abraham's victory over the wicked as if it was his own.[60] After the battle, Melchizedek blessed "bread and wine" as a sacrament for Abraham.[61]

This event was so pivotal for Abraham and the faithful who followed, it is preserved in a mosaic, showing the priest-king Melchizedek in a royal purple cloak offering bread and wine at an altar. The white altar cloth is decorated with Melchizedek's seal—two interlocked squares in gold with a circle in the center. On the left of Melchizedek (signifying the past), Abel offers a lamb. On the right of Melchizedek (signifying the future), Abraham gently offers Isaac in sacrifice—a symbol of how Heavenly Father would sacrifice his Only Begotten Son, Jesus Christ, to redeem us from the Fall.

A vibrant rainbow (the symbol of Zion) rises above them. A heavenly hand (perhaps Enoch's as a ministering angel or the Lord's) is visible through a rainbow arc as if directing Abraham to go to and gather Zion.[62] This mosaic is rich with meaning and highlights how gratitude connects us with Heaven.

Gratitude enabled Abraham and Sarah to create Heaven on earth. They used the wealth of the earth: art, clothing, gardens, gold and silver, food, shelter, and familial love to awaken others in Christ and remind them of why they were here—to grow in experience and return home to our Heavenly Parents. Compassionate messengers, they gathered souls and patiently awaited their own posterity with Jacob.[63]

They cultivated gardens with entrances to the North, South, East and West to welcome travelers from all four-corners of the earth. These gardens served as a symbol of the square, or the earth, with its four corners, or "four quarters" so they could point others to Heaven. After travelers had enjoyed the fruit of the garden, they would thank him. Abraham would exclaim, "Why give me thanks? You should thank He who alone provides food and drink for all creatures." His guests would ask, "Where is He?" and Abraham would look up and answer, "He is the Ruler of heaven and earth," and then teach them of how to give thanks to God above.[64]

They used their time, talents, and energy to feed the hungry, clothe the naked, teach them songs of thanksgiving, and point all men and women—brothers and sisters—homeward to Zion. Gratitude filled their bowels with charity toward all, until the doctrine of the priesthood distilled upon their souls (and the souls they saved) as the dews of Heaven.[65]

Abraham and Sarah understood that Christ's priesthood power is a connecting power, not a controlling power. They treated all with kindness, reminding us we never know if we are engaging with angels in disguise.[66] They lived for the compassionate connection of the doctrine of Christ and His priesthood—lifting others home in truth and love. They also set the stage for an entire nation of people capable of filling the world with hearts that could build Zion.

MOSES AND ISRAEL

Like the former prophets, Moses was called at a time when men's hearts were hard and cold. And like those before him, Moses was mentored by another—his father-in-law Jethro—in the Holy Order of the Melchizedek Priesthood. Moses was called to be "in the similitude"[67] of, or a pointer to Jesus Christ. He gathered and delivered the Lord's people, taught them the law, and worked to purify them to lead them up the mountain Sinai to also see Christ's face.[68]

During his own initial encounter with Christ on Mount Sinai, the Lord opened Moses's eyes that he might see marvelous and wondrous truths. The Lord lifted him up on high and showed Moses the earth and the ends thereof—all the children of men, which are and which were created.[69] Moses saw the past, present, and future, along with all the glory of God, namely our Heavenly Parents' children.[70] This transfiguration was similar to what Enoch and Abraham experienced when they became seers unto the "Most High."[71]

After the "glory of God" withdrew from Moses, Satan came tempting, calling upon him, crying, "son of man, worship me."[72] But having been exposed to truth, Moses could discern between Satan's darkness and God's glory. Moses refused to worship Satan. In turn, the devil ranted, railed, and raged, causing the earth to shake with his fury. Moses at first feared the bitterness of hell emitted by Satan's presence, but he continued to call on Christ until Christ returned to give Moses a promise very similar to that of Enoch's: that he would be "made stronger than many waters."[73]

At first, Moses, like Enoch, feared his inability to speak on behalf of the Lord. However, Moses grew to control the elements with words. Moses spoke to control the forces of nature, defy the wicked with hard hearts, and protect the remnant. Standing uncompromisingly before Pharaoh's mighty power, Moses declared the Lord's foreordained purpose. [74] He used God's priesthood to speak and inflict plagues, desolation, and death, all to deliver the Israelites.

As promised, he was made stronger than many waters and eventually turned the great Nile River to blood.[75] After Pharaoh finally let the Israelites go, Moses's *word* divided the Red Sea so the children of Israel might escape Egypt on dry ground. Like his ancestor, Enoch, Moses used his priesthood authority to realign the temporal reality with the spiritual foreordination, and set the Lord's people free.

Imagine for a moment Moses standing at the edge of the Red Sea, pressed by the throngs of exhausted, hungry, and fearful people behind him. Imagine him looking behind at the pillar of fire separating his people from the Pharaoh and his armies, and then looking back with determination at the impossible barrier of water rippling mercilessly before him, the opposite shoreline invisible from his view.

Amidst that noise, that stress, surrounded by the fear of millions cowering before Pharaoh's armies, it seems Moses heard the Lord whisper to his heart, "*Be not afraid. Speak. Become.*" That spirit of liberation, of power, quiet and still, came to Moses in his heart and mind, providing him with confidence and peace.[76] In the moment

Moses looked at the water and spoke in faith, a miracle occurred "by his word."[77] As he spoke, the waters fled and divided so that the Israelites could walk across the ocean floor on dry ground.[78]

Once the Lord's people were free from the earthly bondage of Egypt, Moses strove to liberate them from the spiritual bondage of "victimhood." The belief that they were victims, and incapable of choosing for themselves. To teach them to act in faith, Christ's light radiated ahead of them as a cloud by day and pillar of fire by night, leading them to the promised land where they could one day rise to Heaven above.[79] During this time, Moses taught them the laws and ordinances of the Lord and prepared them to receive the full blessing of the Melchizedek priesthood, so that they might become prophets themselves, rise up, and see the face of the Lord.

Moses spoke with the Lord "face to face" as a man speaks with his friend.[80] After conversing with the Lord, the same *shekinah* or celestial fire that had lighted the burning bush now burned in and around Moses, and "the skin of his face shone; and [the people] were afraid" to come near to him because he radiated such might and authority.[81] They insisted Moses place a veil over his face to cover the brilliance of God's glory within him.[82] They also insisted Moses remain an intermediary between them and God, terrified that the Lord's presence, face, and glory would destroy them.

This was a unique moment in history. The children of Israel had been saved repeatedly by the hand of the Lord through His prophet, and yet they refused to hear Him, receive Him, or know Him. They refused to awaken and join the Heavens. They preferred to remain fallen, with deaf ears, blind eyes, and fat hearts.[83] Unwilling to accept the restorative and purifying power of Christ's priesthood, the Lord removed Moses—and the power to speak in God's name with the priesthood—from ancient Israel.[84]

But in his mercy, the Lord did not forsake them. He allowed the teachers of thirst, hunger, pain, and consequence to open their minds and to soften their hearts. He did this even though *He* would pay the price himself through the power of His infinite Atonement.

Moses also recognized that all of Israel had the potential to awaken. When the children of Israel refused to seek God on their own and insisted on Moses as their intermediary, Moses lamented,

"Would God that all the Lord's people were prophets, and that the Lord would put his spirit upon them!"[85] He wanted all to feel the power of connecting with and serving God and awakening to their foreordained paths.

Likewise, Moses's path up and down Mount Sinai to meet with the Lord face to face was a path he hoped to model for the Israelites, so that they too could enter Zion and know Christ. But even after Christ led Moses to deliver Israel they remained hard-hearted, were unwilling to unite their hearts as one, and refused to listen to the Lord and receive His healing love. They continued to choose their own paths instead of accepting His path that would lead them back home together as Zion.

In rejecting the ordinances of the gospel, the Israelites rejected godliness, the power to become more like Christ by helping *others* become like Christ. His priesthood unlocks the mysteries of the kingdom and the knowledge of God precisely because it allows us to join hands with the Lord in serving and restoring others, softening their hearts, opening their ears, and awakening their eyes. This power is the power by which we can eventually see the face of God, and live, even if in this life we only see Him in others and recognize Him in ourselves.[86] One group that did this was the Rechabites.

THE RECHABITES RAISED TO THE LORD

Christ foretold of His own rising and His joyful lifting of others "on high" who believe in Him.[87] He explained He has raised up "even as many as have believed in my name" to His bosom in Zion.[88] Personal translation was the exception, not the rule. It was communities that united their hearts that unlocked the power to rise to terrestrial then celestial heights.

Enoch and Melchizedek are the most obvious but not the only examples of communal translation. There are other examples in ancient scripture that suggest multiple Zion*s* have risen from the earth.[89] Traditions suggest Moses and later Alma had communities so united in the laws of love, they were lifted to Heaven. Jeremiah 35 also points to the Rechabites, a people so highly favored of the Lord they were returned to His presence.

The Rechabites had made covenants with God and wandered as shepherds, never planting gardens or building a city, as if seeking the Lord in the stillness of the wilderness. Jeremiah invited some of the Rechabites into the Jerusalem temple at the Lord's command, and told them to partake of wine in the Holy of Holies. They refused, even at the insistence of the prophet, telling Jeremiah their father had made a covenant with God that they would never drink alcohol—and they stood steadfast in that covenant. For their faithfulness, Jeremiah promised them they would be blessed throughout the generations and never want for a man in the presence of the Lord.[90]

The apocryphal record of the "History of the Rechabites" suggests these Rechabites were eventually translated as a community to a higher plane—or a terrestrial state of existence, awaiting the Lord's return to the earth. There they radiate light without thirst, hunger, or pain as their "sight is fixed continuously and unceasingly in the light of the future."[91]

They live in a garden of "pleasant and splendid trees which are filled with lovely, marvelous and abundant fruits" where "sweet and delightful water" flows from the roots. A cloud encircles them "like a bulwark" or covering from the sun suggesting they are above us, and their land is filled with "a glorious light" so darkness and night do not enter it. In this state they possess "a shining appearance and dwell in light."[92] They had been placed on this "holy land" caught up by angels, to the presence of Christ—He being the foundation stone of their home above.[93]

THE CIRCLE AND SQUARE—SYMBOLS OF ZION

The ancients used symbols to share the message of Zion's rising with those seeking it. Symbols were the best way to teach because they transcend the barriers of language and time. So, the message of Zion became universally symbolized with a circle and a square.

The earth was symbolized by a square representative of the number four in ancient scripture with the phrase the "four corners," "four parts" or "four quarters" of the earth.[94] Alternatively, Heaven was symbolized by a circle or "one eternal round"[95], represented by the number three for the Godhead.[96] Isaiah described God as the one "who sits on the circle of the earth" and "spreadeth out the heavens as a curtain."[97] Likewise, the Father and the Son sit on a blazing throne, behind "*circling* flames of fire."[98]

The symbolism takes on a new meaning when Heaven and earth reunite in Christ's restoration. Adding the number three (for Heaven) plus four (for earth) equals seven (the number of completeness and wholeness) In other words, 3 + 4 = 7 (Heaven plus earth equals perfection).

Ancient prophets have used symbols to point to Christ's holy order to unite Heaven and earth. The following symbol is representative of Enoch's purpose and focus—joining Heaven and earth through Zion—and can be interpreted as the Seal of Enoch. It is seen on various temples including throughout the Las Vegas Temple.

This symbol has influenced the world religions for thousands of years. I first learned of this square/circle unity symbol while on a mission in Romania and Moldova. After touring a Romania Orthodox Church in Chișinau, Moldova, I was told by a priest that the Romanian King, Ștefan Cel Mare (meaning Stephen the Great), built the church while defending Romania from invading Muslims. A fierce defender of Christianity, legends tell that he would build a church after each victory and built churches throughout Romania and Moldova. I witnessed many of these churches still standing in the Romanian and Moldovan countryside, despite the Soviet Union's communist-led efforts to destroy Christianity.

The priest explained to me that the churches were intentionally constructed to have a square base, to represent earth with its four corners, and a rotund top, to represent the Heavens as symbolized by a circle. I interpreted this to mean the church now stands as a place where Heaven (square) met earth (circle), demonstrating that Ștefan Cel Mare's battle victories were a gift from heavenly help. These churches remain a symbolic reminder, pointing to the seal of Melchizedekian purpose. This presence of symbols of Zion in Orthodox symbolism reinforces the idea that whispers of Zion echo in all Abrahamic religions—even if suppressed or largely forgotten.[99]

Image 8 *Seal of Enoch*

Similarly, China still has an ancient structure called "The Temple of Heaven," with three circles, in three circles, in a square, where the Emperor (as the "Son of Heaven") would enter the outer square to perform a "border sacrifice" at the border between Heaven and earth. He would progress to the center temple, from the outer square, to the inner circles. To prepare himself to enter Heaven to plead for his people, he would disrobe, be washed, anointed, and then clothed in new robes to enter the three inner circles and then the three circle temple at the center. The "circle altar," the "Fasting Palace," and the "Divine Music Administration" still stand, and circles and squares are everywhere. These symbolic similarities to other religions' processes to commune with Heaven suggest Enoch's ascent to Heaven influenced Chinese beliefs as well.[100]

Melchizedek appears to have designed his own seal incorporating Enoch's, to point to the time when the earth and Heavens will reunite. His seal is made with a circle inside a square and a second square, as depicted in **Image 8** and as shown below in **Image 9**. Melchizedek's symbol can be interpreted as his own earthly Zion rising to join Enoch's Zion above in the Heavens.

As the son of Noah, and as someone who was alive at the building of the Tower of Babel, Melchizedek would have seen Enoch's Zion floating in the Heavens above. The potential of joining Zion in the skies would have been obvious. It is easy to conclude Melchizedek's seal was a symbol of how he was actively seeking to build a Zion below

Image 9 *Seal of Melchizedek*

to join Enoch's Zion and Christ in Heaven above. It also explains why his seal is not just one square around a circle, but two squares interlocking around the eternal circle of Heaven.

Some debate whether the symbol is actually Melchizedek's.[101] Regardless of whether it was a symbol of Melchizedek's own making or later used to symbolize him and his own rising to the Heavens, the two squares surrounding a circle have rich religious symbolism. The symbol answers questions about the scriptures regular use of the phrase "the heavens and the earth" throughout the Old Testament. Why multiple Heaven*s*? Were Isaiah and Jeremiah speaking of the Heaven of Enoch and the Heaven of Melchizedek joined in celestial unity with the Heaven of our Parents above?

The Dead Sea Scrolls may also point to the seal of Melchizedek. The archangel Michael describes a heavenly vision of degrees of fire like the degrees of Heaven. From above, he sees nine mountain peaks: two to the north, two to the south, two to the east, two to the west, and one in the middle. The vision also describes a "city built to the name of my master" that can view "everything done" as if witnessing earth from the sky.[102]

From this skyward position, the description of nine mountains could represent Melchizedek's symbol if each corner of the seal were a

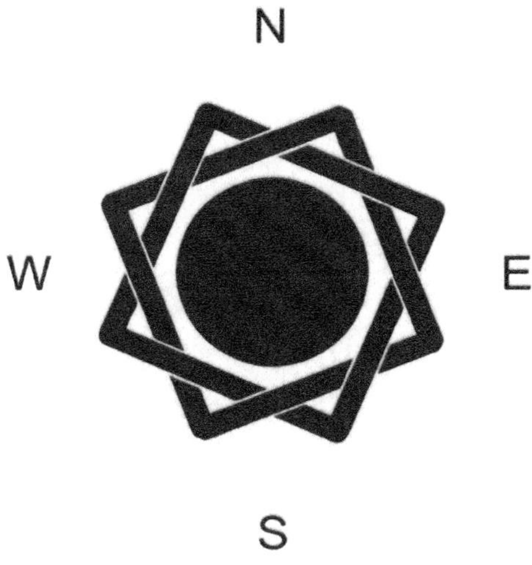

Image 10 *Possible Seal of Melchizedek reference in Dead Sea Scrolls*

mountain peak, and the center circle was the center mountain peak, the city of Zion. From this perspective above, it is almost as if Zion itself is budding up and out as an earthly flower, pointing and rising heavenward, representative of Zion being "lifted in glorious majesty . . . in heaven."[103]

This eight-pointed star is associated with Melchizedek throughout Jewish, Muslim, and early Christian architecture, art, and literature. It has been used in artwork as early as 520 AD, like in **Image 9** and **Image 10**. The symbol clearly held multi-layered meaning for those who used it. In the context of modern revelation, it is hard not to view it as a symbol of the glorious purpose of the Melchizedek priesthood and Christ's invitation to raise pieces of earth to the Heavens to join Zion above.

Ancient artwork of these ideas and concepts also contains other symbols of Zion, including half and full circular rainbows, people radiating light in holy s*hekinah* with circles around their heads, ministering angels surrounding an altar, two temples, and the seal of Melchizedek in the center.

These murals speak of the presence of Zion *above*, while Christ directs earthly affairs through ministering angels, as depicted by the hand above or calling to those on earth to sacrifice their idols or

Image 11 *Basilica di San Vitale in Ravenna, presbytery, left wall, central lunette, 520 AD*

worldly vanities that they might rise up. The layers of symbolism sing of heavenly purpose.

The seal is also clearly a focus of the mosaic in **Image 11**, created roughly five hundred years after Christ's ascension to Heaven. This art contains symbols of Christ's intercession to bring Heaven and multiple pieces of earth together, in Zion. The circle in the squares appears as a celestial star, similar to how the city of Enoch might have radiated from above as it hovered in the Heavens like a satellite, calling men to Christ and reminding them of their foreordained purpose. The seal also shows Heaven (as a circle), and two pieces of earth (as two interlocking squares) connecting as one.

The symbol appears to have been adopted by Jews as early as 1008 AD, in the oldest surviving complete copy of the Hebrew bible in Hebrew (known as the Masoretic text, aka the Leningrad Codex), which has the Seal of Melchizedek surrounding the Seal of Solomon or Star of David. Although the circle above is depicted as a star below, the similarities are strikingly obvious.

The star of David in the center was later adopted by the First Congress of Zion in 1897.[104] Some suggest the star of David was

Image 12 *Leningrad Codex 1008 AD, Cover page E, folio 474a*

allegedly chosen for its *non-religious* connotations.[105] However, the symbolism suggests Zion and the Seal of Melchizedek were woven into the fabric of the souls of ancient believers as well. It is easy to see the connection when considering Moses's pursuit of Zion for himself, and *all* the children of Israel as he worked to reintroduce his people to their Lord. This symbol has lasted through the centuries, and is

Image 13 *Seal of Melchizedek as seen above the San Diego Temple*

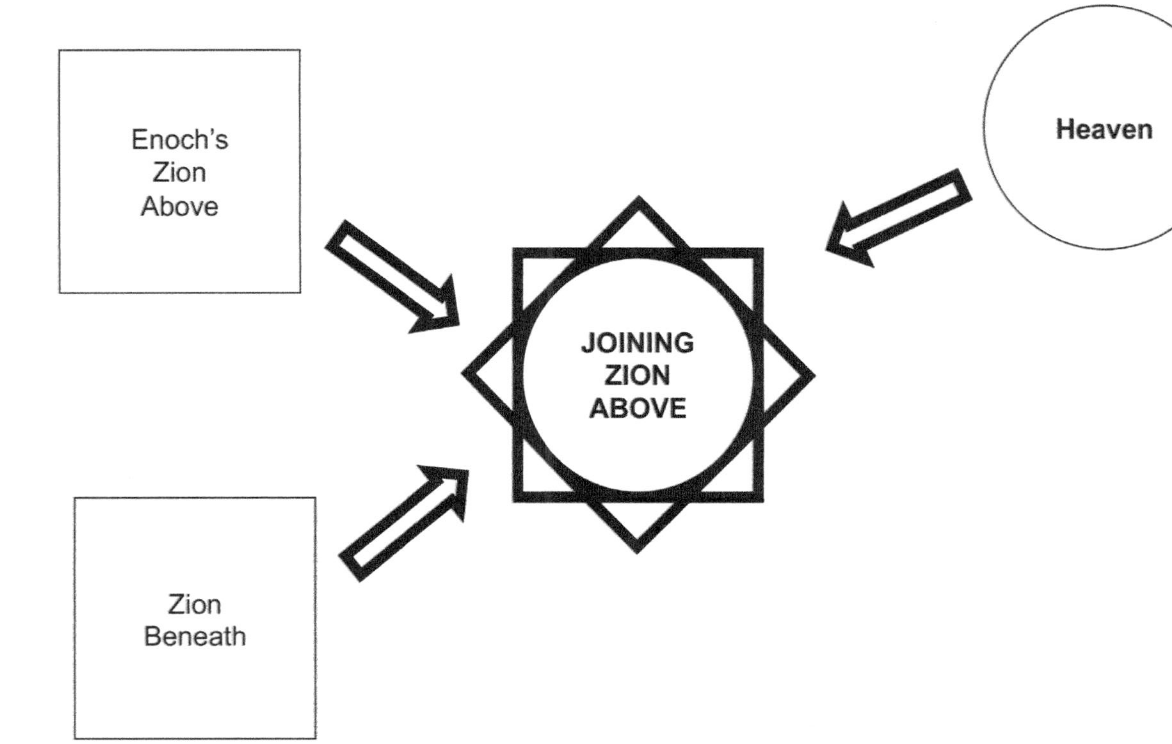

Figure 1 *The Seal of Melchizedek is a symbol of multiple Zion's uniting in the Heavens.*

included throughout modern worship like the San Diego Temple, including from above, as described by archangel Michael.

Taken further with Melchizedek, his seal becomes a representation of how Melchizedek's Zion beneath (also a piece of the earth shown as a square), hoped to be raised to the Heavens above (the circle) to meet Enoch's Zion above (another square). The symbol becomes two Zions from earth (two squares) interlocking around Heaven (the circle) in the eternal oneness and unity of Heaven. When we can see the symbolism of combining the circle and the squares, the seal evokes a deep layered meaning of our communal purpose here on earth—to rise home together, in unity, as Zion (see **Figure 1**).

The Lord states plainly in D&C 84 that He is gathering Zion into one until He brings "down Zion from above" and raises "Zion from beneath."[106] These symbols provide a powerful image of our potential to be united in heart and mind as Zion. When Satan will have no more power over the hearts of men and the earth will sing in purity and light, finally redeemed from the Fall with Christ as their king.[107] We "hasten" or speed up when this will occur as we accept Christ, the founder of Zion.

CHRIST—THE CHIEF CORNERSTONE OF ZION

Throughout the Old Testament, New Testament, and Book of Mormon, Christ is referred to as the "chief cornerstone" of Zion,[108] the "precious corner stone" that we can build our lives upon to be raised up, fully restored from the Fall.[109] But for the wicked His truths are a stumbling block, designed to awaken them as He pleads with them to seek Him in their sorrow.

Christ's Church in these last days uses a symbol that contains an image of Christ under an arch—portraying his rising from the grave as the resurrected Lord. His arms are extended to all, inviting us to find shelter in Him. President Russell M. Nelson reinforced the significance of this symbol in a talk entitled "Opening the Heavens for Help" and noted Christ was standing on the cornerstone, His Church.[110]

This is a glorious new image with ancient symbols. It is designed to invite us to Christ, embrace His truths and His way of being, feel

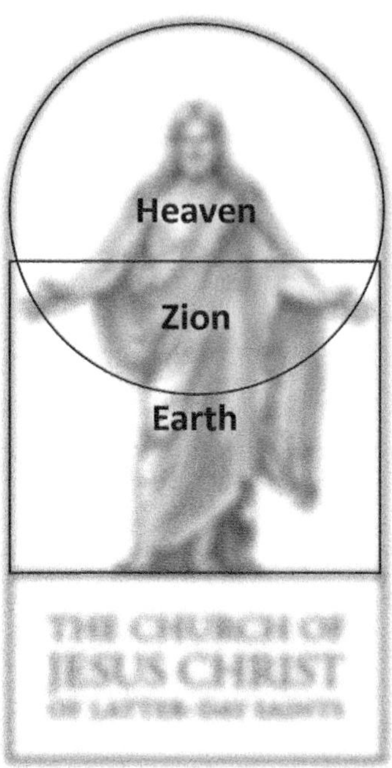

Figure 2
Logo of The Church of Jesus Christ of Latter-day Saints with the Circle and the Square superimposed

His love, and follow Him. Christ perfectly channeled His agency, bridled His physical body, walked on water, conquered death, and raised others and Himself from death's nightmarish sting. He lost Himself in our service that He might find all of us and pierced the veil to pull down from Heaven all foreordained gifts, powers, blessings, and purposes. Christ *is*.

The Church's new logo contains whispers of the symbols of Melchizedek to those that will hear. The arch is symbolic of the rainbow and completes a circle, fitting in the arch above, with a square creating the base. The circle and square converge at Christ's open arms in the center, reinforcing that Christ is the God of Heaven (the circle) and earth (the square) and brings them together in Zion. Symbolic of the Lord gathering "all things in one."[111]

He Himself, is the path that redeems us from the Fall. He joins Heaven and earth between His hands through the power of His at-one-ment. Orson Pratt taught on multiple occasions that Zion is the "*one grand method, for the salvation of the righteous of all worlds. . . .*

Zion is selected and taken from all of them."[112] Zion acts as a foundational step up for the righteous or the stumbling block down for the wicked.

Millions of the righteous remnant have been born as Abraham and Sarah's children and witnessed of Christ. Prophets like Elijah, Samuel, Lehi and Nephi, and John the Baptist pointed to the light of our Savior. Inspired luminaries like Joan of Arc, Michelangelo, Rembrandt, Davinci, Raphael, Columbus and *many others* filled with the power and light of Christ manifest that light in art, science, literature, leadership and discovery. Whether they recognized it or not, they filled this world with evidence of Christ—the Redeemer of Israel—the source of everything that is beautiful, creative and true.[113]

Still, not one of these righteous or inspired children was perfect. Even with an immeasurable prior existence in the presence of God, despite meticulous planning and preparing for this life, honing gifts, and becoming full to the brim with premortal potential, all (except Christ) have sinned and fallen short of the glory of God.[114] Even great prophets like Enoch and Moses had their inadequacies, shortcomings, and failures. They all needed a redeemer, a personal restorer. Christ is that perfect exemplar, the Redeemer, the Restorer, and the Creator—the guardian of our Heavenly Parents' great plan of salvation to awaken us through the veil and redeem us from the Fall. He was sent to save all who would follow Him. He heals us from the pain of our inability to fulfill our foreordained path, and He teaches us to become more like Him in the process. Our Heavenly Parents' divine plan for their children's happiness rests squarely on the shoulders of Christ who is *mighty to save.*[115]

Christ's own path was foreordained, planned from the beginning, and created spiritually in the Heavens before He came to earth. Christ himself declared He came to do his Father's will, gather Zion, and "*raise it up again* at the last day."[116] In ways we cannot fully comprehend because of the veil, Christ's priesthood, His power, and His Atonement already existed and radiated spiritually. Even in the past, they transcended time simultaneously, blessing past, present, and future.

This is how prophets across the centuries foretold His coming, identified the star of His birth, His baptism, His death, and His glorious resurrection. They saw the spiritual creation of His life before He manifest it physically. His perfect alignment between His spiritual and physical self allowed Him to overcome all that separates us from home. Once Christ was born, it was His mission to manifest and couple His spiritual pre-existence with the physical. Once He accomplished His Father's foreordained path, He had "all power, even to the destroying of Satan and his works at the end of the world, and the last great day of judgment."[117] He reigns, endless and eternal, in Heaven as "Alpha and Omega," the "beginning and the end."[118]

We have the same duty to fulfil our premortal purposes by manifesting who we really are. When we fail to live up to our foreordained path, it creates war within us—a dissonance between our bodies and our spirits. Although not the only cause, this dissonance causes pain, affliction, sorrow, heartache, illness, and prolongs our spiritual death, the painful gap between us and our Heavenly Parents, our true selves.

Christ can awaken us and remind us of our divine agency, that through Him we do not need to remain spiritually dead forever. As we look to Christ "in every thought," and "doubt not" and "fear not," He reminds us who we really are until we are personally restored then *raised up at the last day.*[119] Just as Christ was foreordained to be the Messiah, Enoch was foreordained to be the first prophet of Zion. Abram was foreordained to be Abraham. Sarai was foreordained to be Sarah. And you were foreordained to be *you*.

Christ sees us as we are, were, and will be. His heart yearns "wide as eternity"[120] after each of us. He understands us and will care for us better than we can care for ourselves. If we accept it, Christ's love breaks and heals our hearts to open them to receive all from Him and realize He has already descended beneath us to lift us up to Zion.[121]

CHRIST'S FIRST RISING TO ZION

ALTHOUGH WITHOUT SIN AND FILLED WITH LIGHT, OUR SAVIOR WAS judged and condemned by those blind and in darkness. In strict obedience to the laws of love, He loved God, and others as Himself, and descended into the darkness of death to save us all. He remained true to the end from His birth to His crucifixion and through His death.

His disciples on earth despaired. How could He die? He who had saved Lazarus, who had healed so many, who radiated love unceasingly? But, as prophesied—and as created spiritually before it was made manifest physically—on the third day Christ *rose* from the dead, being the first of our parents' children to fully awaken, to fully become.

After He had descended below all things, overcome the world, mastered time, ascended to Zion above, visited his Heavenly Parents, and received all they had prepared for Him—including a perfect body—Christ was fully empowered, perfected, and glorified. His Resurrection—that perfect restoration as the complete circle of His becoming like His Heavenly Parents must have caused a radiating and lasting explosion of light, spirit, truth, power, majesty, and reunion we cannot yet comprehend—a roaring multi-dimensional wave of glory that radiated through the eternities, more moving, more majestic, and more transformative than Moses dividing the Red Sea, Jared moving mountains, or Zion rising to Heaven—more inspiring even than the creation of suns, planets, and our earth herself.

It is difficult in our current state to understand how transformative this moment was. Christ overcame all darkness, all evil, all pain, all opposition. He overcame the veil, overcame death, overcame *all.* He had fully become the master of life, time, space, travel, light, truth, love, glory, and eternity. He had not only suffered with all He atoned for, but He was empowered and enriched by the experiences He shared with them across all time. His spiritual foreordination, His spiritual pre-creation was perfectly coupled with his physical body. He had risen in fullness of glory like our Heavenly Parents. *He was GOD.*

After He rose from the dead, He appeared first to Mary, then to the Apostles and His many faithful disciples. He showed them He had received all the Father had prepared for Him, and He continued to enjoy His physical body, now exalted. He ate honeycomb and fish and bread. He embraced His followers.[122] He loved them, smiled with them, wept with them, reminded them to have faith and rejoice—that He had overcome the world—and showed them the scars He had preserved in His hands, feet, and side. These wounds of betrayal and crucifixion He received "in the household of His friends" became tokens and signs of His descent below the Fall—victory over death, over the world, and the invitation to Zion through Him.[123]

ZION IN ANCIENT AMERICA

Isaiah referred to Zion as a great tent, with curtains spread wide across the earth anchored by divine cords and stakes.[124] He prophesied of a day when Zion would fill the earth and restore the sons and daughters of Zion in gladness. Christ continued this restoration even in death. He returned to our Heavenly Parents above and organized the righteous who had died before His resurrection into armies of angels to chase darkness from the earth.[125] After He resurrected, Christ would descend from Zion above with His angels and plant seeds of truth in the hearts of His followers—then return above in a cloud of glory.[126]

Christ tied Heaven and earth together with threads of light in a grand fabric of purpose and glory with descent and ascent to prepare for the day when He would lift the whole earth back home above. Each community on earth that accepts and obeys the Lord's truths becomes a stake in this great tent of salvation, a tent tied with cords of light reaching to Heaven with Christ as the pinnacle in Zion above.[127]

Days after His resurrection, Christ visited the Nephites, descending in a pillar of light from Zion above. He healed, blessed, and taught them. He showed them the wounds in His hands, feet, and side, healed their sick, blessed their children, and encircled them in light and angels.[128] He would continue to visit and gather the remnant scattered across the earth to bring all His children together into one-fold with Him as their celestial shepherd.[129] Wherever He visited, Zion blossomed. After Christ ministered to the Nephites, they lived in unity and righteousness for two hundred and thirty years.[130]

This peace came because all were focused on Christ as their Lord, rather than worldly possessions, titles, or distractions. They realized His gifts were more precious than anything in this fallen world.[131] Christ established these stakes of Zion to help the saints love the Lord their God and to love their neighbors as themselves.[132]

As they did this, communal translations *must* have occurred. When we live the laws of Heaven, we generate light, and it becomes impossible for us to remain in this fallen world. We literally transform all matter around us until God wraps us up in His power and glory and carries us home.[133] Likewise, when we see others as cocreators of Zion, we can rise up in joy and harmony with those around us. This unity will never come by force or compulsion or political policy. This unity comes into our hearts as a song of the redeeming love of Christ that transforms us until we resonate together in harmony as His Zion.[134]

CHRIST'S FINAL ASCENT

We cannot abide Christ's presence or see His face and live without obedience to the laws of His priesthood.[135] The doctrine of the priesthood is compassionate connection—where our hearts are turned toward each other and united as one—neighbor to neighbor and children to God.[136] Without this heart-to-heart unity the earth will be wasted at His coming.[137]

Christ elevates, purifies, and refines everything around Him. As such, Christ could not stay on this earth in His glorified and resurrected state for long without destroying it and our agency. Thus, after Christ finished teaching the ancient apostles and early saints in Jerusalem, they watched longingly as He was "received," "carried," or "taken up" in a cloud to Zion to the city of Enoch that remained in the Heavens, partially hidden behind the veil. His ascent was so glorious, His followers remained there, "gazing up into heaven," awaiting His return as if they were pleading for Him to return, or for Him to take them with Him to the skies.[138]

Angels assured these yearning Saints, that Christ would return in the way He had ascended: in a cloud of light and song.[139] But they were to be left behind as the remnant, to gather scattered Israel throughout the world and prepare Zion. Before this glorious day could come, when our hearts would be tied together in families and communities into the brilliant tapestry of Zion, there would be a great falling away or apostasy—a final scattering.[140] To contrast the darkness of Satan's world with Christ's brilliance, He would allow the world to descend further into darkness, murder His apostles, and reject Him as the corner stone of Zion. Our ancestors would refuse Christ's healing call and wallow in the dark ages for over a thousand years before a great and final restoration would commence, as the Lord would begin to restore not only His Church but His people.

Moroni, the prophetic author of the Book of Mormon, who lived nearly four hundred years after Christ's visit to America, left us a final invitation and reminder of our destiny in Zion above. He invited all on the earth to "awake and arise from the dust," strengthen our stakes, and become Zion.[141] He ended the Book of Mormon looking forward to his own restoration. He testified that because of Christ, he too would conquer the grave and rise triumphant *through the air.*[142]

Since Moroni's testament, the world has suffered world wars, pestilence, pandemics, disasters, great upheavals, destruction, and fire. But the earth is also experiencing a renaissance, a grand awakening. The song of Zion has continued to sing in faint whispers to the remnant that Enoch, Noah, Moses, and Christ left below and will sing to us as we answer the call of Zion within.

CHAPTER 3 ENDNOTES

1 All the ancient patriarchs and matriarchs "looked forward with joyful anticipation to the day in which we live; and fired with heavenly and joyful anticipations they have sung and written and prophesied of this our day." *Teachings of the Prophet Joseph Smith*, p. 231.

2 D&C 45:10–14.

3 *Teachings of the Prophet Joseph Smith*, p. 51.

4 Psalms 93:1; The Old Testament contains 43 references to the phrase "the Most High." Understanding that Zion was *lifted up*, is it any wonder that the Lord is referred to not simply as the best, or brightest, but the "most high over all the earth"? (Psalm 83:18). These references to height dwindle to seven in the New Testament as if to suggest as the earth aged, we forgot the Lord's current residence is with Zion above in the Heavens as the Lord of the "most High." I also smile at the symbolism of the number of references (43 and 7) as symbols of earth, Heaven, and Zion.

5 Joseph Smith Translation, Genesis 14:32.

6 Joseph Fielding Smith, *Doctrines of Salvation* 2:316 (emphasis added).

7 D&C 49:8.

8 *Enoch and the City of Zion: Can an Entire Community Ascend to Heaven?* David Larsen, 2014, available at https://byustudies.byu.edu/content/volume-531-2014 (last visited 03/04/2020).

9 D&C 124:9.

10 *Enoch and the City of Zion: Can an Entire Community Ascend to Heaven*?, David Larsen, 2014: https://byustudies.byu.edu/content/volume-531-2014 *citing* (Aquila H. Lee, *From Messiah to Preexistent Son* (Tübingen: Mohr Siebeck, 2005), 258).

11 James R. Davila, "Heavenly Ascents in the Qumran Scrolls," in *The Dead Sea Scrolls after Fifty Years: A Comprehensive Assessment,* ed. Peter W. Flint and James C. VanderKam, 2 vols. (Leiden: Brill, 1999), 2:471.

12 David Larsen, "Enoch and the City of Zion: Can an Entire Community Ascend to Heaven?" *BYU Studies*, 2014 https://byustudies.byu.edu/content/volume-531-2014.

13 David Larsen, "Enoch and the City of Zion: Can an Entire Community Ascend to Heaven?" *BYU Studies*, 2014 https://byustudies.byu.edu/content/volume-531-2014

14 Quran 21:85.

15 Quran 19:56.

16 Alma 45:19.

17 Mosiah 18:26–29.

18 Alma 13:12.

19 D&C 88:122.

20 In the book of Jasher Chapter 16:11, Seth the Son of Noah is

referred to explicitly as "Adonizedek king of Jerusalem." He is the same person as Melchizedek, who blessed Abraham after the battle of the Kings. Elyon is regularly translated as "The Most High" *see* https://hermeneutics.stackexchange.com/questions/18674/why-is-elyon-translated-as-the-most-high.

21 *The Blessings of Abraham, Becoming a Zion People*, E. Douglas Clark, p. 139.

22 *See* the definition of Melchizedek, available at www.definitions.com.

23 "When Abraham returned from the war [with Chedorlaomer], Shem, or, as he is sometimes called, Melchizedek, the king of righteousness, priest of the Most High God" (Ginzberg, *Legends of the Jews*, p. 233, [Pinnacle Press: 2017]). *Also* "Jewish tradition pronounces Melchizedek to be a survivor of the Deluge, the patriarch Shem." (*Smith's Bible Dictionary*, p. 393, Holman); "And Adonizedek king of Jerusalem, the same was Shem" (book of Jasher 16:11).

24 *Times and Seasons* (vol. 6, p. 746) speaks of Shem, who was Melchizedek, found by Alma E. Gygi, in her 1973 article titled "Is it possible that Shem and Melchizedek are the same person?"

25 Richard D. Draper, "Sacrifices and Offerings: Foreshadowing of Christ," *Ensign* Special Issue: Old Testament, September 1980.

26 Targum Yonathan and Targum Yerushalmi to Bereishith 14:18–20. Talmud Bavli to tractate Nedarim 32b et al.

27 Psalms 110:2–4.

28 Genesis 14:19.

29 Hebrews 7–12.

30 Alma 13:18–19.

31 Alma 13:1–6.

32 Alma 13:14.

33 Joseph Smith Translation, Gen. 14:34–35, emphasis added.

34 Alma 13:7.

35 D&C 107:48:1–3.

36 Moses 1:39; Joseph Smith Translation, Genesis 14:31.

37 Joseph Smith Translation, Genesis 14:25.

38 Alma 13:29; see also D&C 76; Joseph Smith Translation, Genesis 14:25–40.

39 Alma 13:31 noting "many more things are written" about Melchizedek.

40 The Book of Mormon references a multitude of other books, including the plates of brass, the larger plates of Nephi. A list of the lost, hidden or incorrectly translated scriptures is kept under the post "Additional Scriptures" available at www.HereToChoose.org. *See also* Popol Vuh, p. 5, Sacred Book of the Quiche Maya People—Translation and Commentary by Allen J. Christenson, 2007, noting that "early Christian missionaries burned great numbers of hieroglyphic texts in an attempt to eradicate indigenous religious practices" and persecuted scribes until "the art of

hieroglyphic writing virtually disappeared among the Maya people."

41 Moses 6:5.

42 Paulo Coelho, *The Alchemist* (HarperCollins: 1998), p. 142.

43 *Ibid.*

44 Joseph Smith Translation, Gen. 14:34.

45 Joseph Smith Translation, Gen. 14:36.

46 Genesis 11:29.

47 Genesis 15:17; 17:5, 7, 15, 19.

48 Genesis 17; Abraham 1:2–4.

49 *The Blessings of Abraham, Becoming a Zion People*, E. Douglas Clark, p. 92 (Chpt. 4, fn. 115 citing Genesis Rabbah 39:8, in Harris, *Hebraic Literature, 240,* noting "This is spoke of Abraham").

50 *Ibid. see* fn. 114 (citing Qur'an 26:83–85, In Cragg, Qur'an, 118).

51 Abraham 1:11–12.

52 Abraham 1:5–7.

53 *The Blessings of Abraham, Becoming a Zion People*, E. Douglas Clark, p. 77.

54 *Ibid.* at p. 70.

55 *The Blessings of Abraham, Becoming a Zion People*, E. Douglas Clark, p. 93, fn. 119 (citing Moses 7:24).

56 Abraham 3:22–23.

57 D&C 78:10, 19–21 (emphasis added).

58 *The Blessings of Abraham, Becoming a Zion People*, E. Douglas Clark, p. 133–136.

59 *Ibid.* at, p. 133.

60 *Ibid.*; Hebrews 7:1

61 Genesis 14:17–19; Alma 14:15.

62 For further commentary see *The Blessings of Abraham, Becoming a Zion People*, E. Douglas Clark, p. 92 (Chpt. 4, fn. 116 (*citing* Weitzmann and Kessler, *The Cotton Genesis,* 72, and Plates 2 and 166)).

63 Brigham Young, "Extensive Character of the Gospel, Etc.," in *Journal of Discourses* 6:283, 289

64 E. Douglas Clark, *The Blessings of Abraham, Becoming a Zion People*, p. 200 (*citing* Ginzberg, *Legends of the Jews,* 1:270–71).

65 D&C 121:45.

66 Hebrews 13:2.

67 Moses 1:6.

68 Genesis 32:30; Exodus 24:11; Deuteronomy 34:10; Moses 1:2; D&C 84:89.

69 Moses 1:8.

70 Moses 1:7–9.

71 Moses 1:11.

72 Moses 1: 12–13.

73 Moses 1:25.

74 Exodus 3:14.

75 Moses 1:25.
76 D&C 8:2–3.
77 1 Ne 17:26.
78 1 Ne 4:2.
79 Exodus 40:34–38; Isaiah 4:5 promises of this occurring again in the future.
80 Exodus 33:11; Exodus 19.
81 Exodus 34:29–30.
82 This was the same fire that burned around Abinadi when he was on trial before wicked King Noah, as well as the same fire that it is believed radiated from Joan of Arc while on God's errand to defend France: https://saint-joan-of-arc.com/trial-condemnation.htm.
83 Isaiah 6:10.
84 D&C 84:24-25.
85 Numbers 11:29.
86 D&C 84:19–23.
87 D&C 35:4; The *First Book of Adam and Eve*, CHAP. LXVIII verse 23, in *The Forgotten Books of Eden*, translated by Rutherford H. Platt Jr., 1926.
88 D&C 38:4.
89 Emmanuel Swedenborg, a seer in the 1700s who prophesied of a pending restoration, wrote 18 books of the spirit world and people enlightened through virtue and truth until possessed of a "consequent intelligence and then taken up into heaven." *A Swedenborg Sampler* P. 44, Swedenborg Foundation, www.sweedenborg.org.
90 Jeremiah 35.
91 History of the Rechabites, 11:2–3.
92 History of the Rechabites 11:3–5b.
93 History of the Rechabites 14:1–2.
94 3 Nephi 5:24, 26; Ether 13:11, Moses 7:62, D&C 135:3, Mosiah 27:6; D&C 45:46, and many more. For example, this square as the symbol for earth is also reverenced in the Mayan's oral history which referred to the earth with its "four corners and its four sides" was measured and staked out by the Framer and the Shaper who are the Mother and the Father of life and all creation, the giver of breath and the giver of heart, who give heart to the light of everlasting. Popol Vuh, p. 56–57 Sacred Book of the Quiche Maya People—Translation and Commentary by Allen J. Christenson, 2007 available at www.mesoweb.com/publications/Christenson/PupulVuh.pdf.
95 1 Nephi 10:19; Alma 7:19–20; Alma 37:12; D&C 3:2; D&C 35:1.
96 Isaiah 11:12; 2 Nephi 21:12; Revelation 7:1; D&C 77:8.
97 Isaiah 40:22.
98 D&C 137:2.
99 The symbol of Zion's purpose—to ascend from earth to Heaven—is also manifest as the Mandala in the Eastern religions of Hinduism, Buddhism, Jainism, and Shintoism with the squares and circles configured as a map

of the multiple Heavens and deities above. Willa Jane Tanabe, "Japanese Mandalas: Representations of Sacred Geography," *Japanese Journal of Religious Studies*, 28 (1/2) (2001): 186–188.

100 World Heritage Convention, available at www.whc.unesco.org/en/list/881, last visited 03-04-2022.

101 Alonso L. Gaskell disputed the authenticity of the history of the Seal of Melchizedek, and rumors that Hugh Nibley referred to it as such, in *Religious Educator* Vol. 11 No. 3, 2010.

102 *Words of Michael the Arch Angel*, in *The Complete Dead Sea Scrolls in English*, seventh ed., trans. by Geza Vermes (Penguin Classics: 1998).

103 *Book of Noah*, in *The Complete Dead Sea Scrolls in English*, seventh ed., trans. by Geza Vermes (Penguin Classics: 1998).

104 "The Flag and the Emblem," Israeli Ministry of Foreign Affairs: "The Star of David became the emblem of Zionist Jews everywhere. Non-Jews regarded it as representing not only the Zionist current in Judaism, but Jewry as a whole."

105 Scholem 1949, "The Curious History of the Six-Pointed Star. How the 'Magen David' Became the Jewish Symbol" p. 251 (emphasis added); "Then *the Zionists came, seeking to restore the ancient glories*—or more correctly, *to change the face of their people*. When they chose it as a symbol for Zionism at the Basle Congress of 1897, the Shield of David was possessed of two virtues that met the requirements of men in quest of a symbol: on the one hand, its wide diffusion during the previous century—its appearance on every new synagogue, on the stationery of many charitable organizations, etc.—had made it known to everybody; and on the other, *it was not explicitly identified with a religious association in the consciousness of their contemporaries*" (emphasis added).

106 D&C 84:99–100.

107 D&C 84:102.

108 1 Peter 2:6–8; Job 38:6; Ephesians 2:20; Psalm 144:12; Jeremiah 51:26; Luke 20:17–18, Jacob 4:16.

109 Isaiah 28:16, Jacob 4:16.

110 Russell M. Nelson, "Opening the Heavens for Help," April 2020 general conference.

111 D&C 84:100.

112 Orson Pratt, "Man is the Offspring of God, Etc.," *Journal of Discourses* 17:322; *see also* Orson Pratt, "God is Light, Etc.," *Journal of Discourses*, 19:280.

113 Romans 3:23.

114 Romans 3:22.

115 D&C 133:47.

116 John 6:38–39.

117 D&C 19:1–3.

118 D&C 19:1.
119 D&C 6:36, John 6:36–39.
120 Moses 7:41.
121 Alma 26:37.
122 Luke 24:42.
123 Zechariah 13:6.
124 Isaiah 33:20; Isaiah 54:2; 3 Ne. 22:2.
125 1 Pet. 3:19–20.
126 3 Ne. 11–17.
127 Isaiah 54:2.
128 3 Nephi 11:11–17.
129 3 Nephi 14:1–5.
130 4 Nephi 1:35.
131 4 Nephi 1:3.
132 Matthew 22:38–39.
133 *Teachings of the Prophet Joseph Smith* p. 51, http://scriptures.byu.edu/.
134 Alma 5:26.
135 D&C 84:22.
136 D&C 121:45.
137 Malachi 4:6.
138 Mark 16:19; Luke 24:51; Acts 1:9–11.
139 Acts 1:9–11.
140 Thessalonians 2:3.
141 Moroni 10:31.
142 Moroni 10:34.

BOOK TWO:
ZION RESTORED

CHAPTER 4

ZION ECHOING IN AMERICA

"There never was a people who had more reason to acknowledge a divine interposition in their affairs, than those of the United States."
—George Washington[1]

ZION'S PURPOSE—TO GATHER THE REMNANT AND RISE UP TO THE Heavens—did not disappear with the ancients. Zion has continued to influence and inspire hearts and minds, including those of America's Founding Mothers and Fathers. Zion's call from the Heavens inspired them to build a land worthy of Zion, where a restoration of all things—for the whole earth—could burst forth.

Zion's song continued in the hearts of the Native Americans, the *remnant* of the House of Israel in America.[2] The ancient patriarch Jacob prophesied and blessed his son Joseph to be a branch of Israel that would extend over the wall and grow into a fruitful bow.[3] The wall was the ocean. Although many of the Native Americans warred against each other and worshiped idols, others maintained traditions of truth and peace, including oral scriptural traditions and laws of harmony.

The law of the Iroquois, known as the Great League of Peace, founded in 1142, is the oldest existing democracy, and united six tribes but let them each rule their own people, teaching that all men should have one heart and one mind. This powerful unity inspired the

United States-based system of government and the U.S. Constitution itself.[4] Seeking the peace of Zion, the tribes had a tradition of tipping over trees to expose the roots, burying their swords beneath, and replanting the roots to ensure the roots ensnared the weapons to make it more difficult for them to war against each other, similar to their ancestors who are also recorded as doing so in the Book of Mormon.[5]

The song of Zion called to the open hearts of the pilgrims in Europe seeking religious freedom in America–a land promising unity *and* liberty. God sheltered America as the birthplace of freedom to reawaken to its foreordained potential as Zion. Over the last three hundred years, tens of millions of people have immigrated to the United States, seeking the "American Dream," a chance to follow their own conscience, and to exercise their "inalienable rights" in the hope that they might rise up and improve their circumstances. Although they may not have known it, the potential of Zion was calling to them to follow their foreordained paths to create Heaven on earth.

WHISPERS OF ZION IN AMERICA

Zion's influence on our founding fathers is obvious in the architecture and art of Washington D.C. I gave tours of the U.S. Capitol for Senator Orrin Hatch daily from 2004–2005. At that time, unlike today, Capitol tours took nearly two hours and included a full tour of the original Supreme Court, Capitol Building, the original and new Senate and House buildings, and extensive artwork that commemorated the history of America.

We would descend below the legislative buildings to the heart of the Capitol. While we walked, I would share stories of American purpose. Sharing the rich history and tradition of America's founding patriarchs and matriarchs thrilled me. It also became clear to me on those tours that the United States of America was built on remnant stirrings of Zion.

Perhaps the most iconic symbol of Zion's continued influence on American history is the Capitol of Washington D.C. itself. During my time there, it was common for tour guides to note that the Capitol was built at the tip of a majestic, multi-mile compass and square, symbols of Masonic tradition.[6] I believe the American founders wanted Washington D.C. to point citizens to God. As a result, the National

Mall itself serves as a constant reminder to those who "see with eyes that see" that God is the architect of America where the compass (a circle symbolizing heaven) and the square (symbolizing the earth) meet.[7]

At the center of the National Mall, rising above all who attend the Capitol, is a mural entitled *The Apotheosis of Washington.* Hovering at the center of the Capitol Dome, the painting pulls visitors' eyes heavenward. It depicts George Washington raised to the Heavens, encircled by thirteen women resting in clouds of glory, symbolizing the original thirteen states, holding a banner declaring *e pluribis unum* (of many one). Around them are more female figures representing Liberty and Victory/Fame as well as female depictions of War, Science, Marine, Commerce, Mechanics, and Agriculture. The word "apotheosis" in the title means, literally, the raising of a person to the rank of a god and that a rainbow arches at Washington's feet.[8] Yes, a rainbow, the

Image 14
The Apotheosis of George Washington—*Capitol Washington, D.C., Brumidi, 1865*

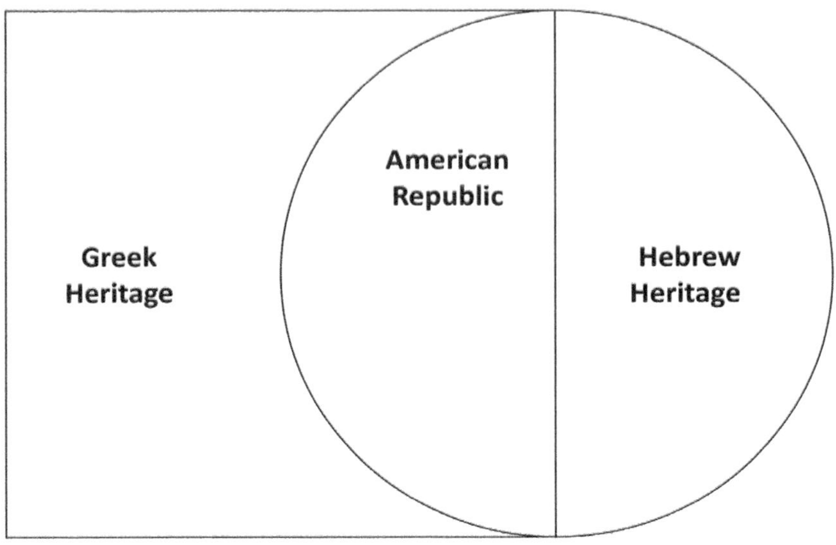

Figure 3 *America is endowed with Greek and Hebrew Heritage.*

covenant symbol of Zion and the bridge to Heaven and our Heavenly Parents' throne.

It is impossible to ignore these symbols of Zion in America's art. Our history is founded on this Christ-centered hope in Zion, and *The Apotheosis of Washington*, rainbow and all, is a symbol of our collective potential: that we can each rise to the Heavens as we allow God to be the architect of our life here and now. Our faith in God and desire to rise up and become our best selves like General Washington—as united individuals—comes from the Greek and Hebrew mindsets of faith and reason that make up our American heritage.[9] The Hafens note in their book *Faith is Not Blind,* even our coins reflect this heritage. They are imprinted with: "Liberty"—from our Greek heritage which birthed democracy, *and* "In God We Trust"—from our Hebrew heritage, sheltered in Jehovah's deliverance. This union of liberty *and* faith is unique to America, and often seems irreconcilable.

Without focus, the Greek and Hebrew heritages tend to war against each other. Just look at American bipartisan politics. Each party acts as if the other is the enemy. While one party teaches liberal independence, the other preaches communal conservatism. But the

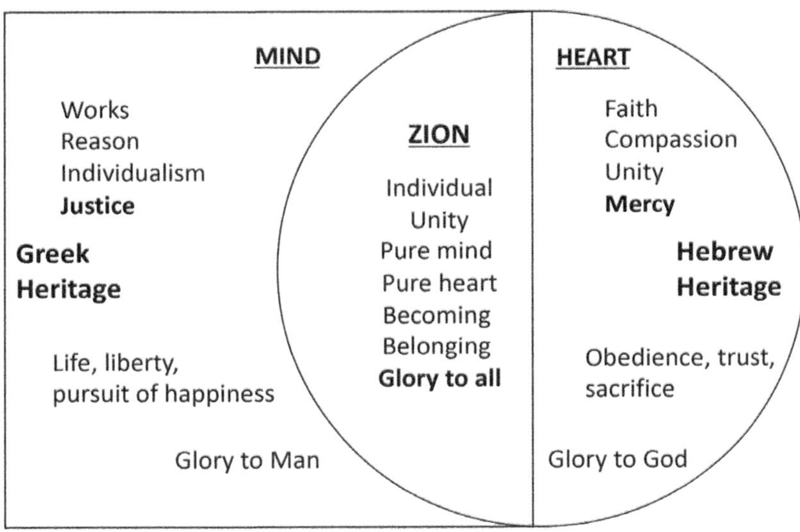

Figure 4 *Zion is the synergy of the heart and the mind.*

beauty of America is that despite what American politicians preach to us, we have inherited the right to both perspectives—the Greek mind for individuality and the Hebrew heart of unity.

America invites us to *become* and *belong* in these United States—to blend our sense of communal faith, trust, and unity with our yearning for democratic liberty, reason and individual identity.[10] Our laws protect the liberty necessary for the self-development prized by the Greeks (becoming) and the communal worship and faith of the Hebrews (belonging). To find clear vision from these two perspectives, we must view them together—like seeing from both eyes. When we see America from each perspective, it reveals itself as a place where we could join our independent-prone minds and our unity-seeking hearts and create Zion where we become *and* belong.[11]

Paul declared that as children of Heaven we are "heirs of God, and joint-heirs with Christ" and that through Him we may be glorified *together*.[12] As depicted in **Figure 4**, we can appreciate that Zion unites the mind and heart, works and faith, reason and compassion, justice and mercy, obedience and freedom, glory to God and glory to God's

Children. Zion allows us to have oneness together—individuality in our community.

Zion is the celestial blend of these strengths counter-balanced against each other that comes as we unite our hearts and our minds. This is why Christ teaches us that His spirit creates liberty *and* order.[13] His truths empower us to be individuals united under the laws of love, where we live in coexistent and cocreative harmony.

In law school I was taught Aristotle's doctrine that "the law is reason, free from passion." I witnessed many insist that sterile analysis—*without* compassion—was the only way to find truth. I felt many law students' analyses of truth became more important than the feelings or perceptions of others. This logic without love prevented unity.

In contrast, I witnessed individuals consumed by unchecked passion, placing feelings above logic. Unbridled, they would follow their emotions regardless of the cost. This proved that passion free of reason is lawlessness.

I saw one example of this while I was working at the U.S. Dept. of Agriculture. I met a bright, energetic young man who insisted he had to experience every emotion life offered to live life to the fullest. He was in and out of several homosexual relationships and often talked about his passions, desires, and appetites as things that would wash over him, beyond his control.

During our discussion, I asked him if he believed we can *choose* how we feel. He looked at me baffled, closed his eyes and with his arms outstretched as if inviting all emotion into his heart said, "I can't choose how I feel. I feel what I experience." I urged him to consider that he could choose how he reacted and what he thought about his experiences and that this would let him control how he felt. He quickly disagreed, insisting his passions were his only guiding star.

Without understanding Christ's works to bring all things into one, we can find ourselves defending only half of the truths Heaven wants to share with us.[14] We can forget that our thoughts and emotions are gifts. The Holy Ghost speaks to us in our minds *and* our hearts. Passionless reason misses half the equation, and loving others without boundaries leads to destructive codependence and enmeshment. True connection with others requires a heart *and* mind, truth *and* love.

Our Founding Mothers and Fathers gave us room to experience these truths for ourselves. They fought for America, sacrificing their own lives to protect our liberty with law. Their sacrifice and vision laid the foundation of a land that would allow for the full restoration of God's kingdom *and* His people. A place where we could find love and truth and build Zion.

THE DAWN OF ZION'S RESTORATION

Even after winning the Revolutionary War, America remained in great commotion. The nightmare of slavery plagued the new world in direct violation of the heavenly principle of agency. Conflict bubbled at the surface. It was a time of great darkness, but also a time of rising light. America was lifting to the song of Zion even in the face of dark opposition, and America's focus on liberty and law was beginning to transform the world. That liberty paved the way for another Enoch-like prophet to rise.

In the Spring of 1820, in the quiet of a grove of trees in Palmyra, New York, Joseph Smith sought God to know what path he should follow to know Christ. Prior to this event he had read James 1:5 in the Bible, which invited him to seek wisdom by asking of God. Joseph wrote that the power of that invitation penetrated his soul, awakening him to action. He sought God in a grove of trees, attempting to pray vocally for the first time. Before he could even speak, Satan attacked him with thick darkness that stopped his tongue. He used all his power to continue to call upon God. Just as he thought he was about to be destroyed, he said, "I saw a pillar of light exactly over my head above the brightness of the sun" that immediately delivered him from the thick darkness that held him down. In that light, Joseph saw two figures standing in the air, radiating light brighter than the sun. These two figures were God the Father and His Son, Jesus Christ. Heavenly Father pointed to Christ and spoke seven words: "*This is my Beloved Son. Hear Him!*"[15]

Like all the ancient prophets and prophetesses called before him, Joseph was called to be a prophet during a time of darkness, when Satan was stirring up the hearts of men to defy the foreordained paths of God. Repeating what he had told ancient prophets before, Christ told Joseph men were drawing near to God with their lips, "but their hearts were far from him."[16] Their hearts were failing them because they were allowing Satan to sit on the thrones of their hearts and create darkness instead of fulfilling the purpose on earth to create light.

Joseph, like Enoch and Moses, was not confident in speech. He was young and uneducated, but like Enoch, in the process of time, Joseph Smith was taught the full order of Heaven. Christ, the Gardener of men's hearts, gave Joseph the powers of Heaven to gather Zion, soften His children's hearts, open their ears that they might hear, and cleanse their eyes that they might see. The God of Heaven led Joseph to commence the restoration of the church, of individuals, and of Zion itself.

As one of the "noble and great ones" foreordained for this purpose, Joseph was raised up as the Prophet of the Restoration, to restore the fullness of Christ's Priesthood and Zion, and Christ's people on earth.[17] As a seer like Enoch, he was given power to see things not natural to the human eye and a clear set of stones in frame-like glasses called the *Urim and Thummim*. Like the *Urim and Thummim* held by Melchizedek of old, the stones empowered Joseph to see *everything*, including the glory of Christ himself.[18]

Christ taught Joseph of ancient Zion and charged him to move the cause of Zion in these last days. After seeing the majestic potential of what has been prepared for us, Joseph likely felt the same pains Enoch and Moses felt as they watched the ancient Israelites harden their hearts and prefer the "bondage of sin" that prevented them from coming to Christ.[19] Knowing of the potential that awaited us, Joseph wept for Zion.[20] But the Lord assured Joseph that he would mourn no longer, and the day of rejoicing would come to the contrite in heart, "for the restoration of his people" so they might stand upon Mount Zion.[21]

To create Zion, our hearts must first be soft, then pure. What is the difference between a soft heart and a pure heart? Soft hearts feel then hear the Lord. Pure hearts are those that follow Him. Our hearts are our keys to the Heavens. When our hearts are pure and united, they seek the joy and growth of others around us. We begin to hear Christ directing our paths. Eventually, our eyes become single to God's work and glory; we see others' divine potential; the Heavens draw near; and we ourselves are filled with light until we also radiate and rise,[22] until like Enoch, Melchizedek, and Joseph, we begin to see all truth, and enjoy things as they are, were and *will be.*

The Lord's voice is to all on the earth to awaken and help each other arise, so He might pour down knowledge from Heaven like a mighty river upon our heads. He is calling to all of us—irrespective of race or religion, color or creed—to come unto Him and gain more light. When we live contrary to His plan and turn inward for our own selfish purposes, we lose the light we have been given.[23] Instead of turning outward like the sun and blessing those around us, we become black holes of self-consumption until our hearts seek our own way and we are lost.[24]

We need each other to radiate and rise. The light we have been given from above grows as we join hands in compassion and common purpose, hear the Lord's song of creation, and join in it as we ascend together. But it is taken away from us when we choose to use our light in a way that prevents others from radiating and rising. This is one reason why Christ warns that many are called but few are chosen: because our hearts become so set on preserving the world's decaying dust below, we abandon our eternal home above.[25]

KNOWLEDGE FROM ABOVE

Joseph Smith continued to receive revelation. Moroni visited Joseph as a ministering angel, triumphant in the air, and guided him to locate and translate the record about Christ's creation of Zion in America: the Book of Mormon. In time, Joseph Smith received the High Priesthood of Melchizedek from the resurrected Apostles Peter, James, and John, men authorized to speak in Christ's name. Joseph was repeatedly visited by Christ as well as Adam, Enoch, Noah, Moses, Elias, Elijah, Isaiah, and many, many more angels.[26]

Joseph went about teaching these truths to all races, especially the remnant of Israel: the Native Americans. As he sought to restore the Church and kingdom of God on the earth, building Zion was Joseph's central melody. He wrote:

> The work of the Lord in these last days, is one of vast magnitude and almost beyond the comprehension of mortals. Its glories are past description, and its grandeur unsurpassable. It is the theme which has animated the bosom of prophets and righteous men from the creation of the world down through every succeeding generation to the present time . . . when all things which are in Christ Jesus, whether in heaven or on the earth, shall be gathered together in Him, and . . . *all things shall be restored.*[27]

As a seer, Joseph could see Zion's pending grandeur as it already had been created spiritually, and he sought to manifest it. He revealed many hidden treasures, retranslated portions of the Bible to recover precious and simple truths that had been lost or corrupted, and brought to light the Books of Abraham and of Moses. He also continued to commune with God and received instruction on how to build holy temples to be raised as refined architectural offerings, each presented as "The House of the Lord" where all nations may come and commune with the Heavens.[28]

Christ, knowing of our spiritual blindness, promised the Holy Ghost would remind us of *all* things, including what we are foreordained to build here below.[29] For example, in June of 1832, the prophet Joseph Smith and Apostles Sidney Rigdon and Frederick Williams prayed to know how to build a temple in Kirtland. In answer, they saw a vision of the temple as it already existed spiritually, very different from the designs of men of the day. This vision of the Kirtland Temple flew over them so they could examine the interior, its designs, and functions.[30] Seeing this spirit matter version of the temple gave them insight into how to frame the temple on earth and allowed them to join hands with the angels to build Zion.

Temples take on a new meaning when we understand the earth's divine destiny is to grow communities fit to be elevated to the Heavens. Temples are sacred places where we are "endowed with power from on High" and learn to be united, so Christ can restore us physically and spiritually, lift us from the Fall, and exalt us above.[31] The Holy Ghost manifests spiritual truths to our spirits. Of all the truths the Holy Ghost "brings to our remembrance," the most powerful truth we rediscover is who we really are, were, and are meant to become in Christ—together. In the temple He invites us to traverse the veil and converse with Him, to awaken to these truths and see each other as fellow journeyers here on earth—striving to be lifted up.

ZIONS TO BE

Joseph Smith taught the "whole of America is Zion itself" and that it would grow until it spanned the four corners of the earth, enriching all nations and all people willing to receive it.[32] Under Joseph's leadership, the Saints immediately went about building and forming temple-centered communities. Joseph designated Independence, Missouri, as the center of the restored Zion of the latter-days and made designs to erect twenty-four temples at the center, two for each tribe of Israel—designated as circles in the square.[33] He divided off half-acre lots, given to rich and poor alike, surrounding these twenty-four temples to ensure people had enough land to grow their own gardens and share in their abundance as neighbors. He planned to replicate this model of communal Zions and "fill up the world in these last days."[34]

This is consistent with John the Revelator's vision of a future Jerusalem containing twelve gates, one for each tribe of Israel and twelve angels guarding the new city.[35] He saw twenty-four elders worshiping Christ from twenty-four temples. It would be a time when Christ would reign as King of kings over all nations and Lord of lords over all churches, forever and ever.[36] These twenty-four temples plotted in 1833 appear to have been Joseph's plans to manifest John's vision and help Zion rise and fill the earth.

Joseph warned that this return of Zion would not just happen. The Lord would try His Saints in the *furnace of affliction*.[37] Christ would purify their gold and consume their dross as they let go of the worldly counterfeits offered by Satan. Progressing in obedience to God's telestial, then terrestrial, and ultimately celestial laws of love and unity until Zion fills the whole earth "will require the concentration of the Saints, to accomplish works of such magnitude and grandeur."[38]

Christ also warned against those who say "all is well in Zion" and believe that the Lord will accomplish His work without the Saints' efforts. Brigham Young taught that building Zion is a "practical work . . . not a mere theory" that required all to join together. Only by careful surrender to Christ, His love, and His law, can we root out "the power of the enemy that is sown within us" that distracts us from what we were "*intended* to be."[39]

Inclusion was a central theme of Joseph Smith's teaching that all God's children, bond and free, black and white, male and female, rich and poor are equal, and "must act in concert, or nothing can be done."[40] We need each other. Each soul that builds Heaven adds to its glory. Race, gender, wealth, and color are irrelevant distinctions before God, for "all are alike unto him."[41] As we come to love others as ourselves, we begin to find fellow journeyers, reaching up to return home to Heaven, to awaken and arise. This perspective helps us keep Christ's commandments to love Him, love others as we love ourselves, and purge poverty from our communities.[42]

In the mid 1800s, this message that each soul is not only valuable but essential to God's kingdom was not something the slaveholders and politicians in Illinois, Missouri wanted to hear.[43] As Zion began to shine, the darkness of the world rose up in tireless, murderous opposition. This is as it always is. Darkness does not comprehend light and rages against it. Constant persecution and destruction by those who feared the saints repeatedly drove them to abandon their designs.

As will happen in the future, those wishing to stay in their fallen, dark, telestial state of self-love waged war against those rising to a terrestrial state of selfless-love. Even in America, where religious freedom is constitutionally guaranteed, men, women and children were murdered, maimed, and molested by wicked men in Missouri and Illinois. The mob's violent attacks on Zion's doctrines of agency and anti-slavery led to their fleeing Missouri when Missouri's Governor Boggs issued an unconstitutional order authorizing mobs to kill, take, and "exterminate" all Mormons in the state.[44]

The state of Missouri warred against the early saints. While Joseph Smith and others looked at the Constitution as a divinely inspired framework, they also viewed it as just the beginning, like a bone framework missing the muscle, sinews and tendons necessary to perform its role of protecting the equality, life, liberty, and freedom it revered.[45] After the extensive persecution they had suffered, the Saints created a council of members and non-members, designed to build up the kingdom of God and draft a constitution that would bridge Heaven and earth and gather all the good of the world unto it.[46]

Joseph Smith was clear that this council for the Kingdom of God, more commonly referred to as the "Council of Fifty," was "entirely distinct and separate" from the Church of God.[47] While the Church of God (with its School of the Prophets) was the spiritual framework for the eternal salvation of the soul, the Kingdom of God (with its Council of Fifty comprised of members and non-members) was the legal framework for protecting agency so men and women could be free to be themselves. He noted the Kingdom of God that Daniel prophesied would fill the whole earth and replace all kingdoms was not the *Church* of God, but the *Kingdom* of God—again, a separate and distinct body and legal framework.[48]

The distinction between God's kingdom where Christ reigns as King of kings, and God's Church, where Christ reigns as Lord of lords, is reinforced by the prophecies of two Jerusalems: one in America (Ephraim) and one in Israel (Judah). This may be why Daniel's prophetic stone cut out of the mountain without hands that would fill the earth is *different* than Nephi's prophecies that although the Lamb's church would be armed with great glory and power, it would be small in number because of wickedness.[49] Constitutionally protected law has reinforced the kingdom of God, and as Daniel prophesied, replaced kings with presidents.

Apostle Dallin H. Oaks, the former Utah Supreme Court Justice, and a U.S. Supreme Court potential, taught in April 2021, that while the world was originally led by monarchies, since the advent of the United States Constitution, only three nations now lack a constitution. Thus, I ask if the stone that Daniel saw *has already* filled the earth, and made space for the Church of God to unite as Zion and rise.[50]

I wonder if the democratic foundation of the United States is Daniel's visionary stone that rolled forth—restored to us by various members of the remnant, a government that gave us separation of powers modeled by remnants of Ephraim with Parliament in England and later Congress in America, and the idea of many nations being one as modeled by the remnants of Judah in the Native American Iroquois with the Great League of Peace. As a result of this foundational shift, we now have presidents—not kings—who rule nations. It seems governmental order itself is evidence of God's movement among men, working to overcome the misplaced enmity of men's hearts by giving them more freedom to protect their rights in democratic nations rather than kingdoms. Joseph Smith created the Council of Fifty for this very purpose—to seek out all governing principles and wisdom necessary for the legal framework of God's kingdom, and strengthen laws to protect the liberty of all—worldwide—so they could choose for themselves what, who, and how to worship.

The Council became a place to openly explore and debate governmental principles and opinions, allowing conflict to be embraced as a rich soil for collaboration and improvement. To foster openness, Joseph invited members of other religions and races to the council, gave each member time to speak and urged them to thrust every sense of bigotry or intolerance from them.[51] The Council and its purpose were so cherished that one member, Charles C. Rich, testified he would not exchange his seat on the council "for any earthly seat or crown."[52]

Despite the efforts of the Council, and the protections for religious liberty promised in the U.S. Constitution, the Saints were driven from their homes, murdered, ravaged and raped. Some defended themselves, but many fled. Speaking of some who died defending Zion, Joseph Smith wept at the glory of their bright mansions he saw in vision.[53] He noted Enoch himself was inspired by visions of such celestial and bright mansions as he built Ancient Zion.[54] Likewise, future Zions would be inspired by what *already exists above*, until they become "the pride, praise, and glory of the whole earth," with gardens, orchards, vineyards, lawns, floral fields and the finest works of art, literature, science, music, and architecture.[55]

These Zions would contain a concentration of the greatest wisdom of the earth, and all inspired truth *yet* to be revealed. Joseph Smith taught that collectively, Zion's harmony would gather to it "anything great, noble, dignified, exalted, anything pure, or holy, or virtuous, or lovely," and "anything calculated to exalt or ennoble the human mind, to dignify and elevate the people." All these glories, beauties, and creations will remind those who visit Zion of their heavenly existence before. The beauty will awaken visitors to their own foreordained purpose, and ignite in them the divine, premortal desire to unite in Zion with joy and restore them until they are "caught up, to associate with that Zion that shall come down from God out of heaven."[56]

Christ, the Lord of Zion, inspired the unique, beautiful, and holy cultures and perspectives of the world. Before we came to earth, Christ foreordained saints, endowed them with power, and commissioned them to awaken and save their neighbors and their families. The Lord is the master architect of a global Zion. We are commanded to bring our brothers and sisters home to Zion, empowered with the spirit, angels, and the very voice of God.[57]

We can find those we knew before. The Lord has planted His remnant saints all throughout the golden field of the earth, and has charged us to find them and gather them home, where they can join together and make manifest their creative forces to erect their corner of Zion. This includes those currently lost because they know not where to find the truth, as well as those lost in the chains of Satan's darkness who consciously chose that hell.

On earth, Babylon tries to convince us that wealth is the possession of lands, homes, objects and things—to persuade us to value these things more than people and disconnect us from the true power of love. But in Heaven, the love of others and love of God governs hearts. Relationships and virtues are more cherished than the dust of this fallen earth, such that mansions, gardens, and treasures naturally spring up for the charitable and virtuous. The greater the virtue, truth and love, the greater the bounty. Because in loving others and God more than ourselves, we expand our hearts as wide as eternity and therefore can receive and enjoy the bounty of Heaven.

We need each other to help return the earth to its paradisiacal state and we need each other *now*. Prophets since Joseph Smith have

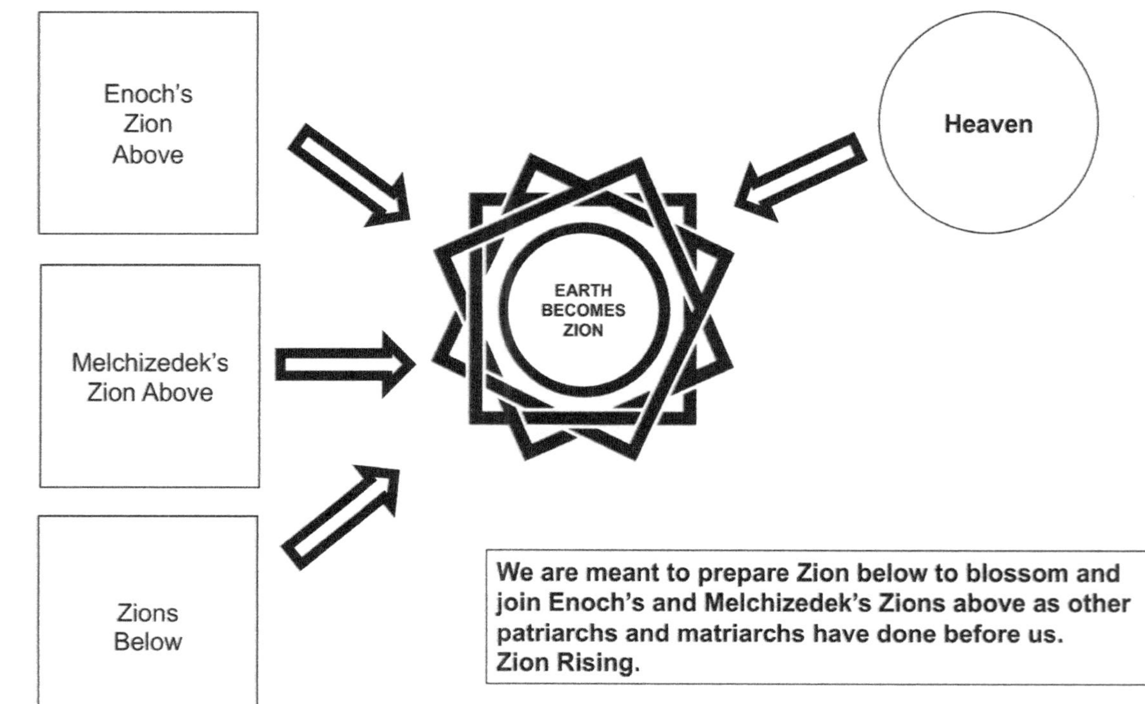

Figure 5 *Zions joining together as one in Heaven. The Seal of Christ.*

Image 15
Seal of Christ, with the twelve Tribes circling Christ the Lord and King, a blossom of unity rising to Heaven above.

echoed this divine and urgent purpose, including Brigham Young, who declared "I have Zion in my view constantly."[58] He explained:

> *We have no business here other than to build up and establish the Zion of God* . . . after that pattern and order by which Enoch built up and perfected the former-day Zion, which was taken away to heaven." Zion "*will come back again*, and as Enoch prepared his people to be worthy of translation, so we, through our faithfulness, *must prepare ourselves to meet Zion from above* when it shall return to earth, and to abide the brightness and glory of its coming.[59]

We are to look "for a modern Zion which shall be after the identical order of the ancient one," he explained. As we answer the call of Zion within us, we will erect magnificent and splendid mansions, edifices, adorned temples, and cities, reflecting "a model of the Zion of old built by Enoch."[60] Apostle George Q. Cannon reinforced this priesthood-based gathering to Zion as an upward gathering, where the Lord, His servants and angels would "draw *up* from the earth, the pure, the holy, the worthy . . . to the society of God."[61]

This gathering would reunite all twelve tribes of Israel around Christ, their Lord and King. He would not only reign over the Church as Lord of lords but over the government of the earth as King of kings.

Recognizing that this reunion would involve future pieces of earth being raised to the Heavens, with the remnant of all twelve tribes of Israel, I see a symbol of "Zion to be" with one more square joined to Enoch's and Melchizedek's. As Christ is the Lord and King of Zion, this symbol of "Zion to Be" can be seen as the "Seal of Christ". In the tradition of the Seal of Enoch and the Seal of Melchizedek, it symbolizes the reunion of heavens and earths into His celestial Zion and contains many other symbols. Each corner represents one of the 12 tribes of Israel, or one of their gates in the New Jerusalem inviting others to Christ. The symbol also buds open like a flower of truth and light reaching skyward to Heaven above, as Zion rises from beneath. And most poignantly, the Seal of Christ appears as a heart-breaking reminder of the crown of thorns Christ wore on the cross, representing His godliness, atonement, and ultimate sacrifice for each of us.

Zion is not merely a place, it is a state of being, a creative coexistence. Zion blossoms when individuals knit their hearts and minds together as one, after being reawakened by Christ's love and truth to their shared purpose, to return to Heaven above. Thus, Zion is wherever God's people reach for and extend their souls to the Heavens, together. This yearning and reaching itself leads them to love one another and forgive one another. It also creates Heaven on earth, spilling over with the blessings of the eternities: art, wealth, health, light, beauty, and song.

But each time Zion begins to gather and then rise and radiate in terrestrial harmony, Satan and his dark angels mount their selfish opposition. Those that sit in darkness—the squinters—often rage against the light, refusing to recognize their fallen state. They prefer their dissonant solos over the harmonic choirs of Heaven. In Enoch and Noah's day, wicked giants loved corruption more than their own blood and sacrificed their own children to idols and howled against Zion's rise. For Melchizedek and Abraham, the wicked kings of the earth warred against Zion as they set their hearts on evil until they bathed the earth with the blood of their children in selfish terror. In our day, those jealous of Zion's beauty will likewise rant against the light. But this opposition serves as valuable contrast to those seeking true and lasting peace, and it gives Zion even greater lift to rise.

CHAPTER 4 ENDNOTES

1 "Letter to Brigadier-General Nelson," 20 August 1778, in Ford's *Writings of George Washington* (1890), vol. VII, p. 161.
2 D&C 19:27.
3 Genesis 49:22.
4 See PBS article: https://www.pbs.org/native-america/blogs/native-voices/how-the-iroquois-great-law-of-peace-shaped-us-democracy/.
5 Helaman 15:9; Alma 24:19, Alma 25:14.
6 *See* https://scottishritenmj.org/blog/the-origins-of-the-square-and-compasses.
7 John 12:40–41.
8 *See* https://www.aoc.gov/art/other-paintings-and-murals/apotheosis-washington.
9 *Ibid.* at p. 51.
10 Bruce C. Hafen and Marie K. Hafen, *Faith is Not Blind*, p. 50.
11 D&C 130:20–21.
12 Romans 18:7.
13 2 Cor. 3:17; 1 Cor. 14:33.
14 Ephesians 1:10.
15 Joseph Smith—History 1:12–17.
16 Isaiah 29:13; 2 Nephi 27:25.
17 Abraham 3:22–23.
18 "Knight, Reminiscences, 2–3"; "Joseph Smith History, 1838–56," vol. A-1, 5, in *Joseph Smith Papers* (abbr. *JSP*), H1:222 (draft 2); *see also* Alma 37:23; D&C 110:3–4.
19 D&C 84:44–51.
20 D&C 21:7–8.
21 D&C 84:2; D&C 21:7–8.
22 Moses 1:39, D&C 88:67, D&C 121:33–39.
23 D&C 93:39.
24 Isaiah 53:6; Proverbs 18:1.
25 D&C 121:33–40.
26 History of the Church 1:39–41, 2:381, 428; D&C 27:12–13, 110:11–16, 128:20–21; JD, 13:47, 17:374, 21:94; and Andrus, *Joseph Smith, the Man and the Seer*, p. 95.
27 Joseph Smith, *History of the Church* 4:185–86, emphasis added.
28 D&C 58:9.
29 John 14:26.
30 *Saints*, vol. 1 Chapter 15, p. 169; D&C 95.
31 D&C 105:1–3, 11.
32 *Teachings of the Prophet Joseph Smith*, p. 362; *see also* Daniel 2.
33 Plat of the City of Zion, circa Early June–25 June 1833 available

at: https://www.josephsmithpapers.org/paper-summary/plat-of-the-city-of-zion-circa-early-june-25-june-1833/1.

34 Joseph Smith to Church Leaders in Jackson County, Missouri, June 25, 1833, in *JSP*, D3:155–56, cited in *Saints* Vol. 1, Chpt. 15 p. 170.

35 Revelation 21:12.

36 Revelation 11:15–16; *see also* "Council of Fifty, Minutes, Apr. 18, 1844," in *JSP*, CFM:128 where Joseph Smith explained, "There is a distinction between the Church of God and kingdom of God [or Council of Fifty]. The laws of the kingdom are not designed to affect our salvation hereafter. It is an entire, distinct and separate government. The church is a spiritual matter and a spiritual kingdom; but the kingdom which Daniel saw was not a spiritual kingdom, but was designed to be got up for the safety and salvation of the saints by protecting them in their religious rights and worship."

37 Isaiah 48:10.

38 Joseph Smith, in *History of the Church*, 4:185–86.

39 Brigham Young, "Building Up and Adornment of Zion by the Saints," *Journal of Discourses*, 9:284a (emphasis added).

40 *Teachings of the Prophet Joseph Smith*, p. 202 (March 30, 1842); DHC 4:570

41 2 Nephi 26:33.

42 Moses 7:18.

43 Dallin H. Oaks, "Defending Our Divinely Inspired Constitution," April 2021 general conference.

44 *See* https://en.wikipedia.org/wiki/Mormon_Extermination_Order; https://www.churchofjesuschrist.org/study/history/topics/extermination-order?lang=eng.

45 "Council of Fifty, Minutes, April 5, 1844" in *JSP*, CFM:85

46 "Council of Fifty, Minutes, March 11, 1844," in *JSP*, CFM:24–25.

47 "Council of Fifty, Minutes, Apr. 18, 1844," in *JSP*, CFM:128.

48 "Council of Fifty, Minutes, Apr. 18, 1844," in *JSP*, CFM:202.

49 1 Nephi 14:120–14.

50 Dallin H. Oaks, "Defending Our Divinely Inspired Constitution," April 2021 general conference.

51 "Council of Fifty, Minutes, Apr. 11, 1844," in JSP, *CFM*:116.

52 "Council of Fifty, Minutes, Apr. 5, 1844," in JSP, *CFM*:89.

53 Joseph Young, "A Scrap of History," p. 1, Sen. Salt Lake City Utah, Printed at the Deseret News Steam Printing Establishment, 1878

54 *Ibid.* at p. 10.

55 Psalms 48:2.

56 John Taylor, *Journal of Discourses* 10:147b.

57 D&C 1:20.

58 Brigham Young, "Building Up and Adornment of Zion by the Saints," *Journal of Discourses* 9:284a.

59 Brigham Young, *DBY*, 443 (citing Moses 7:69).

60 Joseph Young, "Enoch and His City," p. 12, Sen. Salt Lake City Utah, Printed at the Deseret News Steam Printing Establishment, 1878.

61 George Q Cannon, in *Journal of Discourses* 26:241.

CHAPTER 5
ZION *IS*

"Let Zion in her beauty rise; Her light begins to shine." —*Hymns*, no. 41

ZION IS ART

All things denote there is a God.[1] This is true for the miracles created on earth—from the wind, water, trees, birds, to the galaxies and the rotations of the Heavens—and it is true for our efforts to mirror God's creations. The arts were foreordained to draw us to Zion. Enoch himself was the first "great artificer" pointing others skyward with art.[2] Anything that invites us to honor our divine heritage or communicates divine purpose is art. This can include the traditional forms of art—music, dance, painting, literature, architecture—or the non-traditional—science, invention, and medicine. All of these speak of creation.

As children of the Creators, we all yearn to make, create, invent, manifest good, and be a part of Heaven's creation. Participating in the act of creation, even if flawed, awakens us. It allows us to connect with our Heavenly Parents and follow their lead. By embracing our own creative thoughts, hopes, and passions, we are receiving His word and are reminded of our true selves. This is one way we can shake off the dust of the Fall, thin the veil, and receive Christ in our lives. The act of creation itself can awaken us to our relationship with Christ and allow us to hear His song of redemption and creative love within us.

I have often envisioned the revelation of creation as someone standing on a high mountain, arms outstretched, fingers reaching, yearning to connect with Heaven—awaiting a shaft of heavenly light like a bolt of inspirational lightning to course through them and connect Heaven and earth. This is the pure creator's pose—humbly yet faithfully reaching for Heaven.

Spirit is matter with substance, existence, and weight. It is as real as anything we can pick up and feel today, only finer. It continues to exist even after death. We cannot see it now because it is too pure for our natural eyes. But we can feel it with our hearts, the creative seats of our souls, which serve as a divine connection point between the temporal and spiritual worlds.[3]

This spiritual-physical connection means that once we are restored in Christ, we will be able to move across the universe with ease like lightning, capable of visiting any event in history or into the future to enjoy the full beauty of Christ's creations and come to know Him better, and follow His example and be edified by His creations. As we purify our hearts and join Christ in His creations, the Lord will help our creative seats become creative thrones. We will be able to visit where He walked in Jerusalem, peer into the beauty of the Garden of Eden, or witness the glory of the dawn of Creation, "*like the light of the morning*," and "see it as it existed spiritually, for it was created first spiritually and spiritually it remains."[4]

We can also begin to see *what* has been created spiritually that we have yet to manifest, and peer into the future like the prophets of old and today. We can grab hold of that spiritual matter through obedience to and partnership with Christ, and bring it into existence physically—like reeling in lightning from the Heavens to the earth through a rod of meekness. When such creations are manifest, they land with thunderous clarity and vibrate with eternal truth, witnessing of God's purpose and love to all.

Such pure creations remind us that God reigns, that He created the earth for our growth, and that He has paved our path home with His own blood—yearning for us to receive of His height and glory. As we learn to obey His celestial laws—the chief law being loving God and loving others as ourselves in unity—we awaken, as if struck and purified by celestial lightning that fills our system with light.[5] When filled with this light and love, we can channel the power to create in His name and electrify others with the grandeur, power, and glory of God.

To truly create, we must bow to the truth that all things lovely, noble, of good report, or praiseworthy spring from our Heavenly Parents of *all creation* and their Son, the Creator of the earth. True art points us to Him, to Heaven, to home. When we engage in creation *with* Him, we become conduits of the Spirit and reveal, manifest, and uncover His glory and our own. We reveal our premortal gifts each of us was born to manifest to help gather Zion in Christ.

In opposition to this transcendent glory is the celestial counterfeit of Babylon, the whore sacrificed on the altar of the father of lies. Those who offer their gifts to self-glorify, to detract from Christ, and to tread His creations under foot. The fallen world peddles these false creations, after Satan convinces us to sell our creative forces for Babylon's broken imitations, neatly wrapped in the brass and glitter of Hollywood and Broadway and the spectacles of worldly performance. **We are not meant for telestial brass; we are meant for celestial gold.**

We create to awaken others to Heaven above, not entice them to wallow in the fallen dust of earth below. Any of us who have sought fulfillment on the world's stages of vanity will one day remember we all were made for celestial theaters of creation, and that the emotion, drama, and applause we seek in the stories of Babylon are tinkling brass compared to the golden songs of Zion.

Imagine a future world full of art, science, literature, architecture, theater, and music so glorious, so brilliant, it is almost blinding. *This is Zion*. This is our home. Such a future was seen by ancient prophets from Adam, Enoch, Seth, Abraham, Moses, Elijah, Paul, John, and Joseph Smith. It exists spiritually and it will manifest physically as we turn our hearts and minds to Heaven and as we listen to the angels inviting us to join in the dance of creation.

The prophet John Taylor prophesied that the coming Zion would capture up the finest gifts and talents of the world. He prophesied that "if there is anything great, noble, dignified, exalted, anything pure, or holy, or virtuous, or lovely, anything that is calculated to exalt or ennoble the human mind, to dignify and elevate the people, it will be found among the people of the Saints of the Most High God." He declared that this would include arts, sciences, and manufacturers so concentrated in the wisdom of the world and inspired in the wisdom of Heaven that Zion will be filled with such glory, light, and lift that they will be "caught up" when Christ returns with Enoch's Zion above.[6]

Hold this potential in your mind's eye. Your Zion-worthy creations await. They already exist spiritually, and as we build Zion in our hearts, in our families, and in our communities here and now, our communal obedience to celestial law will create such radiance and joy that we will be unable to stop ourselves from rising to meet Enoch's city above as it appears in the Heavens with Christ. Together, we will build Zions after the order of Enoch's Zion, as we "answer to the Zion within" us.[7] This foreordained potential rests inside each of us, waiting to be unlocked and set free.

Zion on earth first started in Enoch's heart. Then it rose in the hearts of others—others who built a community, where the people were of "one heart and one mind [with] no poor among them."[8] These included those "who love[d] the Lord their God and their neighbor as themselves."[9] They became one in mind, united as the "pure in heart."[10]

The unity of hearts and minds in Enoch's Zion enabled creation, light, purpose, joy, and the continual presence of Christ until they were lifted into the Heavens. Since Enoch, Zion has been gathering and rising and continues to rise like blossoms of purity extending skyward.[11] The Lord has been harvesting souls from the earth, lifting up the righteous into His Heavens in communal joy as their communities bloom as flowers of Heaven. What creation inside *you* is crying out to be created, so it might blossom skyward? What gifts were *you* given to add to the glory of Zion and fill *you* with joy?

Such gifts contain foreordained power, and are designed to point our eyes, ears, and hearts to God and remind us of Zion here below. History is full of such examples of artists pointing to a collective before. Here are just a few choice examples:

Michelangelo, the master whose sculptures and paintings have inspired other artists for centuries, acknowledged that things were created spiritually before they manifest physically. He is recorded as saying "I saw the angel in the marble and carved, until I set him free. The sculpture is already complete within the marble block before I start my work. It is already there. I just have to chisel away the superfluous material." Fueled by his ability to make foreordained masterpieces come to life, he later said, "Many believe—and I believe—that I have been designated for this work by God."

Florence Peterson Hansen, a prolific sculptor known for life-size creations, after being devastated by four miscarriages, she focused her creative aching into the "clay babies" she molded with her fingers. She felt the gift of sculpting rise up inside her when the Lord inspired her. "I have never had anything come so easy. Every artist knows when it happens to them because it just takes place before you."

Image 16 *Florence Peterson Hansen with Camilla Eyring Kimball and the prophet Spencer W. Kimball, in front of her statue "Joseph and Emma Smith," at Temple Square in Salt Lake City (used with permission);*

Image 17 *Florence Peterson Hansen at home sculpting an image of Christ holding a little one (used with permission).*

Her son Chad Petersen noted his mother had no ego. She would fast and pray before creating, and invite neighbor children to create with her. "I've been looking forward to getting to the other side to see what else she created" he said.[12]

George Fredric Handel himself noted that when he wrote "Handel's Messiah," it was as if he were possessed from something he had created before. He is quoted as saying, "Whether I was in my body or out of my body as I wrote it, I know not. God knows." [13] A prior stroke had paralyzed his right hand, and he had blurred vision. He could only barely play a keyboard or conduct musicians. Yet, caught up in an urgent need to make manifest those creative forces within, he talked of having visions and is quoted as saying, "I did think I did see all heaven before me, and the great God Himself seated on His throne, with his Company of Angels." With this vision, despite the difficulties of age and disability, in only twenty-four days[14] he composed a fully orchestrated testimony singing of the prophecies of Christ's coming, His life, and His eventual triumph over evil and death.

John Philip Sousa had a similar experience with the Stars and Stripes, which he wrote while at sea. He stated, "Suddenly, I began to sense a rhythmic beat of a band playing within my brain. Throughout the whole tense voyage, that imaginary band continued to unfold the same themes, echoing and re-echoing the most distinct melody. . . . When we reached shore, I set down the measures that my brain-band had been playing for me, and not a note of it has ever changed" as if the music had already been written.[15]

Marie Curie, who discovered radiation and championed x-rays, refused to let fear and difficulty prevent her from understanding truth. She declared "science has great beauty" and "Nothing in life is to be feared, it is only to be understood. Now is the time to understand more, so that we may fear less." She believed in something more and made it manifest through hard work toward her vision, sacrificing her own health to discover tools to enhance the health of others.

Winston Churchill, who used speech and literature to inspire the world to defend freedom against the tyranny of Hitler, also recognized a foreordained purpose and used his talents to rally others to truth. On May 10, 1940, the day Germany invaded Western Europe and Churchill assumed control of the English forces, he wrote, "As I went to bed at about three a.m., I was conscious of a profound feeling of relief. At last, I had authority to give direction over this whole sea, and I felt as though I were walking with destiny, that my past life had been but a preparation for this hour, for this trial . . . I was sure I would not fail." [16]

Yongsung Kim, a current-day artist, paints beautiful paintings of Christ walking on water. I met him in 2019 at Swiss Days in Midway, Utah. While I was there, someone said to me, "Can you believe he paints all these pictures of Christ, and he's actually an atheist?"

I was shocked. I had never heard such a thing and had read he believed Christ taught him to paint! In hindsight, this woman seems now to have either been an atheist herself seeking justification or a mortal angel sent to prompt me. After I disagreed, she said, "Well, why don't you ask him." With that challenge, I did.

Image 18 *The Author and Yongsung Kim—Swiss Days, Midway Utah 2019*

I asked him if God spoke to him about his art. He grabbed me by the shirt and stared intently into my eyes, as if searching for something. Through his translator he said, "God shows me what to paint for each painting. *Each one.*" It was a marvelous experience, and now I know firsthand he also believes in Christ, and trusts Christ has a foreordained path of creation in which he can follow Christ's lead and rejoice.

Some have criticized Yongsung's paintings of Christ for showing too much emotion, but staring back into his eyes as he testified to me of his belief in Christ, I felt he too had felt a portion of the joy and sorrow that Christ feels. I believe Yongsung hears Christ's voice and paints the divine whisperings to his soul to manifest art already created spiritually.

Many other artists sense the divinity within themselves of prior creation. Alan Bradley, who wrote "The Sweetness at the Bottom of the Pie," noted he "discovered characters" while writing them.[17] One author referred to this creative state as a "higher realm."[18]

Another author noted he believed our intentions create the reality that we experience. These words came as he described his creative journey to write a book about physics, although he had never studied physics and had no apparent mathematical aptitude. Despite his lack of prior experience, he *knew* his book "Dancing Woo Li Masters" would be published and well received. He wrote, "I did not need to have faith in these things. I knew them. I could see them."[19]

Pure art gives thanks for and points to foreordained and coming glory. When pursued to awaken souls, art is a celestial conduit that pierces the veil. It communicates to our hearts, ears, and eyes divine *purpose*, reminding us of our time with our Heavenly Parents, their plans for us, and the power of the Atonement of their Son, Jesus Christ.

The scriptures often speak of how an experience is so profound that it cannot be spoken of or described with words of man.[20] Such will be the song, art, dance, speech, and beauty of Zion. Zion's art transcends simple letters as symbols of emotion and truth. When empowered by the spirit of God within us, such art speaks to us, gracing all of our senses, awakening our eyes, ears, and hearts to the creative harmony of eternity.

One day through Christ's Atonement we will be bathed in the glory and light of truth so fully that we will be able to hear the songs of Zion vibrating in our hearts, minds, and souls. It will be the perfect day when we are finally filled with light purified, edified, lifted up home to our Heavenly Parents, and to eternal fire.[21] Despite our trials in life, we will look back fondly on this earth life as a "minor fall," necessary for "a major lift," and sing hallelujah as we enjoy a full personal resonating restoration in Christ.[22]

Our own personal restoration will involve us being restored to the gifts we developed before, including those we were prevented from enjoying because of sin and darkness here below. This restoration will be an awakening in the Atonement of Jesus Christ to the callings, talents and missions we accepted and cherished before coming to earth. It occurs as we discover the relationships we had before, and the promises we made to help each other return home—no matter the distraction and no matter the cost. This life is a dream, a nightmare if we get lost in its trappings, and a vision of joy if we remember our foreordained purposes.

ZION IS LIGHT

Before we can unveil all of Zion's artistic glory, we must ignite the light of Zion in our hearts. Without the light of Jesus Christ and His gospel, each of us would be doomed to the destruction of darkness.[23] Christ's mission is to bring light to us when we sit in darkness, and if we join Him, that is our mission to others as well.[24] The Savior himself said, "I am come a light into the world. He that followeth me shall not walk in darkness, but shall have the light of life."[25]

Each canon of scripture, in all Abrahamic religions, begins with descriptions of *light:* The Old Testament describes darkness, then God speaking to create light.[26] The New Testament describes how Christ is light, and darkness cannot comprehend light.[27] The Prophet Lehi in the Book of Mormon describes seeing a pillar of fire and conversing with God.[28] Joseph Smith saw a pillar of light "above the brightness of the sun"[29] when he first met Christ. The Quran and the Torah initially point to God *as* light.[30]

Christ is the "Father of Lights."[31] He is the true light that lights every person to come below,[32] a light which cannot be hid in darkness.[33] He is the "light of truth . . . he also is in the sun, and *the light of the sun*, and the power thereof by which it was made."[34] Christ is the light that awakens us to our true selves.

Conversely, Satan is a black hole of darkness. Self-consumed like an imploded star, he generates no truth or light himself, but dwells in cold emptiness. Pondering this contrast between God and Satan, I have often asked myself: If Christ is the source of all light, truth, energy, creation, power, warmth, heat, color, movement, strength, understanding, discernment, glory, fullness, unity, harmony, happiness—forever, and if Satan is the epitome of darkness, damnation, entropy, emptiness, blackness, confusion, misunderstanding, disarray, discord, inertia, sorrow, dullness, cold, lack of warmth—forever, then how does Satan have any real power?

Satan's power is limited to that which *we* give him, through obedience to his lies. He darkens our understanding.[35] As Satan seeks to "have *power in us*,"[36] he consumes our light as we obey him. This is the battle for the souls of men—the tension calling each of us to light's creation or darkness's consumption. On one hand, our Heavenly Parents invite us to shine brighter and brighter as we soften our hearts and follow Christ. On the other hand, demons of darkness seek our misery, damnation, and destruction.[37]

Isaiah prophesied of the day when Zion shall rise that the "moon shall be brighter than the light of the sun, and the light of the sun shall be *sevenfold*, as the light of seven days, in that day the Lord bindeth up the breach of his people, and healeth the stroke of their wound."[38] This will be a day when we all sing for joy as the God of Zion reigns over us, letting us become and belong—cherishing the beauty of our individuality *and* our unity in Him. We can awake and be restored to our own foreordained purpose in Christ and be filled with light. His light creates the wealth of Zion within us.

ZION IS WEALTH

Wealth is given to build Zion.[39] But as with all good gifts, Satan seeks to get us to abuse them, worship them as false gods, and become lost in the darkness of his lies. Thus, the love and worship of money as an idol, as our salvation, as more important that the souls around us, corrodes our hearts faster than acid. Wealth is the fruit and burden of divinity. God abounds in the wealth and bounty of eternal life and desires to give us more than we can imagine.[40] There will be abundance, not scarcity in Zion.

The Book of Mormon prophet Jacob urged that as we seek the kingdom of God *first,* wealth will follow. This wealth will be given to unlock the wealth in others, "to do good—to clothe the naked, . . . feed the hungry, . . . liberate the captive, and administer relief to the sick and the afflicted."[41] When we seek the welfare of those around us, wealth naturally follows.

I recall awaking at 4:30 AM one morning as I was writing this book. Fatigued and anxious to go back to bed, I felt an urgent pull to continue studying and writing. A voice came to my heart as clear as a whisper, inviting me to stay awake, listen and write. The voice whispered to me "discomfort is a currency in heaven." It is the same currency of compassion by which Christ bought us with a price.[42]

When we seek the comfort of those around us over the comfort of ourselves, we generate light and happiness within us because we are loving, caring for, serving, and comforting Christ himself.[43] We are joining him in the work and glory of God and helping others become like Him. This is *godliness* and this is Zion.[44]

I have known many millionaires who think of their wealth as a tool of distinction and disconnection. When COVID hit, many were scrambling to find places of seclusion—a farm or ranch they could run away to—more focused on themselves than the greater need of humanity during a global pandemic. While I appreciate the noble desire to protect one's family, wealth is not given to distance from and elevate us above others but to draw us closer to them so we can rise back home even higher, *together.*

Christ tells us the earth is already full with abundance, and there is enough to spare.[45] The wealth of the earth has just been mismanaged, hoarded, and idolized.[46] But the wealth of the earth is meant to build Zion! As we come together as Zion, the Lord has promised us that He will soften the hearts of the kings of the earth to bring their riches to Zion so it may be enriched, exalted, and lifted up. As we soften our hearts and serve each other in godliness, the kings of the earth will bring their wealth to strengthen the Lord's people and cause the "*lifting up of Zion*."[47]

Wealth is the natural byproduct of Zion's rise. As we use our wealth to *love others*, we empower them to live their own foreordained paths—and lift up the hands that hang down and strengthen the feeble knees.[48] As others are given freedom to be their true selves, this creates more wealth. Love is not enablement. Love is not a priestcraft designed to glorify the giver as a false light to the world that they may get gain and praise without seeking the "welfare of Zion."[49]

Rather, this form of love is purposeful. It is designed to uplift, empower and edify and unlock the potential of the receiver. For how many people are kept from their purpose because of poverty and need? How many Einsteins or Michelangelos have remained veiled by poverty?

When we hoard wealth or possessions, we damn ourselves, fracture the community, and impair our ability to join Zion. There are gifts, talents, and wealth that can only be found as we share them and restore our brothers and sisters. This is why Jacob's brother Nephi warned against "the rich as to the things of the world," that "*because* they are rich they despise the poor . . . , persecute the meek," set "their hearts upon their treasures," and make their treasure their god. Nephi warned such "treasure shall perish with them."[50] Laborers in Zion that labor for money likewise "perish."[51] This is why the "rich" man is kept from Zion, because true wealth is not possession but rather connection through serving others as Christ does.

The pursuit of anything other than Zion is vanity. By placing our hearts upon money, we drown in our decaying wealth instead of lifting each other up to eternal renewal as Zion. The earth has more than enough to sustain us all. When we give of our temporal abundance purposefully and in a manner that empowers others instead of enables, we join with the archangels in God's work and accelerate the building of Zion.

ZION IS HEALTH

As we follow Christ, he assures us the "destroying angel will pass over us" [52] and He will give us "health in the navel" and "marrow in the bone."[53] When we realign our spirits with our fore-ordained potential and live consistent with our divine purpose, we heal and strengthen our bodies so we can "run and not be weary" and "walk and not faint" even if we might be dying of a genetic disease or terminal illness.[54] This type of health transcends the temporary fallen state of this world, for it is eternal, everlasting, and who we really are.

As we obtain the priesthood in our families and serve others, we become "sanctified by the spirit unto the renewing of our bodies."[55] This renewal is empowerment in spiritual matter. As we labor for Zion with the Lord, our growth and improvement in the "process of time" includes enhanced physical stamina and strength—so we can run and not be weary and walk and not faint, until we will learn to fly joyfully skyward in the ordinance of resurrection.[56]

On the contrary, when we deny the divinity within us, our spirits ache within our bodies. Although clearly not the only cause of disease, dissonance between body and spirit can cause severe stress, illness, and even physical pain. Without Christ's assistance, the friction between our divine purpose and our natural desires sours our souls. In that state, we can either learn to repent to seek righteousness, or justify our wickedness to prove we're "normal" and not out of sync.

As we age, it is as if we are in a cocoon. Our bodies ache, tire, hunger, and are pained. But this life is not the end; it is the next step in our becoming. There is purpose in our aging. Just like a butterfly struggling to emerge from a cocoon, as we struggle through age, pain, heartache, fatigue, and stress, our eyes open, our ears tune, and our hearts soften—for our wings are forming. Christ is watching over us, nurturing our transformation, calling to us to emerge—and to fly. As we consistently reach to Christ, look unto Him in every thought, doubt not, and fear not, our wings emerge, we will rise triumphant, and soar through the celestial air.

As a lifeguard at BYU, I recall feeling the terrifying weight of old age. I watched a retired professor—Alma Heaton—come in every day to swim. Although his youthful strength and vigor were gone, he remained committed to caring for his physical temple. He would arrive in a wheelchair every morning, sit down on the pool deck, take a deep exhausted breath, then roll and plop into the water. Using all the strength his ninety-year-old frame could muster, he would slowly pull himself along the pool lane lines. He would swim every day for an hour and then, as we lifted him up out of the pool, he would smile in exhaustion and say thank you.

One day, he had a heart attack in the pool! It was a blessing. We were able to save him because we were watching so attentively. But even this did not stop him. He returned the next week, committed to his routine and living life to the fullest. I often watched that happy man, shrunken in his wrinkled body and thought to myself, "I don't want to get that old. I don't want to last that long." My heart ached for him. Likewise, when I meet brothers or sisters struggling with pain or age, arthritis, failing organs, or other ailments, I jokingly declare in sympathy "bring on the resurrection!"

But this progression of our bodies from youthful vigor to old age gives us invaluable experience and invites us to Christ, the resurrection and the life.[57] Christ's gift of physical and spiritual restoration already exists. In a spiritual sense, we are already resurrected. Our spiritual frames are awaiting that glorious day when we shall shake the dust of this mortality from our bones and put on immortal clothing of eternal virtue, flesh, and light.[58]

One example of this is with our hair. As a man in my forties, I have embraced the beauty of my baldness. But in addition to the assurances that we'll have health in our navel and marrow to our bones, and run and not be weary and walk and not faint, I have often pondered on why the Lord promises us that in the restoration, not a hair of our heads shall be lost.[59] Promises and teachings regarding health *and* hair seem to be everywhere.

I trust that the restoration will include awakening to the true glory, health, and purpose of our bodies—created by a loving family with such attention to detail, that even each hair of our head is counted and returned. That one day we will see each other restored to our perfect frames, until not a hair of our heads will remain fallen or lost, but returned to us as a crown and blessing of health.

This restoration of our health, down to our individual hairs, is a blessing of Zion. The laws governing Zion include laws of health. Christ's purpose is to help us perfect our bodies here in this telestial existence, and elevate us to a terrestrial and then a celestial existence. As we progress from one kingdom to the next, Christ writes His truths in our hearts; truths that purify and heal our bodies.

As we labor for Zion, we accelerate the coming of our own triumphant restoration. A day will come when we will see those who have gone before, rise from their graves, alive, full of youthful vigor, wealth, truth and light, awakened and fully restored by the master of Zion—Jesus Christ. This same potential awaits all of us that seek to serve the Lord and others as we build Zion.

ZION IS GARDENS

One of my favorite protein drinks was created by a medical doctor, who on the back of his product says he learned after an early bout with cancer that the higher quality of food we eat the better we feel. I think most of us resonate and agree with that. Although it might taste fantastic in the moment, most of us feel terrible after we eat a candy bar but feel more alive after eating an apple. The nutritional value, the energy, and even the frequency of the food we eat can impact us. In ways we are still learning, in this fallen world, we truly are what we eat.

On this principle that we are what we eat, entire dietary movements have begun insisting we should only eat whole foods or only eat what our ancestors ate. If it stands to reason that eating processed food is less healthy than eating natural food, then it also stands to reason that eating telestial food is less helpful to our bodies than eating elevated or purer terrestrial food, or celestial food.

My sister-in-law—a board-certified nutritionist from Columbia University—notes that the nutritional value of apples is less than half of what it was before World War II. She is very concerned about how our current agricultural practices impact the nutrition of our foods. Our failure to properly nourish the earth's soil, use of pesticides, and genetically modified foods are robbing our bodies of the nutrition we desperately need. Some doctors go so far as to suggest that the fruit and vegetables meant to nourish us are instead warring against us with biochemical lectin barbs like gluten because of our failure to eat in harmony with the earth's natural seasons.[60] All of this begs the question, is the food we are eating inferior to what we *could* be eating in Zion?

After Adam and Eve fell, ancient records suggest they resisted eating any food on the terrestrial earth, afraid that if the forbidden fruit caused them to fall, eating fruit here below would damn them forever. They fasted for forty days until, on the brink of death, Christ revived them and urged them to eat, reminding them even the fruit of this fallen earth was for their nourishment and growth. He then changed their bowels to process food, but they continued to sorrow and fear they would never eat of the pure food of the garden again but would be stuck below.[61]

In contrast, after Enoch was translated to Heaven, he returned and told his children he no longer craved or longed for food of the earth, suggesting that his frame had changed. Enoch rejoiced that his soul did not remember earthly enjoyment and he no longer wanted anything earthly.[62] Likewise, the Lord invites us to come and buy milk without money and honey without price . . . and relinquish the dust and decay of the fallen earth for the living water and bread of Heaven.[63] Christ assures us that once we enjoy this purer form of heavenly nourishment, we will never hunger or thirst again.[64]

Christ's everlasting release of our hunger and thirst is found in the glory of Zion's gardens. Gardens have been a central stage of life since the dawn of creation. Adam and Eve enjoyed the fruit of the Garden of Eden, and were invited to tend to and eat the heavenly garden's fruit. The book of Adam and Eve suggests that after the Fall, the Garden of Eden hovered above the earth. Adam and Eve and their posterity "dwelt on a mountain below the garden" looked up to it longingly. Because the "garden was not far above them" they could hear the angelic choirs and smell its sweet savor on the winds.[65]

Their descendants, Abraham and Sarah, cultivated gardens to awaken others in Christ and remind them of why they were here—to grow in experience and return home to our Heavenly Parents. After travelers had enjoyed the fruit of the garden and expressed gratitude, Abraham would exclaim, "why give *me* thanks? Thank the true host,

He who alone provides food and drink for all creatures." His guests would ask, "Where is He?" and Abraham would answer, "He is the ruler of heaven and earth," and then teach them of how to give thanks to God, and to trust in the dews of Heaven.[66] Likewise, the brother of Jared carried seeds of all kinds and honey bees for gardens to the promised land.[67] The Lord himself compares the house of Israel itself to a vineyard that grows sweet and good fruit when righteous and rotten fruit when wicked.[68] Zion is the celestial fruit of this earth.

Paradisiacal gardens more glorious than we can imagine are the final destination of this earth, with us as the gardeners *and* the fruit of the Lord. Gardens where we labor together, in harmony, learning from each other. As my friend, a former BYU physics professor turned gardener notes, we need many virtues to build Zion. He told me once, "You have virtues I lack, and I have virtues you lack." By laboring together in the gardens of Zion, we can learn each other's virtues and grow as Zion together. Tending to gardens is one of the purest ways for us to learn to knit our hearts together and act in concert so that all are edified of all.[69]

Gardens are also at the center of sacrifice. The Rechabites, commanded not to plant gardens here on earth, were translated to heavenly gardens after proving their sacrifice.[70] Jewish tradition holds they are watching and waiting from their gardens above to help us renew the earth with Christ. Likewise, Christ suffered His terrible atoning sacrifice in the Garden of Gethsemane, was crucified on Golgotha's gardenless and bald hill before He rose triumphant in resurrection from the Garden Tomb.

Gardens will also be the fruit of the pains of our Native American brothers and sisters, the remnant of Israel here in America. I have met those whose grandparents carried seeds for future gardens with them across the horrific Trail of Tears, when they were uprooted from their ancestral homes of the eastern United States. They have started growing their seeds, and reintroducing fruits and vegetables that have been forgotten for generations, already beginning their redemptive work. My friend, Yvvonne Curley, a Navajo leader says her grandmother's seeds are now blossoming in one of hundreds of gardens she has helped Native Americans plant across the deserts of Nevada,

Arizona, and Utah. I believe she has already begun the path to help Christ restore the very earth, and each other, with such gardens.

Our yearning for the fruit of terrestrial gardens is one reason why we will eventually turn our swords in to plowshares and spears into pruninghooks.[71] We will awaken to the truth that the fruit of Zion is more precious than any lucre of Babylon. As we dig our fingers into the nourishing soil of mother earth, we will cultivate connections and purpose to heal our wounds and awaken our hearts. By laboring for each other, the Lord will cause us to blossom as a well-watered garden, until Zion's wilderness flourishes like Eden and Zion's deserts, bountiful like the garden of the Lord.[72] Our ability to replenish and restore the earth itself will accelerate until Israel buds, blossoms, and spreads to "fill the whole earth with fruit."[73]

ZION IS TIMELESS

Time is undeniably life's scarcest resource. I know many who have gathered success, wealth, fame, and power, only to realize they traded their time for that which will not last.[74] Even so, the Lord declares "time is measured only unto man" and time will cease when Christ redeems this earth from the Fall.[75]

The past, present, and future are continually before Christ and under His control.[76] Time is His tool, not an obstacle. The Lord speeds up time or lengthens it to hasten the work of the righteous and confound the wicked. Our righteousness, receptiveness, and gratitude affect whether time is a blessing or a curse.[77] The Lord told Joseph Smith his days were known and would not be shortened.[78] Our days are also known, and if we accept what the Lord has prepared for us, we will see Him perform wonders. Time is His tool to elevate, purify, and bless. He will deliver us, extend us, restore us, and lift us, "in the process of time" as we walk with Him in faith.[79] Only in this way can he remove all elements that would corrupt the eternity of Heaven, for Zion is meant to resonate in timelessness—the earth being a starting place below for us to grow in love and truth through Christ until we rise and radiate with a celestial frequency and song for eternity.

As a young law student, I felt the Lord bend time to bless me. During that time, my wife gave birth to our first and second child. I worked at the White House as a policy clerk in the Office of Science and Technology Policy under President Bush then President Obama. I wrote an article for the *Catholic University Law Review*, led a moot court competition as a vice chancellor, and was the deacons' quorum advisor for our ward. My days would start at 5:00 AM and end at 11:00 PM. I would commute to school two hours each day, and on Sundays I would fill our little Jeep with members from West Africa, take them to church, and make a second trip for my wife and children. Those years seemed impossibly *full*—completely beyond my personal capacity.

Each day I would look at my stacked calendar and plead, "Lord, help me!" And He did, because He is master of time. Those years were some of my happiest. I felt the Lord take me by the hand and magnify, extend, or shorten my time at His will to bless me and my family. It gave me great joy to see how much the Lord could do with me as I surrendered my will to His—because Christ's power is beyond time.

When Christ performed His Atonement, it *transcended* time, blessing not only those in the past, present, and future but also those *before* time itself. Likewise, it had redemptive power in the premortal existence and will continue to elevate all who accept Him into the future. As He works to teach us of His wonders and invites us to participate in His redemptive works, time will become our tool as well. Even something as simple as the energy of our prayers has the power to enrich the future *and* the past.

In 2000, a medical doctor in England conducted a double-blind study about prayer. He randomly assigned the names of 3,363 hospital patients struggling with sepsis into two groups—those to be prayed for and a control group not to be prayed for by his experiment participants. Those prayed for—on average—had decreased fevers, symptoms, and shorter hospitalization. Those not-prayed for were unaffected.[80]

What makes this study so remarkable, is that the patients were from the *past*. Those prayed for *in the past* were healed by the faith of those praying for them in the *future*. While there are a thousand variables that affected each of the ill, prayer can be one of the most profound of those influences because we have the ability with our hearts to influence not only what is around us presently but what has and will exist.[81]

This may sound like mystical, new age mumbo jumbo to some. But those who understand the doctrine of eternity and the timeless effect of Christ's Atonement can appreciate that this was no different than Christ suffering for the sins of Adam and Eve and all their children, thousands of years *before*, as well as for the sins of those yet to be born thousands of years *after*. Clearly, time is irrelevant in the divine arithmetic of Christ's Atonement.

Christ invites us to use our hearts to transcend time and help Him heal each other's wounds, calm each other's fears, and link hearts across eternity as Malachi promised. I believe this is why the hearts of the fathers and the hearts of the children will turn to each other. Fathers and mothers who have gone before, and their children remaining below, will seal the creative power of their hearts together to create Zion here and now and restore Mother earth, her people, and all things—*across all time*.[82]

A hint of how Christ's Atonement not only restores us but also transcends time is revealed in how Christ restored Abram to Abraham. After Christ promised Abram posterity as the stars in the Heavens and all the land he could see, Abram asked for a sign. Christ commanded Abram to take three animals, each three years old, cut them in two and lay the pieces in a straight line, for a covenant.[83]

As night descended, Abram was attacked by "a horror of great darkness"—similar to the darkness Joseph Smith battled before his own First Vision experience—and was warned that his descendants would be cursed and scattered. But he then saw Christ as a "burning lamp" or a "smoking furnace" coming toward him. Abram on one end and Christ as the light on the other "passed between" the divided animals and exchanged places in "at-one-ment."[84] Thus, Christ restored Abram to Abraham to help him fulfill his foreordained purpose as the father of nations.

Since Adam and Eve, animal sacrifice had long been a symbol pointing our hearts to the Atonement of Christ. The words for "cut" and "covenant" come from the same word in Hebrew.[85] Thus true sacrifice contained cutting, but this was more than a sacrifice, it was a covenant, where those making this covenant would pass down the middle of the torn animals which served as a multi-layered symbol of God's work of sanctification.[86]

On this first symbolic level, the gory visual of the animals being torn asunder, divided, and broken, was a visceral demonstration of the death of those in Israel who would not keep the Abrahamic covenant and deny Christ. On a second level, the yearning following the division is symbolic of the scattering of Israel, after they were saved from Egypt. On a third level, the animals torn asunder is an unignorable visual of the heart-rending gap between Heaven and earth, children and Father, as we await our reunion and gathering in Christ, who bowed down as the perfect, unspotted, and infinite sacrifice.[87] A reunion that would again occur with Christ creating a path to restore us so we can find Him, like he did with Abram's animals, like He did with the Israelites in dividing the Red Sea, and like He will do for the Jews when He divides the Mount of Olives in two at His Second Coming to save them from death.

Each of these symbols give richer meaning to how Christ through His restorative "at-one-ment" would reunite that which had been torn, scattered, and divided, gathering and making whole all who accept Him. Each of these symbols underscores the painful reality of the bloody gap between us and Christ, which makes the reunion with Christ more sublime. This promise would include the children of Abram who Christ promised would come out blessed by the hardship with "great substance," restored to their lands and the gospel and finally join Heaven and earth and lift each of us from the Fall.

Following this symbolism, is it possible that Christ atoned for all of us in a similar way, in a way we cannot fully understand but can sense in our spiritual bones? The prophet Abinadi taught that Christ would *see* those He saved as He saved them.[88] Is it possible, Christ likewise saw and joined each of us—one by one like He did with Abraham—while Christ suffered in the Garden of Gethsemane—even though our births would occur thousands of years in the future? Similar to how Christ's light passed through Abram as a covenant to restore him as Abraham, did we somehow walk through Christ to likewise be restored while He suffered in the Garden of Gethsemane?

I also ponder whether Christ's Atonement was not just one way, but that by bearing our stripes and drinking the bitter cup of our darkness and overcoming *our* sins, was Christ somehow enriched by our individual life experiences without the damning guilt of them, because our sins were not His choice, and, by saving us from them, He learned from them—and had His heart expanded by them because of His love for us. Was His divinity extended as He turned our adversities into bread and our afflictions into water as His own heart stretch wide as eternity?[89] Did He gain divine experience in turning our individual darkness into collective light? Did this exchange with each of us through Christ's At-one-ment, allow Him to rise to the heights of *Elohim*, understanding male and female, sinner and saint, the whole and broken—across all time?

Regardless of how Christ performed His infinite atonement, one thing is clear, He did not let the dark and painful experience of cleansing us with His blood, distract him from His purpose. He kept His eye single to the glory of God while saving His fallen brothers and sisters. As Christ performed His Atonement and stood under the crushing weight of our sins, pains, and anguish, He did not let discomfort eclipse His goal. He found peace and power in His purpose: *us*, His children, Zion—the lost He was there to save.[90] Christ is calling to us across time to join Him in that purpose of saving His seed and to use our wealth, our talents, our gifts, our very lives to join hearts as brothers and sisters and sing as Zion.

ZION IS SONG

THE PINNACLE OF CREATIVE SPEECH IS SONG. WE WERE ALL MADE TO sing. Some Native American tribes believe that we each have our own song that only we can sing. It is a song given us by the Creator, a piece of our identity and purpose. They believe in songs that if sung purely, create or destroy. For example, a funeral chant will only be sung after someone has died for fear that it would actually cause a death.[91]

This belief in the power of song is consistent with ancient scriptures. Adam and Eve and their descendants sang praises to God even after the Fall. This included Seth and Jared who sang to the Heavens to purify their people and keep their focus on Heaven.[92]

Song has always accompanied Zion, and our songs bring down blessings from above.[93] The Jaredites sang praises and worshiped God as they crossed the oceans from Babel to the new world. Their songs of praise lifted their boats to rise from the depths of darkness of the ocean.[94] Song lifts our hearts, reminds us of Heaven, and is the most celestial act we can perform with our lips. Pure song, empowered by a pure heart, glorifying Heaven, creates Zion.

Song is the most powerful way for us to draw our hearts *and* our lips to God, and there are countless examples of God's power in song.[95] The walls of Jericho fell at the sound of a few hundred trumpeted voices.[96] Angels filled the Heavens with light and song at Christ's birth.[97] Likewise, Christ himself likely sang with the Apostles at the last supper, before He was crucified. After His resurrection and ascension, the ancient saints *sang* the book of Hebrews to purify themselves to enter the presence of Christ above.

Songs of pure hearts *and* lips create Zion and let us commune with the Heavens. Christ delights in the righteous songs of the heart which are a prayer to God in Heaven above. [98] Joseph and his wife Emma lived this truth. Emma Smith gathered hymns for the first hymnal. Joseph attended singing schools and founded a choir which has become known as the Choir at Temple Square.[99] He encouraged all saints to refine their musical harmonies, teaching our musical talents increase as we obtain the Holy Ghost, until we join the choirs of Heaven. Calling Zion together was the purpose of the Saints' music.[100]

Song persisted even after Joseph's martyrdom. As the pioneers relocated to Utah, Brigham Young championed song and the arts, teaching that music could break the monotony of deprivation and physical labor. "Tight-laced religious professors of the present generation have a horror at the sound of a fiddle," he declared, probably remembering his puritanical upbringing. "There is no music in hell, for all good music belongs to heaven."[101]

Conversely, the Lord notes that all eternity is pained by earth's silence that we are now suffering, caused by the powers of darkness here below.[102] We are created to sing, and songs sung with sincere hearts and lips become a prayer that elevates, enlightens, and glorifies God, ourselves, and those who hear. Joseph Smith taught that as the Saints learned to sing with their whole hearts, their songs and anthems would "*soften into celestial melody, melt the hearts of the Saints and draw them together*," as if pulled by heavenly magnetic stirrings.

Then would "Zion of the Last days . . . become beautiful" and be "hailed by the Saints from the four winds, who will gather to Zion with songs of everlasting joy."[103]

The songs of Zion will call to each of us to awaken and remember why we are here and what we chose to be before descending. Heaven's melodies will stir within us a remembrance of our deepest divine desires: to rise up, radiate, and return home. Zion will be the place to gather together and sing the "song of redeeming love,"[104] where hearts that have broken here below are changed, healed, softened, and permanently purified for glory, where we can look others in the eyes, see as we are seen, love as we are loved, and share the joy of our rising and awakening in Christ.[105]

Heavenly union is magnified when we join *together* in song. Our yearning for unity takes on new meaning in light of the global pandemics and quarantines and governmental rules against gatherings. It has been easy to feel alone and isolated, hidden behind the medical masks of fear. But Christ has promised us that we will rejoice and sing after the harvests, scourges, and plagues are over.[106] He assures us of a time when He will stand in our midst and together we will sing *this new song*:

D&C 84

99 The Lord hath brought again Zion;
The Lord hath redeemed his people, Israel,
According to the election of grace,
Which was brought to pass by the faith.
And covenant of their fathers.

100 The Lord hath redeemed his people;
And Satan is bound and time is no longer.
The Lord hath *gathered all things in one.*
The Lord hath brought down *Zion from above.*
The Lord hath brought up *Zion from beneath.*

101 The earth hath travailed and brought forth her strength;
And truth is established in her bowels;
And the heavens have smiled upon her;

And she is clothed with the glory of her God;
For he stands in the midst of his people.

102 Glory, and honor, and power, and might,
Be ascribed to our God;
for he is full of mercy,
Justice, grace and truth, and peace,
Forever and ever, Amen.

Although set as verses, there is no evident rhyme or rhythm to these words in English. The melody and music must be hidden, awaiting a day when we will sing with new hearts in our native tongue—the language of creation—the language of Enoch and Adam. I wonder if, similar to how the voice that announced Christ to the ancient Americans started as a piercing whisper and grew as people yearned to understand, this song will likewise begin as a whispered lullaby until it crescendos into a Heaven-filling chorus of release, as the Saints unite in Zion's harmony and abandon the world's dissonance. When we hear this song of Zion, it will be familiar to us and fill our hearts with awakening fire, as its chords purify us for the choirs above.

If Christ's words can create the earth, surely His redemptive songs will ignite it. These powerful words ring of redemption, grace, Heaven's smiling glory, and Christ returning. They foretell time ceasing, Satan being bound, and of the earth being fully restored, awakened to its premortal glory and turned to a sea of glass, fire, and joy.[107] I wonder if learning to sing this song will accelerate this event, as saints join their hearts and voices in collective transcendence, lifting the hearts of Zion skyward.

CHAPTER 5 ENDNOTES

1 Alma 30:44.
2 *The First Book of the Secrets of Enoch*, Chpt. I verse 1, in *The Forgotten Books of Eden*, translated by Rutherford H. Platt Jr., 1926.
3 Brigham Young, in *Journal of Discourses* 14:227, 231a–231b, "Our Present Life, Etc." (citing Moses 3:5); *see also* D&C 131:7
4 *Ibid.*
5 D&C 105:1–3.
6 John Taylor, in *Journal of Discourses* 10:147b (citing Joseph Smith Translation, Gen. 9:21; Moses 7:27) emphasis added.
7 Joseph Young, "Enoch and His City," p. 12, Sen. Salt Lake City Utah, Printed at the Deseret News Steam Printing Establishment, 1878.
8 Moses 7:18.
9 Mark 12:30–31.
10 D&C 97:21.
11 John Taylor, "The Work of God, Etc.," *Journal of Discourses* 23:235, noting "there have been Zions before."
12 Phone interview with Chad Hansen regarding his mother Florence Petersen Hansen, October 20, 2020.
13 Dana Taylor https://supernalliving.com/2012/12/24/legend-of-the-angelic-inspiration-of-handels-messiah/.
14 *Ibid.*
15 "Marching Along," *Recollections of Men, Women and Music*, January 1, 1928.
16 Sterling W. Sill, "Motivations," BYU address, https://speeches.byu.edu/talks/sterling-w-sill/motivations/.
17 Bradley, "Introduction," *The Sweetness at the Bottom of the Pie: A Flavia de Luce Mystery.*
18 Steven Pressfield, *War of Art*, p. 103.
19 Gary Zukav, "Introduction," *Dancing Wu Li Masters: An Overview of the New Physics*, p. xxvii.
20 Helaman 5:33; 3 Nephi 17:15.
21 D&C 50:24.
22 Leonard Cohen, "Hallelujah," song, Passport Records, 1984.
23 Robert D. Hales, "Out of Darkness into His Marvelous Light," April 2002 general conference.
24 Luke 1:79.
25 John 8:12.
26 Genesis 1:3.
27 John 1:5.
28 1 Nephi 1:6.
29 Joseph Smith—History 1:16–17.

30 Quran 2:17, 257. In biblical Hebrew, light in the phrase יְהִי אוֹר (yəhî ʼôr) is made of two words. יְהִי (yəhî) meaning "to exist" and אוֹר (ʼôr) meaning "light"; compare Genesis 1:3.
31 D&C 67:9.
32 D&C 93:2.
33 D&C 14:9.
34 D&C 88:77.
35 Ephesians 4:17–19.
36 D&C 93:49.
37 Ephesians 6:12.
38 Isaiah 30:26.
39 D&C 6:6–7; D&C 11:7.
40 D&C 39:17–19.
41 Jacob 2 18–19.
42 1 Cor. 6:20.
43 Mosiah 2:17.
44 D&C 88:67.
45 D&C 101:75.
46 D&C 104:17.
47 D&C 124:9–11.
48 D&C 81:5.
49 2 Nephi 26:29.
50 2 Nephi 9:30.
51 2 Nephi 26:21.
52 D&C 89:21.
53 D&C 89:18.
54 D&C 89:20.
55 D&C 84:33.
56 Spencer W. Kimball, "Our Great Potential," April 1977 general conference.
57 Rob Gardner, *Lamb of God*, Release date, March 8, 2011, spiremusic.org.
58 Isaiah 46:4.
59 D&C 89:18–20; Luke 21:18.
60 Steven R. Gundry, *The Plant Paradox: The Hidden Dangers* (HarperCollins Publishers: 2019).
61 *The First Book of Adam and Eve*, Chpt. LXV verse 23, in *The Forgotten Books of Eden*, translated by Rutherford H. Platt Jr., 1926.
62 *Ibid.* at Chpt. LVI–LVII.
63 2 Nephi 26:25; Isaiah 55:1; Psalms 105:39–41.
64 John 4:13; Matthew 5.
65 *The First Book of Adam and Eve*, CHAP. XI versus 7–11, in *The Forgotten Books of Eden*, translated by Rutherford H. Platt Jr., 1926.
66 *The Blessings of Abraham, Becoming a Zion People*, E. Douglas Clark, p. 200; D&C 121:45.

67 Ether 2:1–3.
68 Jacob 5.
69 D&C 88:6.
70 Jeremiah 35.
71 1 Thessalonians 5:5; Isaiah 2:3–4.
72 2 Nephi 8:3; Isaiah 51:3.
73 Isaiah 27:6.
74 "Time is clearly not our natural dimension. Thus it is that we are never really at home in time. Alternately, we find ourselves wishing to hasten the passage of time or to hold back the dawn. We can do neither, of course, but whereas the fish is at home in water, we are clearly not at home in time—because we belong to eternity." Neal A. Maxwell, "Patience," BYU address, 27 November 1979.
75 Alma 40:8; D&C 84:100.
76 D&C 130:7.
77 Genesis 6:3; Moses 8:17; Joshua 10:13.
78 D&C 122:9.
79 Moses 7:21.
80 Leibovici, Leonard, M.D., "Effects of remote, retroactive intercessory prayer on outcomes in patients with bloodstream infection: randomized controlled trial." *British Medical Journal*, vol. 323 (22 December 2001): 1450–1451, available at: https://www.ncbi.nlm.nih.gov/pmc/articles/PMC61047/.
81 *Ibid.*
82 D&C 77:9.
83 Genesis 15:5–10.
84 Genesis 15:8–18; Joseph Smith Translation, Genesis 17:3–12.
85 The Hebrew word covenant " תירִבְ " comes from the root meaning to cut.
86 Jeremiah 34:18–19 which contains similar references to passing between a divided animal as a symbol of an everlasting covenant.
87 Jacob 5; Judges 19–21.
88 Mosiah 15:10–15.
89 Isaiah 30:20, Moses 7:41.
90 Isaiah 53:10; Mosiah 14:10: prophesy by Isaiah that when God makes Christ's "soul and offering for sin" through the Atonement "he shall see his seed"; see also Hebrews 2:16: noting because of the Atonement Christ was one with us and "took not on the nature of angels" but "took on him the seed of Abraham."
91 *Introduction* to *The Forgotten Books of Eden*, Rutherford H. Platt Jr., 1926; *see also* https://www.britannica.com/art/Native-American-music. Note that "Native Americans trace the ultimate origin of their traditional music to the time of creation, when specific songs or musical repertories were given to the first people by the Creator and by spirit beings in the mythic past. Sacred narratives describe the origins of specific musical instruments,

songs, dances, and ceremonies. Some ritual repertories received at the time of creation are considered complete, so that by definition human beings cannot compose new music for them."

92 *Second Book of Adam and Eve*, Chapt., X:4, *The Forgotten Books of Eden*, Rutherford H. Platt Jr., 1926.

93 D&C 25:12.

94 Ether 6:5.

95 Isaiah 28:16.

96 Joshua 6:1–27. Note the numerical symbolism, that the walls fell on the *seventh* time the trumps were played on the *seventh* day.

97 Luke 2:12–14.

98 D&C 25:12.

99 Joseph Young, "Vocal Music," p. 14, Sen. Salt Lake City Utah, Printed at the Deseret News Steam Printing Establishment, 1878.

100 Our current hymnal contains the word "Zion" 157 times, with the "Israel, Israel God is Calling" alone using "Zion" 18 times.

101 Brigham Young, in Journal of Discourses, 9:244.

102 D&C 38:11–12; this makes me question if hell rings with silence.

103 Joseph Young, "Enoch and His City," p. 12, Sen. Salt Lake City Utah, Printed at the Deseret News Steam Printing Establishment, 1878.

104 Alma 5:14.

105 Helaman 3:35.

106 D&C 84: 96–97.

107 D&C 84:100–102.

CHAPTER 6
THE OPPOSITION

"The time is soon coming, when no man will have any peace but in Zion and her stakes."
—Joseph Smith 1

THE PEACE AND GLORY OF ZION DOES NOT JUST OCCUR; WE CREATE it with pure hearts and minds. Terrified of Zion's rising glory, Satan prods and entices the natural tendencies of our bodies to harden our hearts. He works to destroy our unique talents and erase our divine individuality because building and raising Zion as promised by Daniel will "call into action the energy, skill, talent, and ability of the Saints."[2] We all must do our part.

So, Babylon and all the actors on Satan's stage rage against Zion's majesty by attacking those who can create it. After Satan and his hosts lost the war in Heaven and were cast down to earth,[3] the Lord cursed Satan to a life of traveling on his "belly" and "eating dust the rest of his life."[4] This curse was symbolic and literal damnation. Heavenly Father clipped Lucifer's wings of lift and light, which until his rebellion had allowed him to move about the Heavens.[5]

Still damned here below, Satan continues to wage war against our Heavenly Parents' plan. His every effort is to rob us of the joy and peace of rising as Zion. He does this by teaching us to use our own agency against ourselves to blind our eyes, deafen our ears, and deaden our hearts. He works tirelessly to ensure that even the elect will be deceived and to persuade us to remain lost, forgotten, and alone.[6]

I have seen the devastating effects of Satan's war firsthand. I grew up in what many referred to as the heart of "Zion"—the college town of Provo, Utah (affectionately called "Happy Valley"). I could see Brigham Young University and the Provo Temple from my home, and four other temples from our mountain view on 1450 East. I would hike the "Y" Mountain in the summer and cool off from the Provo heat with rich ice cream from the BYU Creamery. Surrounded by believers, in my teenage mind, everyone seemed to be on the same team.

The unity of Provo I enjoyed in my youth seemed to evaporate over the following twenty years. In 2018, I attended my twenty-year reunion at Provo High. I had been married to my gorgeous wife for fourteen years, and God had blessed us with five happy children. I had worked on Capitol Hill for Senator Orrin Hatch and in the White House for President Bush and President Obama, had graduated from law school, and was working for a tech company in Las Vegas.

I felt far removed from those I loved in Provo. I was excited to reconnect with many of my friends and their families. Imagine my sorrow when I discovered that, although just twenty years earlier in 1998, when ninety percent of Provo High students were faithful members, by 2008, more than half appeared to have left the Church of Jesus Christ or become antagonistic toward it.

What had happened? Why did more than half of my friends—strong, hopeful, happy, rich-in-potential Saints—turn away from Zion? Why were many of them now apathetic, bitter, angry, or upset with their lives? Like how God asked Adam in the garden after eating the fruit, I felt my heart ask itself, "*ayekah*?," meaning in Hebrew, "where is your light?"

I pondered on this for weeks after my reunion. I looked at several of my own family members who had also spurned or grown apathetic to God. I felt I was witnessing a great battle for the souls of men and women, and hard-hearted casualties had fallen all around me. I yearned to understand why they had left and, more importantly, how could I help them return?

I believe those who reject Zion, Christ, and the fellowship of the Saints do so because of unresolved *pain* and *fear*. These two thorny weeds, if unchecked by the healing of Christ's truth and love, bear fruit of darkness, thorn and thistles that manifest as selfishness, addiction, contention, ingratitude, and apathy. Satan entices hearts heavy with pain and fear to surrender their light for the false release of addiction, justification, distraction, and self-betrayal. But the gospel of Jesus Christ is the *only* place to find lasting peace and healing. While we disappoint, fail, injure, and destroy, Christ's love and peace *never* fails. He is the sure way home.

Satan often convinces us the only way to overcome pain is to kill the nerve, not heal the wound. I have hardened my own heart at times when I let a painful experience eclipse my view of the Savior instead of helping me focus on Him. Christ helps us see that the pain of affliction and the heartache of adversity can be for our good if we turn to Him. When we are in pain, He reminds us of our past and calls us to our future, teaching us that He alone understands the pain, sorrow, darkness, sickness, and solitude of each of His children on earth because He is above all things, He descended below all things, and He calls us up to His throne on high.[7]

On the contrary, just as Enoch saw, Lucifer weaves chains of darkness to ensnare the whole world.[8] Working to get us to forget who we are and drag us to a deeper sleep, his most crippling bonds are the lies he convinces us to tie around ourselves. When we experience difficulty, pain, sorrow, fear, anger, and contention, he whispers that the opposition we feel in life is God's displeasure with us, rather than obstacles we can climb to rise back home.

Satan and his followers are trying to convince us we are not sons and daughters of Heavenly Parents, made in their image and foreordained to become like them, but that we are crippled, temporary, worthless, tainted, and filthy beyond cleansing—that we are *nothing*. His tools have wreaked havoc on the agency, mission, and purpose of our Heavenly Parents and their children. Below are just a *few* examples of the tools Satan uses to harden hearts, blind eyes, and deafen ears to the truths, light, and glory that awaits us.

THE DARKNESS OF FEAR

WHILE SENSING FEAR CAN ALERT US TO DANGER, WALLOWING IN FEAR creates darkness. Unless we choose to warm our heart in light, faith, and repentance, fear will stop our hearts cold, and our creative seats will rage in self-destruction. By persuading us to focus our hearts on our fears of what could be, rather than trusting in what has been ordained to be through Christ, Satan leads us away from our personal and collective celestial potential—the divinity inside us.

When we believe fear, we begin to prize our lives more than those around us until we become swollen in our own darkness. If we're not careful, Satan can then persuade us to disconnect from those around us who are offering us chances to know Christ by serving Him through serving them.

When our hearts fear, they fail and *create* darkness. All living during the COVID-19 world have seen or felt the effects of fear. Many who used to welcome a warm handshake or embrace shrunk from it. Others once energized by large groups and gatherings felt trapped in their homes, isolated and alone.

As Melchizedek is said to have taught alchemists, "there is only one thing that makes a dream impossible to achieve: the *fear* of failure."[9] If we let it, fear cripples creative light and clips our wings before we even try to fly. Fear blinds our eyes to our potential and leads us to treat others around us as less important than our fear. As we overcome fear, we can join hands and hearts to rise together in foreordained purpose, rather than shrivel into solitude and a dark sleep from which we may not awaken.

The Lord teaches us faith and love overcome fear and bring confidence. When we begin to feel charity and choose thoughts of virtue our *confidence* will "wax strong in the presence of God," and in this place of compassion for others, "the doctrine of the priesthood will distil upon [our souls] as the dews from heaven."[10] *This doctrine of the priesthood is compassionate connection*—unified purpose in helping each of us rise to the divinity within us.

Our divinity continues inside us, despite being fallen, because of our connection to Christ. The act of becoming like our Heavenly Parents *is* like learning to walk on water.

Imagine Peter's determined courage and enthusiasm when he leapt out of the boat and to join the Lord on the water. We often focus on how Peter became afraid and the Lord had to rescue Him. But this misses the reality that once Peter's fear was quelled, Peter walked again on the water! Through Christ, Peter overcame his fear, and was able to rise up with Christ, redeemed, lifted, and empowered.

Just like Peter saw Christ walking on the water and yearned to join His Lord, we are all invited to come out on the water and be with God. When the winds and the waves crash upon us, when the storm whines and its lightning rages, we all have a choice. We can focus on what we don't have, or we can focus on what we do have. We can focus on how the boat is out of control or uncomfortable, or we can look out on the water and see the Lord calling to us, the Prince of Peace, unchanged by the storm. Though life is full of storms, each of us is meant to walk on the water, hand in hand with our Lord.

We may not be able to control the storm-tossed sea, but we can always control where we look. If we look to Christ in every thought, doubt not, and fear not, we *will* walk on water. And we will laugh through our tears at the joy of it all. We unlock this divinity and bounty within us by keeping our eyes fixed on Christ. As we watch Him do the impossible and trust Him enough to step out over the boat into the storm-tossed sea when He calls to us, we learn to "look unto [Him] in every thought; and doubt not, fear not."[11]

This is why Satan does everything to keep us from seeing our Savior, and from trusting in His miracles. Fear of pain, fear of regret, fear of loneliness, fear of inadequacy—they all obstruct our view of Christ's hand calling us out onto the water. What is your fear? What is keeping *your* heart back? Finding our way to Zion with others is our purpose. Believe. Choose to let that purpose and love for others replace all fear.

THE LIE OF PAIN

Pain is a universal weight in the human experience. Even after it passes, the apprehension of it can send shivers up a spine. This is especially true if we believe pain means the Lord does not love us. The Lord often allows pain to be our teacher, even though He knows the weight of healing our pain will be a greater burden to Him. I experienced this form of education while serving as a missionary in Moldova. Christ allowed pain to soften my heart and draw me to Him. It was one of the greatest gifts I have ever received, but it threatened to be my greatest poison.

It began one morning while playing basketball (yes—almost every terrible mission story starts with this phrase). I went up for a rebound and came down hard on my knee. It twisted incorrectly, and I fell to the ground. I tried to stand but collapsed again in severe pain, unable to walk. I was terrified. I had felt prompted not to play that morning, but we had little to do, and although I had felt prompted not to, I chose to play anyway.

My missionary companions rushed me to the nearest hospital. Moldova is a beautiful country home to sincere children of Israel. These people are kind and wise and have open hearts. But decades of Communism robbed them of much of their wealth, and, as a result, the hospital I came to had little to no diagnostic services. As I lay there disabled, another patient thrashed on a gurney next to me, covered in blood, screaming in Russian that he was going to die. I felt as if God was punishing me for not listening and my pain was evidence of Heaven's disfavor.

The doctor took an X-ray, but having no X-ray paper, printed it on normal paper, and determined I had simply sprained my knee. He injected my knee with pain killer, slapped a cast on it and told me I would be fine in a few weeks. I later learned I had torn the cartilage (meniscus) on both sides of my knee cap in what surgeons at the time referred to as a rare "double bucket handle tear." I had torn out two pieces of cartilage the size of my largest fingers that were now floating in my knee. The loose cartilage had lodged itself between my knee bones and made it impossible for me to walk.

I returned home to the U.S. the day before Christmas for knee surgery. For the three months that followed I despaired, worried that my own mistakes had led me there. My heart began to harden, bruised by my experience. Then I remembered a lesson my grandfather George W. Pace had taught me a few months before I left on my mission. The lesson softened my heart, and I saw Christ reaching out to me—offering me the bread baked in adversity and the water purified in affliction.[12]

The lesson was based on a talk by John R. Lasater that illustrated the tenderness of how Christ as our shepherd knows each of us by name and that we are more precious than money to Him. Lasater wrote of an experience where, while journeying with the Moroccan king's motorcade on behalf of the U.S. government, the trip paused after one of the vehicles hit a little lamb:

> An old shepherd, in the long, flowing robes of the Savior's day was standing near the limousine in conversation with the driver. . . . The king's vehicle had struck and injured one of the sheep belonging to the old shepherd. [By law because] the king's vehicle had injured one of the sheep belonging to the old shepherd, he was now entitled to *one hundred times* its value at maturity. However, under the same law, the injured sheep must be slain and the meat divided among the people.
>
> My interpreter hastily added, "But the old shepherd will not accept the money. They never do . . . *Because of the love he has for each of his sheep.*"
>
> It was then that I noticed the old shepherd reach down, lift the injured lamb in his arms, and place it in a large pouch on the front of his robe. He kept stroking its head, repeating the same word over and over again. When I asked the meaning of the word, I was informed, "Oh, he is calling it by name. All of his sheep have a name, for he is their shepherd, and the good shepherds know each one of their sheep by name." [13]

As predicted, the shepherd refused the money and left with his small flock of sheep, with the injured one tucked safely in the pouch of his robe. Like this good earthly shepherd, Christ knows each of us by name and calls to each of us to allow Him to carry us home. Similar to how the shepherd refused one hundred times the sheep's value because of his pure love for his sheep, Christ loves each of us, and He will not give us up—especially when we are injured.

My grandfather told me he too had witnessed a shepherd in Israel carrying a lamb on his shoulders with a broken leg. When asked about the lamb's leg, the shepherd responded that he himself had broken the lamb's leg. "What? You broke the lamb's own leg? Why?" The shepherd explained that this particular little lamb had a hard time hearing his voice. To save him from the dangers of wolves or getting lost, the shepherd himself broke the lamb's leg, knowing he would bear the burden of carrying the lamb on his shoulders as it healed. The shepherd knew that in doing so, the lamb would come to trust the shepherd, learn his voice, and come to follow him.

As I lay in my bed one night, with my entire leg throbbing after surgery, my soul feeling crippled and alone, I felt Heaven was punishing me until the tender truth of this lesson poured over my heart. I was the lamb with the broken leg, and I was not alone. Christ, my Shepherd, was carrying me on His back, healing me, inviting me to hear His voice and follow Him.

I healed. I returned to Romania and Moldova a few months later to finish my mission. To this day, I have no lasting effect of the knee injury. But the impact of this lesson on my heart was eternal. I came to know that the Lord knew me and was calling to me, that He would carry me when I fell and that, in doing so, I would learn to hear Him better. If I would listen to His voice, he would feed my soul with His bread and water, and I would never hunger or thirst again. I could be awakened in Him.

Even though Christ carries us to awaken us, it is up to us to stay awake. Over twenty years later, pain was used to soften and teach my heart yet again. I had started a new job and was working ten- to twelve-hour days, sitting at a desk and eating very poorly. My work paid for all my meals, and I reveled in the dessert foods I had rarely enjoyed in my youth. I recall on at least two occasions eating an entire Costco-sized bag of peanut M&Ms while I worked late into the night writing legal pleadings.

The spirit consistently warned me to drink more water, exercise, and take care of what I ate. The warnings were obvious, but I did not listen. I even recall one month hearing at least three times, alerts on the radio to drink more to avoid back injury. Each time, I was so focused on my work, on proving I was good enough by performing, that I ignored the clear warnings.

One morning I awoke feeling awful. My body ached, my mind was numb, and worst of all, my heart was not at peace. I felt a slave to the constant call of refined sugar. In anger-filled purpose, I pled with God. "Please help me stop eating sugar," I cried in the shower that morning through hot tears. I was done being crippled and trapped.

I learned that day to be careful what I pray for because the Lord *does* answer prayers. I also learned that if I offer a prayer with a sick heart, the Lord will first have to cleanse my heart before He can bless my soul. I didn't know it then, but the Lord started me on a decade-long journey of pain to awaken me and cleanse my darkened heart.

That same night, I came home late, unsettled, unbalanced, and unhappy. My wife, sensing I had over-extended myself at work (again), suggested I go for a bike ride. I used to ride my bike to work before taking this new job. She could tell that my balance was "off," and that I was going to take her peace from her in search of my own if I didn't go do something to rebalance myself.

I went out that night still angry—angry about work, angry about my lack of happiness, and angry about my enslavement to sugar. I can still remember the feeling I had as I pushed my body harder than I should, fueled by that anger. I awoke the next morning to the greatest pain of my life. A gnawing, unsettled ache began in my lower left back and ran down my leg. Constant tension filled my hip that was impossible to release, as if I needed to crack a joint but couldn't.

It remained constant for months. I couldn't sleep. Then I couldn't walk. Then all I could do at times was crawl. It was overwhelming and debilitating. I quickly learned the pain increased whenever I ate refined sugar. My prayer had been answered.

My poor wife saw me descending into a pit of pain and darkness and could only watch as it consumed me. I thought I could push through it, that I would get better. I kept telling myself I had always healed before. I had been blessed with a body that would do what I told it to do. It was just a matter of time until the pain would go away and I'd be back to my normal self.

Eventually, I got an MRI and found I had ruptured a disc in my lower back. Bits of disc material were impacting my nerve endings, causing me constant pain. I refused surgery for months. Finally, I succumbed to the idea of surgery when the pain was so unbearable, and I started considering much darker thoughts, questioning the purpose of life.

After surgery, the pain left for a time but returned more intensely weeks later. I remember walking into the surgeon's office for a post-operative diagnosis, devastated and discouraged. I saw many other people the waiting room, with the same symptoms, their faces contorted in pain, limping, unable to move. However, all were at least twenty-thirty years older than I was. I saw one woman in her sixties, bitter, consumed by her pain and raging against her children who were with her. Her face was full of enraged sourness, like a wounded dragon intent on releasing the dark fire within—even if it meant burning herself and those she loved.

Seeing her venom, I realized I had a choice. My surgery had not worked; the pain remained. But I could choose what I did with it, as I had with my knee. I could let the pain turn me into a victim, or I could rise above it. I could let it harden me or I could let it soften me. I began to abandon my angry complaints and started seeking answers.

It took me years, but I now see my breaking as one of the greatest gifts of my life. As I let Christ into my pain-shocked heart, I realized He was teaching me empathy, and waking me up to see others around me, and saving me from future dangers. In time I found Pilates and learned to strengthen my core. I learned how to walk correctly and about the muscles I had been given but neglected to use. I also learned to stop eating other things. He taught me line upon line and food by food. He would warn me with a voice that said, "You don't want to eat that," or even "don't eat that" when a food would intensify my pain.

A few months before COVID-19 hit, the Spirit led me to cut gluten, soy, peanuts, and milk from my diet. I lost 40 pounds in three months and later learned that those foods cause inflammation. I started taking turmeric regularly, a natural anti-inflammatory. I worked out daily. In my own process of time, I started to be restored both physically and spiritually. When I contracted COVID-19 in 2020, because the Lord had taught me to change my lifestyle (starting over a decade prior), I avoided serious complications.

My back pain has not entirely gone away. It returns at times as a reminder when my heart and mind are in the wrong place. When I become too focused on the wrong thing. When I seek my worth in my profession or the opinion of others, the pain returns. It has become a "thorn of the flesh" reminding me to wake-up and return my focus to Christ and my real purpose.[14]

If you feel overwhelmed by pain, I want you to know I have also lived in that black pit. The darkness can seem unbearable at times. I remember taking slow walks after my surgery to try and release some of the tension. I would look up to the Heavens, see the stars, and wish to be whisked away, lifted up to a celestial place far from my pain. I now know that place is Zion. I don't need to be carried away for release, for I've learned that the peace of Zion can happen here and now as I hear Him.

All experiences are an invitation to come to know Christ and to be lifted back up to Him. This is especially true for pain. But these things will only be an invitation if we choose to feel Christ's compassion and love. If we are able to believe, we'll never feel pain alone. Christ knows our pain better than anyone. He suffers it *with* us, *beside* us. He weeps with us. He aches for us. And He is calling to each of us to release us from it, *pleading* with us to let Him heal us and fully restore us in this life and on into the glory of the next.

Christ's compassion comes because He has descended far below all darkness and pain and found a way out for you. His path is designed for your pain, your sorrow, your aching. We are His work and his glory. He not only lets us learn from pain, but He personally paid the price to ensure we learn from it and are not scarred by it. Satan knows this and will do everything he can to keep us from finding Christ in our pain. We can ignore his lies and let our sufferings draw us up to Christ. We can let the experiences soften us and fill our heart with compassion for others until we feel Christ's love for all around us.

CORROSIVE CONTENTION

When our hearts struggle with unresolved pain or fear, it causes a wide array of problems, from addiction or apathy to entitlement and pride. All of these heart pains eventually lead to Satan's most destructive fruit—contention. Any form of contention in our hearts wars against Zion.[15]

Contention is different than conflict. As I have worked on billions of dollars of transactions and litigation debates over the years, I have found that conflict can be the richest soil for innovation, discovery, and ultimate unity—even between opposing parties. With this mindset, conflict fosters creation. We can keep the laws of Heaven and love God, our neighbors, and ourselves and defend ourselves from those who would harm us, if we remember there is a difference between conflict and contention.

Contention is not simply conflict or a difference of opinions but devilish by design. It is meant to be personal, a direct assault, to hit someone where it hurts—in the heart. This is true even when we feel we are justified in attacking another or using anger to defend ourselves from an attack. Contention is perhaps the easiest trap to find myself in if I lose myself or forget my purpose. The good news is Christ's love and truth can awaken anyone wrestling with contention—if we accept it.

I remember sitting opposite one of the most contentious lawyers I had ever met while handling a multi-hundred-million-dollar lawsuit. I had spent at least three hundred hours talking to this attorney. Her contentious spirit made my entire legal team wince. She was one of the most intelligent, aggressive, and *angry* lawyers any of us had ever encountered.

I spent one morning preparing for another ten hours with this attorney. Hopeful to find peace in the face of contention, I pled with the Lord to show me how to do my job in "the Lord's way." I knew only the Lord could deliver me and ensure contention did not poison my heart.[16]

Several miraculous things occurred. First, the Lord started with *me.* He softened my heart until in my mind's eye, I saw her as Christ sees her—a woman with a glorious past, a fallen present, and glorious potential future. Through this lens, I saw this lawyer as a young child—sensitive, intelligent, looking for peace—rather than the aggressive lawyer before me.

This transformation in my own heart occurred when I discovered that the expert witness, an industry-famous data center designer named Peter Gros,s was actually from Romania. We had only ever talked on the phone, and it was not until I heard him speak in person, that I could hear his almost negligible Romanian accent.

When it dawned on me, I smiled and asked him, "*Vorbiti Romanesti*?" ("do you speak Romanian?"). His eyes widened and we both laughed. He was not expecting me to know Romanian any more than I was expecting him. I saw this moment—orchestrated long before I showed up to the deposition—as evidence that God does have a plan for each of us.

Peter was intelligent, kind, and peaceful with me *but also* with the opposing attorney who many would view as "the enemy." His presence softened both of us. In doing so, my own intentions toward her changed. I no longer saw her as an object to defend myself from but as a human worthy of compassion. I reminded myself she was a wife, a new mother, and a daughter of God that had chosen Christ before coming to this earth. She was a spirit child of our Heavenly Parents. She had faith in Christ and came below, trusting He would save her, despite herself.

She was once a baby in her parents' arms, a toddler that learned to walk, a teenager with hopes and dreams. She is a god-in-embryo. I realized I would likely meet her in Heaven and wince at my own interactions with her. Who was I to treat her as less than her potential?

As my heart continued to soften that day, the spirit in the room shifted, and her own mood shifted in response. Her tone softened, and she shocked me when she said in passing, "I'm beginning to realize that litigation isn't real life. There are much more important things." The deposition was the most peaceful I had ever experienced. The Lord had delivered me by softening my heart and hers in truth. For a few moments—we both had reawakened to who she was. God was working with me as much as he was working with her.

When we see others as they really are—when we remember our role in the universe as cherished children of God, loved by divinity, destined for glory, no one in their right mind would treat a child of Heavenly Parents with disdain, malice, or avarice. Satan knows this and uses contention to blind our eyes to the divinity of those before us and our divinity within.

Divinity is the ability to radiate light when surrounded by darkness, to turn brass to gold, adversity to bread, affliction to water, poison to nourishment—hate to love. Christ's love transforms us, not just because it awakens us to who we really are but helps us see how precious all are around us, and how we can all interconnect as a foreordained Heaven on earth.

Life tests our divinity to see if we will return hate for hate, evil for evil, railing for railing, war for war—or—turn the other cheek, choose charity, and see those that attack us as precious, albeit wounded and fallen. Christ's compassion not only brings Him everlasting peace but peace to all willing to receive. His very presence elevates, perfects, and restores.

This is the divine heritage of the followers of Christ: to turn sickness to health, sin to sanctification, war to peace, darkness to light, and burning gold from the dark lead around us, until all the sickness, sin, war, and darkness are rid from the earth and our streets are paved with gold. We do this through the transformative and restorative power of charity, which is Christ's atoning and elevating pure love. He loves all of his children, and all those who accept His love *become* His.

His love heals us, restores the brightness we lost when we fell, and helps us become the sons and daughters of God and see others as Christ sees them, until when He returns we shall see Him as He is and be like Him, celestially radiant, pure, burning bright with eternal divinity and godliness. Our natures will be changed and our very presence, like Christ's, will liberate, elevate, and illuminate all around us.

It is only in this way that we can prove ourselves. This earth was given, and Christ's blood was shed to allow us to learn to practice the full measure of agency and be healed when we err. He is inviting us to see how to be divine even when surrounded by evil. When we are faced with war, hate, darkness, and sickness, we are being given an opportunity to awaken this divinity within us, this ability to choose Christ and become like Him. Thus, problems, sickness, obstacles, opposition, are for our benefit—at His dreadful but necessary cost. They are invitations to look to Christ, to doubt not, to fear not, to walk on water, until He has fully instructed us on how to awaken and become—TO BE like the great I AM—until we rise back home to Heaven above.

Zion is already inside us waiting to be restored. By driving contention from our lives and seeing others eternally, even when they rage against us, we allow the Lord to accelerate our own individual restorations. The sooner we join Christ in the restoration of ourselves, families, cultures, and the world, the happier we will be. For Zion continues to rise—no matter the opposition.

CHAPTER 6 ENDNOTES

1 *Teachings of the Prophet Joseph Smith*, sel. Joseph Fielding Smith [1976], 160–61.

2 Joseph Smith, in *History of the Church,* 4:185–86, citing Daniel 2:34–35, 44–45.

3 Revelation 12:8–10.

4 Moses 4:20.

5 Orson Pratt taught that we should "look forward to that state of more advanced happiness when this *mortal shell* shall be laid off; and when we, in the spiritual state, shall be enabled to enjoy those enlarged powers of locomotion which we have reason to expect" and travel at the speed of spirit, not just the speed of light. "That we may *fly swiftly to other worlds on missions.*" Orson Pratt, Journal of Discourses 3:97.

6 Mark 13:22.

7 D&C 88:6.

8 Moses 7:1–41.

9 Paulo Coelho, *The Alchemist* (HarperCollins:1998), p. 141.

10 D&C 121:45.

11 D&C 6:36.

12 Isaiah 30:20.

13 John Lasater, "Shepherds of Israel," April 1988 general conference.

14 2 Corinthians 12:7.

15 3 Nephi 11:29; the word "contention" is mentioned 82 times in the Book of Mormon.

16 Alma 23:23; Alma 24:21.

BOOK THREE:
ZION RISING

CHAPTER 7
ZION RISING IN YOU

"As many as will not harden their hearts shall be saved in the kingdom of God."
—Jacob 6:4

PRESERVING YOUR ETERNAL IDENTITY AS A CREATOR

Brigham Young taught the "greatest gift" God grants His children "is the gift of eternal life; that is, to preserve their identity—to preserve themselves before the Lord." There is something about Christ's existence even His very name that carries power and affects everything around Him. We invoke His name to sanctify, heal, and bless. As the great "I AM," Christ elevates all around Him.[1] He defines His circumstances and experiences, rather than letting His circumstances or experiences define Him. He transforms lead to gold, water to wine, and darkness to light. Moses warned the Israelites to stay off of Mount Sinai where Christ dwelt until sanctified "lest he break forth upon them" because only the sanctified could withstand the Lord's presence.[2] His mere presence is so powerful, even prophets had to be changed (transfigured) to not wither and die before Him.[3]

Is it any wonder we needed the galactic distance of the Fall—the physical and spiritual separation—to give us room to prepare to meet Him? We need space and time to purify our hearts so we can *be ourselves* in His brilliant, burning, and radiant glory. It is only by obedience to *divine* law—where we love others as ourselves—that we ensure the earth is not "wasted" at His coming.[4] We preserve our eternal identities by gathering light and intelligence into our souls, and gain confidence before Him as we unite our hearts in virtue, truth and compassion.

THE CREATIVE POWER OF HIS WORD

Our Heavenly Parents taught Christ how to create and destroy with His words.[5] He created the universe, men and women, and all things on the earth by the power of His word, for Christ's "words cannot return void . . . [but] must be fulfilled."[6] In Genesis, Christ speaks to create light, and John later referred to Christ as "the Word." His word is so powerful, Christ himself describes it as quicker than a two-edge sword, capable of diving asunder of both joints and marrow.[7] His whisper pierces our hearts to the center, even when we cannot fully understand or hear His words.[8]

Christ invites all of us to be mighty in word, like Him. He restored Enoch from a stuttering lad into one whose word moved mountains, turned back rivers and made lions roar. He restored Moses from a man slow of speech, into someone who declared to Pharaoh and the mighty Egyptians, "Let my people go!" Moses became a prophet who sent down curses of Heaven and divided the Red Sea with a word. Christ's restoration of His people, His mighty work and wonder, is to enable *each* of us to speak in His name and create Heaven on earth.[9] For just as Christ created the Heavens and the earth with His word, we can also create with our words.

Brigham Young taught we were created to command "the creation and redemption of worlds . . ., extinguish suns," and by our very breath, "disorganize worlds, hurling them back into their chaotic state."[10] This power to create with a word begins with the things we tell ourselves, in our hearts. When we align our hearts and lips, we also create by our word. Is it any wonder that Satan, to stop the First Vision from occurring, tried to bind Joseph Smith's tongue as he began to pray, so that Joseph could not speak, as if Satan knew stopping Joseph's tongue could delay Christ's releasing pillar of light?

The Mayans taught that God's *word* brought about creation of the earth.[11] The fantasy and fiction of Hollywood and Broadway spin stories of characters like Elphaba in Wicked or Harry Potter the young wizard, that possess the power to create or destroy with words. Enoch's ability to speak and command rivers, mountains and lions shows us that power in word is not fiction, it is eternal reality. As children of Heavenly Parents, our speech can also create or destroy when empowered with faith and generated with a pure heart.

Japanese scientist Masura Emoto, demonstrated the creative power of our lips and hearts with a fascinating experiment involving jars of rice and water. He wrote the words, "I hate you" on one jar, "I love you" on another, and then completely ignored a third jar. After thirty days, the rice he said "I love you" to began to smell sweet; the rice he said "I hate you" to began to stink; but the rice he ignored turned black. He concluded we create with our words, and that even criticism is more enriching than utterly ignoring something.[12]

We have conducted the same rice experiment with my children several times and it has worked *each* time. Many critics claim to have debunked this experiment. Some insist the rice is merely influenced by what bacteria makes it into the rice jar before it is sealed.[13] However, their attacks reinforce the truth that these effects only occur when our hearts *and* our lips are aligned. Words without belief are empty. But words with faith will not return empty.[14]

Satan works tirelessly to convince us to use this power of the word against ourselves. He has become the very darkness he warned us against premortally. Although Satan cannot read our thoughts and hearts, he whispers poisonous distortions to us in ways that sound truthful.[15] Like warping our reflection in a mirror, he twists our interpretations of our experiences in an effort to convince us we are lost, fallen, broken, and unredeemable. He seeks to erase our eternal identities with these lies.

As children of the Creators, who taught Christ to create with His words, we also create with our words, *especially the words we tell ourselves*. Recognizing that Christ has the "words of eternal life," Satan seeks to interrupt our rejoicings and prevent us from hearing the words of eternal life that Christ is singing to us to help us be peaceful and happy.[16] He does this by deceiving us to use our creative powers of speech to tell ourselves false stories about our experiences to smother our gifts, joy, and light. He persuades us to attach false meaning to our life events and convince us that somehow they mean something about us.

Satan starts his attacks in our youth, seeking to persuade us to create darkness with what we tell ourselves. I remember a debate with my three-year-old daughter one evening. She was happily draining a tub after she finished her bath until I offered her a green towel instead of her favorite purple towel. She began to wail. Reminding myself that the best opportunities for connection occur when someone is upset, I channeled patience and asked her why she didn't want the green towel.

"I want purple!" she cried.

Still trying to understand what was making her so upset, I asked more gentle questions. She finally whimpered, "If I use a green towel, I'll turn into a boy!" With three older brothers and only one older sister, she believed colors were gender specific. I scooped her up and told her that she was my little girl, her Heavenly Parents' little girl, and that nothing she did on earth would change that, not what colors she wore or what people told her. She snuggled into me and now happily uses the green towel, understanding—at least as far as colors are concerned—that what she experiences does *not* define her identity.

These lies Satan whispers to us as children influence us throughout our lives until we learn to root them out and destroy them. How often have we defined ourselves by something other than our true identity? How often have we said, "I'm not good at math," or "I'm a terrible reader"? What we tell ourselves affects us. If we can open our hearts, we can explore what we are telling ourselves about our experiences and discover the lies that prevent our hearts from being soft and bright. My wife and I have taught and counseled hundreds of our brothers and sisters over the years about how to chase darkness from their hearts.

Whenever we would meet with them, we would ask them what they hate. Within minutes, this discussion would point to an experience they had in their youth that was still bothering them, something they were reminding themselves about and telling themselves subconsciously hundreds of times throughout the day, a story about who they were because of that painful or troubling experience.

One night we met with an institute brother. He was intelligent, handsome, bright, energetic, and full of enthusiasm for life, but he was also deeply pained, as if trapped by some barrier or wall. After opening up, he finally explained he feared he had made a very poor decision years ago when he told a young woman he loved that his career was more important than marriage at that time. Heartbroken, she eventually married someone else. He was devastated. He was terrified he had lost his one chance for love and would never reach his potential.

My heart filled with compassion for this young man, and I expressed sorrow for him. We explored why he had pushed her away in the first place. He could feel the compassion I felt radiating from the Savior for him and as it touched his heart, he began to identify several painful early childhood experiences. I expressed sorrow for him, and could see why he would choose to feel wounded by those experiences! I asked him how he felt, and what these painful experiences meant about him. He sat and pondered his emotions in silence, with drooped shoulders, until he shrugged and said, "It means God doesn't care about me."

As soon as he said the lie out loud, his eyes widened in shock. He realized he had been repeating that Satanic message to himself with each difficult experience. Camouflaged like a weed in the grass, the lie had buried itself deep in his heart, to the point where he began to believe the dark thought was his own. Satan had convinced him to use his divine power of speech to speak that lie over and over and over, until had become his constant internal narrative. It had poisoned his heart and created a dark shadow over his daily walk.

But, as soon as he had spotted and named the lie, his spirit of light immediately rejected it. He pulled out the weed, and bright truths flooded him, healing his wounds. He spoke them out loud, rapidly, and with building energy, letting the core truths rise up inside him and fill his temple with light. Truths that Christ *does* care. That Christ would miss him if this young man chose not to return home. That he was a star in God's Heavens. I testified to him that he was not just destined to be a star in God's Heaven but a maker of stars. He felt

Steps to keeping your view clear and removing lies that Satan uses to eclipse your view of Christ.

Step 1	Step 2	Step 3	Step 4	Step 5
Identify Experiences	**Acknowledge Feelings**	**Have Compassion**	**Name the Lie**	**Speak Truth to See Christ**
In that experience I was:	How did I feel/interpret that experience?	Hear Christ say to you.	What are you telling yourself about this?	Banish the lies with truth
Attacked Wounded Abused Ignored Used Deceived Objectified Idolized Judged	Angry Depressed Wounded Overwhelmed Upset Disappointed Unseen Unloved Unwanted	That was hard. That was painful. That was not ok. You're not crazy. It makes perfect sense you would feel that way. Those feelings make sense.	I'm not enough I'm worthless No one can love me I'll always be alone God hates me	Christ defines my worth. Christ's Atonement heals. I choose the miracle. Christ still loves me. Christ knows how I feel. He still loves me.

Every experience is an invitation to know Christ, look to Him and live – to see Him – doubt not; fear not.

Figure 6 *Steps to seeing Christ in every step.*

liberated, realigned, and enlivened. The day after this experience, I read Psalms 147:3–5, which assures us Christ not only heals us but knows each star and calls them all by their names. Christ knows us. He is reaching to heal us and awaken us to the majesty of His Heavens.

Whenever we define our worth by something other than our relationship with Jesus Christ, we refuse true joy. Whether it be possessions, pride, power, popularity, position, pleasure, or pain, if we believe our experience defines us, if we base our perspective of who we are in those momentary emotions rather than in our relationship with Christ, we perpetuate a lie and deny our true identities. We create darkness where there should be light, and our hearts turn cold and harden in that darkness.

How do we do chase away that darkness and remain children of light? How do we keep our eye single on God's glory and ensure there is no darkness within us?[17] We look unto Christ in every thought, doubt not, and fear not and remove the lies that eclipse our view of Him.[18]

My wife and I have found this to be the most effective path to staying centered in truth and keeping our vision clear of lies that fill us with darkness, and distract us from our true worth and joy in Christ:

Step 1—identify a painful experience that is still bothering you.

Step 2—acknowledge how you feel about that experience; the more honest you are, the more you will be able to see how those feelings (and what you're telling yourself about them) are affecting you.

Step 3—accept compassion from someone who cares about you or from Christ himself.

Step 4—identify the lie attached to that experience and name it.

Step 5—as soon as you have identified the lie, then fill your heart with truth and light.

We have millions of experiences every day. Every experience is an invitation to see Christ. From a warm hand to hold, to a stubbed toe; from delicious food, to food poisoning, all experiences are gifts offered by Heaven to help us see, hear, feel and understand Him. When we keep our hearts soft, and accept compassion from others, our experiences allow us to connect—to understand how things feel—so we in turn can have compassion for others facing similar growing experiences.[19]

When we harden our hearts, we blind ourselves to the connection with Christ each experience holds. While soft hearts connect in empathy, hard hearts stiffen in enmity. Satan knows this and seeks to attach false meaning to our experiences. He delights in warping our perspective. Satan seeks to sour even common experiences and convince us they are our most stressful moments: a screaming child, a deadline at work, a broken phone screen. He suggests these imperfections, these moments of dissonance or mortal jarring are evidence that God does not love us, or that we are unworthy or worthless. He sows seeds of doubt, annoyance, and anger until they grow deep into and harden our hearts.

How do we keep our hearts soft when they are stressed or ache? How do we stay in light and truth when surrounded by darkness? How do we ensure we treat others as divine, not as objects, when others are objectifying us? Two words: Love and Truth. Christ applies love *and* truth to help our hearts stay soft and pure. Compassion is deceptive if it is not based in reality. Likewise, truth is cold and damning without love.

The loving truth is that the Lord wants to bless us with *everything*. Christ remains in Zion above, calling to us, inviting us to feel, hear and see Him in each experience. He is inviting us to obey the laws of the terrestrial kingdom, then the laws of the celestial kingdom (the foremost of which is unity in love[20]), all the while growing brighter and brighter, and rising higher and higher until we radiate with His truth and love.

He has promised us the riches of eternity and "the things of this earth . . . even an hundredfold, *yea more*."[21] But He will not force these blessings upon us. *We* choose how much we receive, and in turn how happy we are, how much light we have, and how close we come to Him. In other words, He will give us the riches of eternity, the keys of the kingdom, light and knowledge, as quickly as we are willing to *receive* them and abide the laws of those blessings.[22]

Our willingness to be enriched with His grace is tied to the softness of our hearts—our active surrender to His plan, His will, His law. Worthiness is receptiveness, and receptiveness is a function of the heart. We can learn to stay in a place of gratitude and receptiveness, even when it feels to us like the world is conspiring against us, by following the example of Christ.

This is one of the greatest skills we are invited to learn here on earth—to be at peace within our own hearts despite outside influences—to be educated by our experiences, not hardened by them. Christ was able to stay at peace, compassionate and centered in His celestial purpose, even when living in a fallen telestial world. We are likewise here to learn to possess a Christlike serenity in purpose, enriched by the difficulty of our own experiences, not damned by them.

Although buried by the pain of the sins of the world, betrayed by His friends, falsely judged, spit upon, tortured, and crucified, Christ stayed focused on His purpose: you and me, all of us. I believe one of the ways Christ stayed centered despite being surrounded by a maelstrom of hell, evil, hate, and darkness was that He never let fear replace His purpose. He never became more concerned for Himself than His mission to save each of us. On the contrary, He willingly gave His life for us, and conquered death in doing so.

Heaven is created by people who have learned to be at peace within themselves, and with others, *regardless* of their circumstances or experiences. They have learned that possessions, pride, power, popularity, and pleasure, are irrelevant to eternal beings who live the laws of Heaven. This can be a hard lesson to learn. I know from the countless times I have failed and winced at my own natural reactions. But I have also learned that each moment can be accepted as an invitation to come closer to Christ and fully enjoy His Atonement and rise upward to His radiating presence by feeling His love and obeying His laws. Conversely, each moment can be a choice to deny His laws, reject His love, and distance ourselves from His light, love, and law and descend downward, deeper into darkness.

Zion is built and rises in our hearts, moment by moment, as our hearts create our reality around us. Our experiences are invitations to come to Christ and let Him show us the truth about ourselves and those around us. He uses our experiences to light the way back home—like stairs to Heaven—raising us until He can reintroduce us to our Heavenly Parents. As we choose to see each experience in gratitude, humility and joy, we choose to see Christ. As we choose to see others as precious souls to connect with rather than objects to abuse or act upon, we choose to become more like Christ.

OBTAINING A PERSONAL RESTORATIVE AWAKENING IN CHRIST

We have all heard the phrases, "it was meant to be," "you were born for this," or "déjà vu." These phrases are not just jargon, they are rooted in the collective sense that we have a purpose from before—that we are here to fulfill a plan and awaken something within us.

Before we came to earth, we saw Christ spiritually create a future kingdom wherein we could cherish the beauty of our individuality *and* our unity in Him. He taught us to pray for the Lord's will to be done, on earth as it is in Heaven, that His kingdom might come.[23] We can not only join that kingdom here and now but we can also build it as we awaken and are restored to our premortal potential, in Christ. Christ explained becoming like little children and following Him *is* His doctrine.[24] It is so simple and so important that He emphasized it twice! Christ can help us regain the soft-hearted nature of our childhood but retain the wisdom of our experiences. This is personal restoration.

The restoration of *people* is a common theme in the Book of Mormon.[25] The prophet Nephi longed for the day when his children would be restored from their fallen state. He testified that this personal restoration was for *all* nations, *all* kindreds, *all* tongues, and *all* people on the earth. Likewise, Alma taught his sons at length of the plan of restoration.[26] He taught the restoration rewards the seeker of righteousness and condemns those who refuse to repent, for that which we "send out shall return unto us again and be restored."[27] Alma rejoiced in the restoration of his enemies.[28] Likewise, the prophets Mormon and Moroni taught of and worked for the restoration of their people in Christ.[29]

The Prophet Joseph taught the importance of knowing that the paths we pursue are approved of God is critical. Without that knowledge, we "grow weary" in our minds, and faint.[30] Likewise, following the path Christ has laid out for our individual lives enlivens us and helps us grow brighter and brighter until the perfect day when the saints will shine in the kingdom of Heaven.[31]

By the power of the Holy Ghost, we can know all truth, discerning all things as they are, were, and will be.[32] This includes knowing the surety of the little steps and the monumental steps we make throughout our lifetime.[33] We can know our path is straight and true as surely as prophets of old did who testified with assurance that they *knew* the Savior would come, that they *knew* He would be born of Mary, and that they *knew* He would redeem His people, thousands of years before His birth.

Knowing we are living with foreordained purpose can bring calm confidence. We can view major events in the world like hurricanes, pandemics, and other natural disasters as evidence that God is in control and preparing the world for His return, stirring up the hearts of men to look to Him and awaken. We can have faith these events are part of our Heavenly Parents' effort to bring us home with Christ who is always guiding, inviting, and healing.

Knowing we have foreordained paths can also bring confidence in personal and individual choices. We can trust that God does care and has a plan for us. He will help us decide who to marry, what career to pursue, and how to live in a way that is receptive to the blessings of Heaven. This type of faith leads to radiant hope.

The reason faith is a hope for things which are not seen but are real is because with faith we can begin to sense, hear, and see what already exists spiritually. John Taylor noted that this prophetic awareness of spiritual foreordination can "bring certain ideas, thoughts and reflections to our minds. An intelligence of this kind is not a phantom, it is a reality."[34]

Even with the confidence that comes from knowing we each have a foreordained path, each of us in some sense has experienced the terror of drowning, of being lost under the weight of reality. At times, our responsibilities, our fears, and our emotions can feel like great waves crashing upon us until we drown, buried by them. As we slip beneath the surface of these crushing forces, we might feel as if we are about to be swallowed up, forgotten, nothing.

Satan strives to deceive us into believing that we are what we experience here below. That somehow our experiences mean something about us. The Father of lies whispers to us that things that disturb our peace and happiness mean something about us and should eclipse our view of Christ. He attempts to poison our hearts with lies that hardship means Christ has forgotten us, forsaken us, or no longer reaches out to us.

But Christ is always above us, calling to us, His hand outstretched, just as He did with Peter, inviting us with a gentle smile to rise up and join Him upon the water. When we grasp His hand through faith, repentance, and obedience, He pulls us up above our fear and reminds us of our true identity. By exercising faith in Him, we can come crashing up through the surface of darkness, lifted by His love—as He teaches us to walk on the stormy water.

With our hand firmly in His, we can feel the water dripping off our faces, the warmth of the sun piercing the storm clouds around us, and open our eyes and see Him. In that moment, we might laugh and cry, as if seeing pure joy for the first time. Then, we walk on the water.

Warmed by the power of Christ's compassion, we become charged with the purpose of saving others from their own depths of darkness. In these moments, we can feel for the first time like our true selves, having undergone a personal restorative awakening in Christ where we allow our divine identities to overcome any darkness and restore us until we are fully awake, aligned with our true selves and with Christ.

This awakening is typified by accounts throughout the scriptures where people are given new names after awakening in Christ. Shem became more like Christ until He assumed Christ's own title of Melchizedek. Abram and Sarai awoke as Abraham and Sarah. Jacob awoke as Israel. Saul awoke as Paul. The Lord takes the gap between our reality and our foreordained potential and bridges it with His grace, to bring alignment between us in our current fallen state and that divine being who we really are, as He sings our true names in His kingdom.

RIBBONS OF LIGHT TO GUIDE US HOME

Our Heavenly Parents and their Christ strike the perfect balance between respecting our agency and doing all they can to help us return Home and become like them. Although we have forgotten, they remember the premortal conversations we had with them of our fears, hopes, and dreams before descending to earth; the covenants we made with each other and with them; and how the overarching principle of agency requires us to choose how much of Heaven we receive here below. They still see the plan of salvation they spiritually framed for us like blueprints to teach us how to build Heaven on earth. They still see how much and how often we will fail to reach that perfection and accept their heavenly gift. But they knew we would and planned for it. Our errors can become part of the plan, as we accept the personal atoning grace of Jesus Christ and reach skyward. His truth, light, and love can change us all and help us change each other.

Revelation or manifesting is the act of showing something that exists but is not seen, usually something in the future. How else could God have his prophets prophesy if things weren't created spiritually before they are created physically? As we open our hearts with gratitude and charity, we expand our hearts to receive those creations, like the prophets before us. Similarly, the Holy Ghost can then bring "all things to our remembrance," including memories of who we really are, what already exists spiritually, and how to be our true selves.[35]

At times we all feel like we are in the dark. We may question our life's purpose, or whether we are doing what we were sent to earth to do. With charity and gratitude, we can reveal our individual purpose, flowing like a ribbon of light before us, guiding us up Mt. Zion on the foreordained path we created spiritually with Christ before we came to earth.

I witnessed an example of this while on my mission in Romania and Moldova. We were approached by an Orthodox priest seeking his purpose. His sincerity surprised me. The first Orthodox priest I met in Romania broke my name tag in half in front of my face, enraged that I was teaching someone in his neighborhood. As such, I was wary of this black bearded man dressed all in black.

But this priest was different. He looked up at me with a quick smile and declared he was on vacation and looking for the true church. He explained he was forced into the Orthodox ministry as a child because he was the second son. His oldest brother was sent into the military, and his younger brother was sent into medicine. As the second son, tradition expected him to serve God, even in the faithless cold of Soviet Communist rule which had largely banned religion.

For decades, he was starved and beaten by supervising priests if he did not read the Bible ten hours each day. He could not reconcile the stark contrast between the power of the word in the scriptures he felt and the anger and fear of his teachers. He told us he knew the Orthodox church was *not* true and that God would hold him accountable if he did not find the truth.

We taught him of how Christ began the restoration of the gospel with Joseph Smith and gave him a Book of Mormon. He feasted on it and rejoiced in Moroni's promise that by the power of the Holy Ghost we can know the truth of all things.[36] He said he had never read anything so clear in all his years of study—that the Holy Ghost testifies of *all* truth.

He read and prayed with us, asking if the Book of Mormon was true. He received an immediate answer. The joy of this truth filled his whole face. He had finally found the purpose he had been seeking. He committed that night to be baptized, even though his family would likely kill him if he left the Orthodox faith. Despite the opposition, he was not afraid—purpose replaced his fear.

He shaved his thick black beard, cut his hair, borrowed a white dress shirt from a missionary, and was baptized the following week. We never heard from or saw him again. Whether he was hiding, or his concerns about his family's vengeance came true, we never knew. However, his conviction was obvious and unwavering, even in the face of death, and I trust he has found peace and joy in Christ.

Similar to this experience, I recall visiting my childhood Patriarch Jae R. Bailiff in Provo, Utah with my sweetheart shortly after we were married. Years before, when I was a teenager, he had laid his hands on my head and declared my potential future in my patriarchal blessing. Over a decade later, when I told him I planned to be a lawyer, he looked distraught. I felt it was as if he was saying with his empathetic eyes, "oh not that path." His eyes couldn't hide his concern for me. I wondered if he felt I had chosen a hard path, or abandoned a better one.

In a way, I felt because he had seen my potential futures, he had greater empathy and love for me. He saw me as my past self, my current self, and my future self. Even though he felt for the welfare of my soul, he would not override my will or decision-making authority. Like Patriarch Bailiff, our Heavenly Parents will not override the agency they have sparked within us. They want it to grow to levels of celestial brilliance until we become like Christ. This only happens as we spread our own wings of light to fly back home. So, out of reverence for that agency, Christ speaks to us in a whisper, inviting us to follow the foreordained paths that *we* chose with Him and our Heavenly Parents before the world was. He stands ever hopeful, calling, hand outstretched, anxious to reveal the paths we chose before but unwilling to destroy our will to make our lives "fit" into His plan.

In this way, our future blessings can appear before us as ribbons of light, drawn out as spiritual measurements of our potential here on earth. As we live day by day, our ribbons weave together with the ribbons of the lives of those around us, intertwined as a physical, living, breathing, dynamic tapestry of light—a rainbow tent for Zion. But the tapestry is not perfect until God's grace, if we let it, arranges and purifies the colors we leave in our wake into a masterpiece of a glorious rising return to Heaven above. The ribbons of those who live with pure hearts, and use their agency to gather and lift their neighbors with an eye single to God's glory, are filled with light, and grow brighter and brighter until the perfect day, and God reveals the radiant glory of Zion in them, around them, and through them.

Imagine a future where, through personal revelation, each of us is so fully aware of our unique talents, gifts, strengths, and weaknesses that we pursue them fearlessly, like this priest. A future where we all trust that the unique corners and edges of our character were designed to fit with others like pieces to a celestial puzzle of Heaven. A place where we do not act in awkward self-awareness but are empowered with the truth that our individuality is godly, and that we each have a critical role to play in Christ's plan.

Imagine a future where we join our gifts together, accept our weaknesses as potential strengths and act in concert to help lift each other to God's presence. As we follow God's laws, starting with the commandment to love God and our neighbors like ourselves, we can lift and ignite ourselves and each other, like the city of Enoch—rising in a blaze of glory.[37]

We are on a mission to reveal our ribbons of light and manifest them physically—line upon line, precept upon precept, like joining together the seven colors of the rainbow, until the earth is full of a tapestry of glorious ribbons of our interwoven lives, evidencing Zion and its truth, harmony, and light. As we live righteously, we couple our spiritual pre-creations with our physical actions as if leaving a ribbon of light in our wake. Our unique ribbons colorfully shine next to others as we form the grand tapestry of Zion.

As we follow and manifest our ribbons of light, we will hear God whisper to us to turn to the right or to the left, to pause or to charge ahead. As we purify our hearts, acknowledge our failures, and seek forgiveness and cleanliness in Christ, we will hear the angels calling. Even now, they are bidding us to join them on this side of the veil as they work to bring about the salvation of *all* of Heaven's children.

Our individual ribbons of light can guide our steps throughout the day—radiating the choices we can make to manifest what we created spiritually with Christ before coming to earth. He weaves these ribbons into a masterful tapestry of diversity and color to create the tent of Zion with each ribbon playing an essential and invaluable role in the foreordained glory of Heaven. The most glorious and impactful arrays of life light ribbons are those created in families, through marriage.

ZION IN MARRIAGE

Recognizing that Christ interlinked us in a way that would save any that would choose to be saved—and potentially save all of us—is it any wonder that Satan strives to remove individual ribbons of light from the fabric of salvation that is the tent of Zion? From the devastating and violent effects of murder, rape or abortion to the debilitating and muting effects of poverty, addictions or intoxications, Satan strives to block us from fulfilling our missions here on earth, thereby removing individual threads from the tent of Zion. When Satan succeeds, Christ and his saints must fill the gaps left by those who refuse or are prevented from manifesting their true purposes here on earth.

But Christ, the master of Heaven and earth, time, and eternity, can overcome all. He will restore His children, help them awaken from the darkness and return to the light. His salvation will transcend time and repair the torn fabric of Zion's tent, heal the broken hearts, and bind up the wounds of those Satan sought to destroy. Christ invites us to participate in that work and glory now, through personal revelation, and join Him as saviors on Mount Zion.[38]

In other words, we are not meant to follow and manifest our ribbons of light in the tapestry of Zion alone.[39] We discover them by serving those around us. My wife helped me reveal my ribbon of light as I choose where to go to law school. After I was accepted to Catholic University of America in Washington D.C., we packed up all our possessions in a U-Haul and started the trek from Las Vegas to D.C. Halfway there, I received a call from UNLV and was told that I had been given a scholarship. We were shocked but felt prompted to keep driving to attend school at Catholic.

My wife's parents—natives of Las Vegas—urged us to turn around and attend UNLV. They even offered to buy us a house to ensure future grandchildren were close to home. To someone like me who had grown up with very little, it was a *very* tempting offer. But as we prayed, we felt the ribbon of light leading us on to Catholic. Even so, I began to question if we should turn around. Returning made logical and financial sense. Just to be safe, we decided to attend Catholic for a week but not to unpack the U-Haul.

Law school itself was terrifying, and law school at Catholic—where I knew no one—doubly so. After a week of competitive pressure and considering the expensive tuition, I was convinced law school would be much easier (and cheaper) in Las Vegas. After arriving, we discovered the apartment we planned to rent was not available. A scholarship and a "free" house in Vegas surrounded by family, seemed like a "no-brainer." After long, *stressful* discussions, we slumped back in our U-Haul to head West. I was sure God was leading us back to the safety of comfort and convenience of Zion.

However, halfway back to Vegas, that ribbon of light we had been following—disappeared. Literal storm clouds circled overhead. Construction and traffic blocked our path. It began to rain. My wife and I started to bicker, then to fight. Darkness filled our little U-Haul cabin.

My wife—through tears—suggested we turn around, stop, and pray. We pled with the Heavens and asked if God would make the correct path clear before us. We chose to head back to D.C., and the clouds parted, sunshine poured down on us, and the road ahead cleared. Our U-Haul cabin filled with light. We had found the ribbon of light again! I went back to Catholic, mustered the courage to face the new terrifying experience of law school, and grew to love every moment.

Countless miracles followed that one decision. I worked under two U.S. presidents in the White House, published an article in Law Review, was a vice chancellor for the Communications Law Moot Court and graduated *cum laude*. As for that free house? We avoided the disaster of my in-laws buying us an overpriced home before the housing bubble crashed with the Great Recession of 2009. That one decision to follow the ribbon of light, made all the difference.

Zion is not a solo. We each have a unique and important role to play, and God wants us to find oneness while retaining our uniqueness. One of the most powerful examples of this oneness coupled *with* uniqueness can occur in marriage as men and women become one.[40]

When two marry, it is like planting two trees next to each other, joined in purpose and called to bear fruit. A healthy marriage is one where those trees find strength in being close together, but not enmeshed. Strength comes as the trees intertwine their ancestral roots, and interweave their branches as they reach up to Heaven, and bear fruit together. But their trunks must retain their uniqueness and independence to enjoy their individuality and agency. In this way, the two are both one *and* individual as they rise skyward finding their nourishment and purpose in reaching toward the sun.

This is not the codependent version of love the world preaches, where one tree consumes another or intertwines itself so fiercely into the trunk and branches of the other tree that the two are indistinguishable. True love is *not* like the famous line from the movie *Jerry*

Maguire where he says, "you complete me." This desperate yearning to find wholeness in someone else risks making another human our god in a way that erases our own identity. When we define our happiness, our worth, our purpose, on anything other than our relationship with Jesus Christ, we will be unhappy. This is true even if we define ourselves by our spouses.

For us to find joy in unity, we must first have joy individually, in Christ. Confidence with others, and with God comes as we center ourselves in Christ.[41] As our hearts resonate with peace in Christ, we create that same peace around us. Christ teaches us we attract what we are: wisdom receives wisdom; truth embraces truth; virtue loves virtue; light cleaves to light.[42] Thus, when we are what we seek we find true connection, peace, light, virtue, joy, and interconnect as Heaven.

This cleaving is most sacredly symbolized in marital intimacy. As marriage therapists and apostles have observed, intercourse itself is the perfect metaphor of oneness.[43] While it is true that procreation is the pinnacle of *physical* connection, the oneness of marriage only comes with spiritual, emotional, and intellectual connection.[44] A physical body can be made by parents who share flesh, but the sheltering love of parents is the capstone of creation. Every child *deserves* to be raised by two loving parents, and the world needs each child and their gifts to shine now more than ever and overcome the darkness.

ZION IN FAMILY

This power to overcome darkness explodes exponentially when we unite hearts in families. How do we create Zion in our families? We love—first those closest to us who often cause us the most discomfort and pain: our spouses, children, siblings and parents. We love them as we support them in their becoming—by creating a safe and beautiful place on earth for them to belong—a family. Think of how powerful and frightening this is. We are responsible to literally bear one another through procreation by bringing little bodies down from Heaven into this world, and then we are responsible to raise them back up in righteousness and love. We are responsible to chase away contention so the Spirit may dwell in their physical temples and help them become their true divine selves. In our own small way, building Zion in our families is how we get to practice being Heavenly Parents.

Loving our own like this comes naturally for some of us. For others, it can be more difficult. I am sure some of us have felt this way at times as we "deal" with our families. I remember teaching a man on my mission the doctrine of eternal families. He looked at me genuinely perplexed and said, "Why would I want to be with *them* forever. I hate my family."

Painful enmity between family members is not new. It divided Cain and Able, Isaac and Ishmael, and many more. In each case, the rage between brothers, despite the tenderness of glorious parents, has burned and boiled in war and hate for thousands of years.

Zion is cleansed of such hatred when we keep the laws of Heaven and love others as ourselves, even when they hate us. Those family members we might view as impediments to our joy, are often the very relationships we need to unlock our true potential. We need each other, and when we learn to love even those who hurt us so we can receive Zion within until Zion begins to rise and radiate around us.

When I consider how we can all receive personal revelation to become instruments of Zion, I want to shout *Hallelujah*! The Lord's plan is great, marvelous, and strong. And we each have a critical role to play in the final scenes of the Lord's plan. We can see the divine light of Christ in each individual we encounter. He saved and saves, healed and heals, lit and is lighting the world with His truth, glory, majesty and joy, and He is working to save each of us.

Everything we need to create this grand awakening is *already around us*—already created spiritually. Christ is offering it. The angels are singing of it. It is up to us to receive it, create it and be it.[45]

STANDING IN HOLY PLACES

Christ assures us that even with the disasters and calamites of these last days and the wars that will rage around us, if we follow Him, we will be able to stand in holy places, unmoved until He comes again.[46] Our hearts not only play a role in finding this safety while we await His return—they help us create it. As followers of Christ and children of our Heavenly Parents, our hearts can affect the matter around us—creating peace despite war. This sanctification of the elements around us starts with restoration and renewal of the elements around our spirits—our physical bodies and their distinct parts.[47]

Christ has taught us that as we follow Him, His laws, and His priesthood, we will not only run and not be weary, and walk and not faint but our bodies will be renewed, and we will be lifted up as if on eagles' wings.[48] This restorative lift involves regaining our spiritual senses, including our ability to *hear*, and eventually our ability to *see* as we did before the Fall. Christ has urged us to let our "eye be single" so we can be filled with light and comprehend all things. His reference to our eye in its singular form, is not just a reference to our physical eyes, but our spiritual eye. Our eye is our first method of sight, lost when Adam and Eve fell. Our eye acts as an instrument of input to receive truth, knowledge, wisdom and light from above, which is why if our eye be single, our whole bodies will be filled with light until we too—like Christ—radiate celestial rainbow fire and chase darkness from us and comprehend all things.[49]

As we regain the ability to be able to comprehend all things, will Christ teach us how to command the elements, wind, waves, trees, and even the matter around us until we can reorganize our own matter in resurrection, reuniting the clay of our bodies around our spirits to the degree of glory we are willing to receive? Remember, Christ has promised us that if we have faith in Him, we will be able to do what His apostles saw Him do and even greater things.[50] It seems to me one of these greater things is the ability to reorganize our matter into a celestial body with our spirits, which is why Christ says if we have a celestial spirit, we will be quickened by a celestial body, and likewise with a terrestrial body if quickened by a terrestrial spirit, or a telestial body if quickened by a telestial spirit. Our spirits are quickened—or animated—by whatever spirit we are willing to receive.[51]

This elevating and quickening power doesn't stop with our bodies. As our hearts and our very bodies become purer, quickened by His spirit, we begin to have the ability to elevate the matter around us and make it purer as well. Thus, we create the Heaven or hell we inherit with the spirit we create in our hearts.

This belief and desire to have spirit affect the matter around us is not new. We bless our food, our newborn children, and those who are sick. We also bless homes, churches, and temples, seeking to make them holy and imbue them with heavenly light—dedicating them and even consecrating them to God. As we follow Christ and become more like Him, we can sanctify the matter around us with something as simple as prayer—as our hearts and our lips align in humility before the Lord.

My wife tells a story of when she attended the Washington D.C. Temple as a teenager and was so impressed with the spirit she felt there, she pled with the Lord it would never leave her. As she returned to her hotel room with her fellow students, the longing to return to the holiness of the Temple increased until she secluded herself in the bathroom of the hotel and pled with the Lord. As she humbly sought Christ in prayer, she has told our children she felt the same spirit she felt at the Temple fill that little hotel bathroom. Her prayers sanctified that place for her, and in doing so she not only stood in a holy place, as Christ invites, but her heart and prayers made that place holy. This ability to affect the matter around us becomes earthshaking, as we do it together. This is why Christ is inviting us not only to unite our hearts in our homes and our churches, but also calling to us to look up and unite our hearts with the hearts of the fathers and mothers who have gone before—the angels singing above us—calling to us to purify our communities' earth so they can become holy and rise home to Heaven.[52]

ANGELS TO HELP US RISE AND RADIATE

Joseph Smith taught "Men and angels are to be coworkers" in revealing Zion.[53] As we join Christ in His work and glory and teach others of the path back home to Heaven, we join the angels as "Saviors on Mount Zion"[54] and "restore" each other in Christ, and saying "to the prisoners, Go forth; to them that are in darkness, Shew yourselves."[55] In Hebrew, this act of awakening or becoming is known as "galah" (לָא), where we reveal, uncover, or rediscover the divinity in ourselves and others until we all dwell "in all high places" of Zion.[56] The angels are here to help us rediscover ourselves and our heavenly wings of light, so we can rise up as Heaven on earth.

If we are open to it, manifesting our true selves includes learning the will of Heaven through angels and dreams. We are constantly in the presence of heavenly messengers and beings, including Christ who tells us He is in our midst and we cannot see Him.[57] The Lord will send messengers of those we know and love, who can "touch our hearts by teaching us through someone we love and respect."[58] Our ministering angels are our relatives and ancestors from before, and they can see us better than we can see them and know us better than we know them. They see the spiritual matter we cannot discern and come with messages, light, and truth about our Heavenly Parents' plan and yearn for us with greater emotion than we feel for ourselves.[59]

Christ sends ministering angels to our bedsides in the quiet of the morning to speak truths and share light.[60] Our angels will also come to us in our dreams. The ability to receive dreams can be enhanced as we show the Lord, we will hear Him. We can do this by keeping a pen and pad of paper by our bedside, praying as we retire, and then writing down every detail we can recall from our dreams when we awaken. We will then see our dreams communicate truths about the future.

I experienced this while I wrote these books. I awoke early one morning to three women full of light and the most beautiful music I had ever heard. They walked into my room and laid books behind me as I slept. They radiated fire and the books themselves burned brightly, as if burning from within. I could tell the books were heavenly, heavy, and full of purpose. The heat the angels and the books emitted penetrated my back and healed it for days afterward. I can still see the event clearly in my mind, seared there by *shekinah*.

The dream was so real, I immediately sat up in bed to see who had entered my room. I looked around and found it still and empty, but the golden song lingered in my mind, a song of Zion. That evening, I received a book in the mail: *Enoch and His City*.[61] I vaguely remembered ordering it. It had the same ancient looking pages of the burning books held by the lead angel, and I immediately knew it was a fulfilment of my dream. I will never forget the experience, or the invigorating burning and song that filled my room and woke me that morning, as I was blessed by those beyond the veil. Angels *are* among us.

Enoch and all the ancient prophets and saints raised to Zion have remained engaged as ministering angels, their hearts yearning after us for five thousand years. Their songs ring of redemption. They have been moving about the Heavens and earth with celestial zeal and fire to prepare us for the terrestrial order and the Second Coming of Christ, so the earth can rest and they can return to it.[62]

This pattern of ministration occurred after the wicked Lamanites were converted by Ammon and his brethren in the Book of Mormon. They recognized their sin, earnestly sought forgiveness and then were called to join in Christ's work through revelation and ministering angels.[63] As we repent and become receptive to what the Lord has prepared for us, of course angels are going to descend to invite us to join them on the errands they are also anxiously attending and serve as Christ's hands on this side of the veil.

Our future joy, wings, and peace *already exist*—it is simply up to us to receive them. Heaven's messengers are singing to us. We can hear their celestial song and be reminded of our purpose, like discovering our ribbon of light guiding us along our way in this life as we choose to listen. Charity, gratitude, and revelation open our hearts to the bounty of Zion already inside us—waiting to rise.

This is in large part because Zion is being gathered on *both* sides of the veil. Many have lived and died who were "blinded by the craftiness of men" or "kept from the truth because they knew not where to find it."[64] Yet Christ's power conquers even *after* death. Hearts on both sides of the veil will connect, and together, use the creative powers of their hearts to purify the matter around them and heal the earth.

Those righteous men and women who *would have* accepted Christ but were unable to do so because of the wickedness of others will be gathered in to act as ministering angels from behind the veil. *They will be restored.* They will join Elijah and call to their own children, turning their hearts of the living and the dead to join together in eternal life.[65]

There are angels all around us, actively working beyond our sight. They are our ancestors, our children to be, all who yearn for us. They are whispering to us of who we were before we came to earth, who we are now, and who we are meant to become in the eternities.

They are whispering of *Zion. And* we can join hands with them and build—*now.*

Life is like a stage for the mortal. We live our lives, rarely seeing—but at times sensing—the audience. Our loved ones beyond the veil, obeying the great commandment of loving others as they love themselves, are pleading for us and rejoicing with us as we choose the light. They mourn with us when we fail, sin, or hurt. When we die, we walk off the stage, through the veil, to the audience above. We will see they look a lot like us, for they are our family from before and for eternity.

Anxious for our well-being and happiness, these ancestors attend us as ministering angels. They bring light to us in our dark hours and joy in our sorrow. They help us bring to pass those things that were created spiritually before. And we likewise help restore our ancestors by receiving ordinances for them vicariously (on their behalf), unlocking the power of godliness.[66]

When we empower our ancestors by doing ordinances for them in the temple, they return in gratitude—as chariots of fire—to empower *us.* They act as guardian angels on our behalf and open the windows of Heaven for us until with united hearts we tie earth and Heaven together in love.

RECEIVING ZION NOW

Our inheritance in Zion already exists spiritually and awaits us. We are invited to eat of the Lord's abundance, drink His living water, and never hunger or thirst again, and let our souls delight in fatness.[67] We are invited to sing and bring down Heaven. As we obey the Lord's laws, we justify then sanctify this land and elevate it as Zion enriched by the Lord's creative power.

What are we waiting for?

The only limit to the blessings of eternity is our unwillingness to *receive* them by obedience to the laws that govern them.[68] The Lord is clear: we obtain celestial glory as we receive and live according to celestial laws of love, truth, and light. If we are only willing to receive and be quickened by terrestrial law, then we will have terrestrial glory. And so on with telestial law and glory up to celestial law and glory. Our receptiveness to God's laws is the true measure of our worthiness.

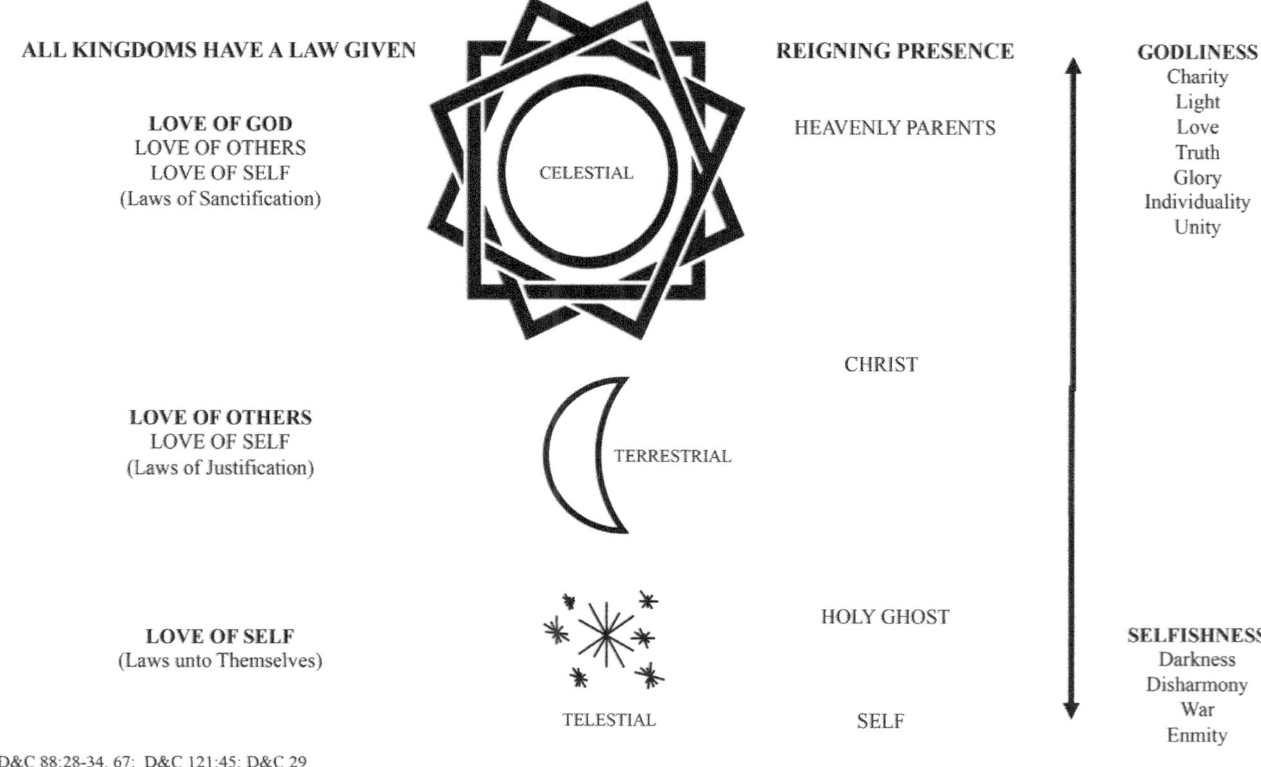

Figure 7 *The Laws of Love and Associated Degrees of Glory*

Oftentimes in life we find fleeting ideas, things, and relationships that we believe will bring us peace, safety, and comfort and cling to them to the point that we cannot receive anything else. But Christ invites us to open our hearts and our hands and surrender that dust for the gold of eternity. As with Enoch, He is working in us to expand our hearts as "wide as eternity" so that we can receive ALL He and our Heavenly Parents have.

The sanctified who expand their hearts, find restoration in Christ and help build Zion in truth and love. And as we join these saints, we will add to the building of Zion below which will be raised as our "inheritance among the Saints of the Most High."[69] But those who reject the Lord and His law, and fight against Zion, even if they have the priesthood, will have no inheritance in Zion. In other words, we claim our inheritance in Zion by obedience to divine laws and by using our health and our wealth to love and serve those around us. If we hoard and covet our own wealth, health, and talents, we will never have the thrust or lift to rise back home.

Christ declared to Joseph Smith, "all kingdoms have a law given" and "that which is governed by law is also preserved by law and perfected and sanctified by the same."[70] When we obey just laws, we are elevated and protected by them. When we violate just laws, they condemn us, and we rebel against them, seeking excuse from their judgment.[71]

All laws of the kingdoms of the Heavens are self-contained in the first two great laws of Heaven: to love God with all our heart, mind, and strength, and love others as ourselves.[72] Upon these two commandments hang all laws, all scriptures, all covenants, all purpose.

We currently live in a fallen, unloving, *telestial* world. This is why those who are quickened by *telestial* law even struggle to love themselves. Obedience to this commandment alone leads to imbalance. It is like stopping on the first rung of a ladder without grasping the rungs above for balance and direction. The result is selfishness, greed, and self-destructive dissonance with who we are meant to become.

If love of self is not guided and inspired by the next step of learning to love others, love of self alone will lead to disharmony with others. If we only love ourselves, we will never be able to enjoy the true beauty and divinity of those who surround us. Conversely, loving ourselves can be hard for many of us who feel we are not enough and have been poisoned by Satan's lies that an experience we have suffered somehow defines us and erases our divine worth. But when we recognize that our love of self is designed to give us the ability to love others, divine purpose overrides the imbalance, disharmony, and fear.

We choose to be quickened by *terrestrial* law when we love others and ourselves. This less glorious telestial world celebrates those who live terrestrial law, those who give of themselves and sacrifice their health and wealth for others. Great leaders like Mother Teresa, Gandhi, Martin Luther King Jr., and many more have demonstrated they can love themselves *and* others. These luminaries have a heightened existence, greater capacity for love, and the ability to rise above their difficult circumstances because they know love of others transcends hardship.

However, love of self and others is also not the pinnacle law. Without expanding the love of others to encompass love of *all* others in our Heavenly Parents' kingdom, enmity between Heaven's children remains. This leads to division between families, cities, nations, and even Heaven itself. When we place our love of a child, a spouse, or a celebrity, over our love of God, we are refusing to accept the fullness our Heavenly Parents' grand vision for the entire kingdom; a vision that recognizes each child is infinitely precious. In loving something or someone more than our Heavenly Parents, we also refuse to receive all our Heavenly Parents have.

We demonstrate our love for our Heavenly Parents when we help others come home. This is why Christ declares, "inasmuch as ye have done it unto one of the least of these . . . , ye have done it unto me."[73] This is godliness: joining our Heavenly Parents in their celestial purpose of helping others on their path to immortality and eternal life. Godliness is helping *others* become like God, as that is the pinnacle of our Heavenly Parents' purpose with us.

This is why the first great commandment to love God with all our heart, might, mind and strength, is the summation of *all law*. It is only by eventual, full-hearted obedience to this celestial law, loving God and ourselves and all others, that we fulfil the measure of our own creation, and we see our purpose in joining God in His work and glory: to help all our Heavenly Parents' children, all of our brothers and sisters *become*. This is glory, and this is God's work.[74]

Thus, obedience to celestial law is how we receive and rise to celestial eternities and are carried home to God,[75] being "quickened by a portion of [their] celestial glory [to] receive of the same, even a fulness."[76] And we do it together. Together, we have already been empowered to use the lift and light generated by obedience to divine law to ignite and elevate Zion *throughout the world*.

CHAPTER 7 ENDNOTES

1 Brigham Young, in *Journal of Discourses* 6:330 (citing D&C 14:7); see also Exodus 3:14–15; John 8:56–59; D&C 29:1; 38:1; 39:1.

2 Exodus 19:20–24.

3 Moses 1:11–14; Matthew 7:12; Mark 9:2.

4 D&C 2:3; D&C 138:48–49; D&C 121:45.

5 Genesis 1:3–4, 14; Abraham 4:3–4, 14; Moses 2:3–4; Moses 3:7; D&C 38:3.

6 Moses 4:30; John 1:1; Mark 11:12–25.

7 D&C 6:2, 11:1–4; 12:2; 14:2; 33:1.

8 Helaman 5:30; 3 Nephi 11:3; D&C 38:12; D&C 85:6.

9 D&C 1:20.

10 "The Order of Progression in Knowledge—The Way By Which Saints Become One—Aptness of Men to Remember Evil Rather Than Good—a Characteristic of Saints is to Remember Good and Forget Evil—Our Affections Should Be Placed on the Kingdom of God Above All Other Things," A Discourse by President Brigham Young, Delivered in the Bowery, Great Salt Lake City, June 15, 1856., p. 357, reported by G. D. Watt.

11 Popol Vuh, p. 61 Sacred Book of the Quiche Maya People—Translation and Commentary by Allen J. Christenson, 2007, available at www.mesoweb.com/publications/Christenson/PupulVuh.pdf.

12 Masaru Emoto, *The Hidden Messages in Water* (2005). *See* https://en.wikipedia.org/wiki/Masaru_Emoto.

13 *See* https://foodretro.com/debunking-the-rice-experiment/.

14 Isaiah 55:10–11. Incidentally, modern physics terms the effect of an experimenter getting what they want *the observer effect*. For years scientists have debated whether light is a wave or a particle and have found that light will appear as a wave or a particle depending upon what the observer expects. I wonder if this is undeniable proof that Christ is trying to teach us how to use our hearts to affect the matter around us and that we will receive that which we seek.

15 D&C 6:16; D&C 33:1.

16 John 6:68; Alma 30:22.

17 D&C 50:2; John 12:36; D&C 88:67.

18 D&C 6:36.

19 D&C 88:67.

20 D&C 105:3–5.

21 D&C 78:19, emphasis added.

22 D&C 88:32–33; D&C 111:11.

23 Matthew 6:10.

24 3 Nephi 11:35–39.

25 2 Nephi 30:8.
26 Alma 41:1–15.
27 Alma 41:1–15.
28 Alma 37:19.
29 3 Nephi 5:22–26; Mormon 9:36.
30 Joseph Smith, *Lectures on Faith*, 68.
31 D&C 50:24; D&C 115:5; Daniel 12:3, Matthew 14:34.
32 D&C 93:30.
33 Moroni 10:3–5.
34 John Taylor, in *Journal of Discourses* 18:306.
35 John 14:6.
36 Moroni 10:3–5.
37 The prophet Russell M. Nelson has repeatedly invited us to know our purpose through personal revelation and by finding a quiet place to study and pray about questions, we can "grow into the principle of revelation." "Revelation for the Church, Revelation for Our Lives," April 2018 general conference.
38 1 Kings 8:1; Hebrews 12:22; D&C 76:66; D&C 84:2–4.
39 Moses 3:18.
40 Genesis 2:24; Abraham 5:18; Moses 3:24; 1 Corinthians 11:11.
41 D&C 121:45.
42 D&C 88:40.
43 Dean M. Busby PhD, Jason S. Carroll PhD, Chelom Leavitt JD MS, *Sexual Wholeness in Marriage: An LDS Perspective on Integrating Sexuality and Spirituality in our Marriages*, p. 35.
44 Jeffry R. Holland, "Of Souls and Symbols and Sacraments," BYU address, 1988.
45 Christ pointed to the glory of the birds, and the lilies of the field when speaking of temporal needs, and reminded us that our Father already knows what we need, and as we seek the kingdom of Heaven, all we need will be ours. 3 Nephi 13:32–33.
46 D&C 87:8.
47 This includes the ordinances in the temple, where we are symbolically washed and anointed, and consecrated to God's kingdom.
48 Isaiah 40:27–31; Exodus 19:4; Isaiah 91:1–16; Matthew 23:37; D&C 84:33.
49 Matthew 6:22; D&C 82:19; D&C 88:67; "*A Swedenborg Sampler, Heaven and Hell*," pg. 58, Swedenborg Foundation, noting that when people are purified by Christ's love, they emit the "light of a flame," until they radiate heavenly colors, like a rainbow.
50 John 14:12–14.
51 D&C 88:26–32.
52 This can also happen with objects as discussed in my book on Zion's Relics. Think of Moses's staff, the Urim and Thummim, John Lowe Butler's cloak,

the Liahona, the water that was stirred by angels in John 5:4, the clay made by Christ in John 9:6, etc., etc., etc. Our spirits affect the matter around us, for good or for bad. For a discussion on spiritually imbued relics see remarks by Heber C. Kimball, "Its Value—Worth and Virtue of Sacred Relics—Resurrection—Confidence in Our Leaders," *Deseret News*, delivered in the Tabernacle, Great Salt Lake City, March 15, 1857, as reported by: G. D. Watt.

53 *Teachings of the Prophet Joseph Smith*, p. 84.

54 1 Kings 8:1; Hebrews 12:22; D&C 76:66; D&C 84:2–4; D&C 36:2; Obadiah 1:21; Nephi also declared that we will be blessed as we seek to bring forth the Lord's Zion, and if we "endure unto the end they shall be lifted up at the last day… how beautiful upon the mountains shall they be." 1 Ne 13:37.

55 Isaiah 49:9; Galatians 6:1.

56 Isaiah 49:10.

57 D&C 38:7–8.

58 Richard G. Scott, "How to Obtain Revelation and Inspiration for Your Personal Life," April 2012 general conference.

59 Joseph F. Smith, in Conference Report, Apr. 1916, 2–3; see also *Gospel Doctrine*, 5th ed. (1939), 430–31.

60 Our ancestors, future descendants, and those "spirits of the just" who remain concerned for our welfare in the spirit world "are not far from us, and know and understand our thoughts, feelings, and emotions, and are often pained therewith." *Teachings of the Prophet Joseph Smith*, p. 326; When our eyes are "touched by the Lord" and purified like Enoch's, we can see these angels as plainly as we see others now. Widtsoe, John A. (ed.) (1925) *Discourses of Brigham Young*, p. 577.

61 Joseph Young, "Enoch and His City," Sen. Salt Lake City Utah, Printed at the Deseret News Steam Printing Establishment, 1878.

62 Orson Pratt, "All Nations Believe, Etc.," in *Journal of Discourses* 17:145, 148a–b; Moses 1:39.

63 Alma 11.

64 D&C 123:12.

65 Malachi 4:6.

66 D&C 84:10.

67 Isaiah 55:2; 2 Nephi 9:51.

68 D&C 88:32.

69 D&C 85:7, 11.

70 D&C 88:34–36.

71 *See* Helaman 5:1–3, when the Nephites rebelled against their laws, rejected the prophet leader Helaman, and elected Cezoram, because "they were a stiffnecked people, insomuch that they could not be governed by the law nor justice, save it were to their destruction."

72 Matthew 22:37–38.
73 Matt 25:40.
74 Moses 1:39.
75 D&C 105:5.
76 D&C 88:29.

CHAPTER 8

ZION RISING IN ALL THE WORLD

"Verily I say unto you, Zion must arise."
—Jesus Christ, D&C 82:14

GODLINESS—AWAKENING AND RESTORING OTHERS IN CHRIST

Paul invites us to love and help one another "fulfill the law," "awaken," "cast off the works of darkness," and put on the "armour of light."[1] Gathering, loving, and awakening others to their divine potential is godliness, and it elevates and illuminates all of us. We can be fully restored as we channel Christ's love selflessly to help restore others. While we do not have scriptures that detail exactly how Enoch, Melchizedek, and others purified their people into communal Zion, we do have powerful examples of later prophets who used truth and love to others awaken and open their eyes, ears, and hearts.

One such example is that of the prophet Ammon and King Lamoni as recorded in the Book of Mormon. King Lamoni and his people were described as fierce and hardhearted. They had abandoned the Lord and were in great darkness. They were so lost that their belief in God had devolved to a place where they had forgotten they were children of Heaven, believing instead in an unknown "Great Spirit." They did not even know the word "heavens."[2]

Approaching someone in this state of darkness and telling them to *see* is like yelling at someone who is drowning to "stop drowning!" They cannot hear you, and even if they can, they can do nothing to help themselves alone—they are *drowning.* All their senses are seized in panicked fear until they don't even know which way is up. We all have been there at times. We all need someone to help us find which way is up.

I worked as a lifeguard in my teenage years at a hectic water park. After rescuing fifty people from drowning, I stopped counting how many "victims" I pulled from the water. I learned that when it comes to drowning, most people *want* to be saved and are willing to accept help. However, it is impossible to save someone who is drowning—physically or spiritually—who does not *want* to be saved. That is exactly why Satan works to persuade us to believe that we are unsavable, lost, alone—not enough. He convinces us to tie our own hands behind our backs and wallow in our own despair. In these situations, the rescuer must often descend below the victim with love, anchored to truth, and invite them up to safety.

When any of us is drowning, we need a life preserver of love, anchored in truth. We need someone to tell us they understand we're hurting, lost, or afraid. King Lamoni was in a similar state of "drowning" and he knew it. The contention that was arising from their inability to hear, feel, and see each other was so prevalent that Lamoni was regularly slaying his own servants because enemies were stealing his flocks.

To open Lamoni's heart to truth and light, Ammon first opened his own heart. He loved Lamoni, served him and his people and had compassion on them. He performed miracles in service to them—as a lion of the Lord—stopping those who came to scatter the king's sheep, only using force as necessary to defend himself, and smiting off all the arms that were raised against him.

Lamoni was so amazed at Ammon's power and service that he sat in silence for an hour unsure what to say. Ammon did not have to tell the king he was drowning. The king's own heart already knew he was in darkness and needed redemption. Although Ammon could discern King Lamoni's thoughts, Ammon asked questions to keep Lamoni's heart open. Ammon asked what Lamoni knew of Heaven *above.*

The king replied that he knew nothing about the Heavens! Satan had been working to rob the Lamanites of the truth about the Heavens above.[3] So, Ammon taught in simplicity that the Heavens were where God dwells and all his holy angels, as he *looks down upon his children*. He taught King Lamoni of the Fall of Adam and Eve down through the history of the earth, and how Ammon and Lamoni's common ancestors came across the ocean to America led by the hand of the Lord, seeking a promised land.

These doctrinal truths struck Lamoni to his core and stirred within him a yearning to awaken and repent. Lamoni prayed for mercy and forgiveness in Christ and fell to the earth, "asleep in God." After three days, Lamoni rose and declared he had seen Christ.[4] He had been awakened and to his ability to rise back home.

As we serve as emissaries of Christ and gather others, we are fulfilling Isaiah's prophecy that the Lord will send "kings" as "nursing fathers" and "queens" as "nursing mothers" to bring Israel's sons in our arms, and daughters on our shoulders to Christ.[5] I experienced a powerful gathering moment as I flew from Las Vegas to New York in 2019. As I was boarding the flight, I felt prompted to compliment the shirt of the man standing in front of me. He turned and smiled as we started a conversation. Over the next five hours we became fast friends.

We laughed and joked with his friends about their journeys to become men and find their path to fulfillment and happiness. As we interacted, I could feel the spirit of Israel burning in them. It was clear they were sent here to accomplish unique missions . . . to fulfill the measure of their creation and help build Zion.

The Lord has planted His warriors of light, like these men, *all over the world*. They are already members of God's kingdom that will build Zion. They are our brothers and sisters from before but have yet to awaken to the divinity within them, though many feel it stirring. They respond when they feel light radiating in others, and I trust one day I will meet them in Zion.

These men reminded me that the most important thing in our lives are the souls within our sphere of influence. Like C. S. Lewis's observation, "it is a serious thing to live in a society of possible gods and goddesses. . . . There are no ordinary people."[6]

Image 19 *From left to right: Okeno, Sam, Ney, and Stanley—"Kings" of Queens, N.Y.*

Surrounded by children of God, is it any wonder we are called to help them awaken and gather their precious souls to Zion? As the Apostle Paul taught, because of the veil it is as if we are peering at life through a darkened glass.[7] We can only catch glimpses of the glory of those around us. One day soon, the veil shall be taken away and dark scales of blindness will fall from our eyes, until we "behold our faces as in a glass" and see as we are seen and know as we are known, having received of His fullness and of His presence, light, and grace.[8]

Through Christ, we can gather out from among all nations the righteous remnant, those on Christ's salvation team, reserved for today, who have yet to be fully awakened by His light; teammates who wear Christ's jersey but are "hid from the world in Christ with God" awaiting the "restoration of all things."[9] Once awakened, they in turn will act as saviors on Mount Zion and bring others to Christ. These future saints are waiting for us to fulfill our own premortal covenants to find them, love them, teach them truth, and bring them home.

ZION RETURNING WITH CHRIST

Although no man knows exactly when Christ shall return, there are libraries of books written about the Second Coming of Christ—compendiums containing comprehensive catalogues of the signs and wonders that will appear to the righteous of His pending return.[10] These signs include dark times that await the wicked who reject Him. At the center of all the destruction, decay, disaster, and despair of the last days, is the impurity of men's hearts. As we look unto Christ in every thought and "doubt not, fear not,"[11] we can keep our hearts filled with the harmony of Zion—and create it around us—even as the world rages in dissonance.

Christ himself revealed the method and pattern of His glorious return with Zion, and the evils and darkness that will precede it. Speaking to Joseph, He invited us to come unto Him and "reason" with Him as the prophets of old.[12] If we open our hearts and ears to him, we—like the ancient prophets—can obtain a promise to see Zion in the flesh.

The Lord then prophesies, as He did "unto men in days of old," of the signs of His coming, when He will descend in glory in the clouds of Heaven to fulfill the promises made unto our fathers and accomplish the "restoration of . . . scattered Israel."[13] The signs of Zion's and Christ's return will start with the gathering of the remnants from among all nations. [14] There will be wars and rumors of wars, the whole earth will be in commotion, and men's hearts will fail them, such that people will see the destruction on the earth and say that "Christ delayeth his coming until the end of the earth."[15]

The light of the fullness of the gospel will break forth among them that "sit in darkness," but many will "receive it not" and "turn their hearts from [Christ] because of the precepts of men."[16] Then, an "overflowing scourge" and a "desolating sickness shall cover the land."[17] There will be earthquakes in "divers places and many desolations."[18] Men will turn their hearts away from God despite his warnings, "the love of men shall wax cold and iniquity shall abound."[19] These signs are already occurring, and have been for some time.

Since 1960, scientists have noted that the entire earth has vibrated with mini-quakes exactly every twenty-six seconds, as if the earth is shivering or humming in preparation to release its rising blossoms of Zion into the skies.[20] In addition to these mini-quakes, since 2004, earthquakes have been increasing in frequency and intensity.[21] This escalation has only continued during the last sixteen years and has begun to rock generally stable areas. In 2020, a 5.7 magnitude earthquake hit Salt Lake with such force that it shook free the trumpet of Angel Moroni on the Salt Lake Temple. Even though we live on a bed of granite in the Las Vegas valley which generally protects against the propagation of earthquakes, the quakes in 2020 shook our home as well—such that a side gate for our house no longer closes straight.

As Enoch saw in vision, it appears the earth is groaning, calling for release from the wickedness and darkness of men. These quakes suggest the earth is readying itself for Christ's return. Are we?

SIGNS OF ZION'S RISING

The pandemics, tornadoes, earthquakes, hurricanes, murder hornets, riots, wars, grasshopper swarms, and devastating pestilence filling the world, are evidence of Christ's preparations to return. Christ compares the signs of His Second Coming to fig leaves. For fig trees "shoot forth their tender leaves" as a sign that "summer is now night at hand" and the time for harvesting is almost over.[22] To understand this prophecy, it is important to understand the symbol of the fig tree.

Fig trees of Christ's time and location were different than any other fruit tree. While other fruits grow leaves *then* fruit, the fig tree of Jerusalem does the opposite. It grows its fruit first, then sprouts leaves. The leaves are a signal to the world—a sign—that the fig tree has fruit and the time for harvesting has come.

When the Savior cursed the fruitless fig tree with leaves, He was symbolically cursing the House of Israel for showing off their leaves like they had fruit when they had none.[23] The sin was similar to how Christ told Joseph Smith that men were drawing near to Him with their lips, but their hearts were far from Him.[24] In essence, men's hearts—their creative seats connecting their spirits and bodies—were corrupted. Instead of their words *and* works drawing them closer to Christ and bringing forth fruit meet for Zion, they were further distancing themselves from Christ and creating darkness. Christ's response was to curse the fig tree. Likewise, Christ chastens His people with destruction, hoping to soften their hearts and awaken them to Him. He effectively gives them one last chance to purify their hearts before His return.

When we see the signs of this chastening, the plagues, natural disasters, and desolations, we are seeing the fig leaves, telling us summer is at hand and Christ is returning quickly and we should continue "looking forth for the great day of the Lord to come,"[25] trusting that He is about to make manifest His wonders and safety in Zion.

As the world descends further into the chaos before Christ's return because of this final chastening, all who will not take their swords against their neighbor will flee to Zion for safety. Zion itself will be the only place of peace and gather "out of every nation under heaven . . . the only people that shall not be at war one with another."[26] Just as with Enoch's removal from the wicked of his time, removing the pure hearts of the righteous will allow the hard hearts of the wicked to implode in self-destructive war and darkness. Conversely, those living the higher laws of love will begin to create elements of Heaven around them.

The Jews will feel the call to "go *up* to Zion unto the Lord." As they return, the prophet Jeremiah promised the Jews' bountifulness and prosperity would also return. They will build up Jerusalem on its former heap[27] and gather all of Israel to old Jerusalem "out of the north country"[28] to "come and sing in the *height* of Zion, and . . . flow together for the goodness of the Lord, for wheat, and for wine, and for oil, and for the young of the flock and for the herd: and their soul shall be as a watered garden"[29] and likewise "singing with songs of everlasting joy."[30]

But even after all the Jews are gathered and build a new temple, many Jews will still deny the Christ. They will cling to the traditions of the fallen nations, preferring darkness and dust over the ordinances of light and lift, rejecting the Messiah as that "imposter" who was crucified by their fathers.[31] Their continued rejection will bring to conclusion what the scriptures calls the "time of the Gentiles" after which "the arm of the Lord [will] fall upon the nations."[32]

Joseph Smith warned one of the signs of this time would be the disappearance of rainbows, signifying the "coming of the Messiah is not far distant" and "the end cometh quickly." [33] At this time, the Lord will send upon the earth an "overflowing scourge"[34] to awaken the wicked from their "tables . . . full of vomit and filthiness"[35] because they have "erred through wine, and through strong drink are out of the way."[36] Instead of intoxicating themselves in the darkness of their own paths, Jerusalem and those seeking safety there will drink the cup of the Lord's fury and suffer desolation, destruction, famine, and the sword.[37] These destructive forces are offered in mercy by a tender parent designed to awaken all who will soften their hearts and receive light and intelligence.[38]

These scourges will include war. Neighboring wicked nations of the world, jealous of the power of Jerusalem and offended by its brightness, will come to battle against it. For the "nations that live in the regions round about Jerusalem will gather up like a cloud, and cover all that land round about Jerusalem."[39] The armies that will rise against them will be so numerous, it will take seven months to bury the dead and seven years to burn the fuel brought to war against them.[40] This is the battle of Gog and Magog.[41] There, in the valley of Jehoshaphat, east of Jerusalem, "they will lay siege to the city" for forty-two months to obtain its wealth of gold, cattle, and goods.[42]

But even with these odds, the Lord will not leave His people comfortless. His hand will remain outstretched in mercy. He will continue to call to them, hopeful to awaken them and restore them. He will send two prophets, described as two "sons . . . as a wild bull in a net . . . full of the fury of the Lord" who will defend Israel from those gathered to fight Jerusalem.[43] These two "anointed ones that stand by the Lord of the whole earth" will mourn for Jerusalem and be given power to defend the city and her people.[44] They will comfort the people from the famine, war, and the destructions they endure and wage war against the attackers.[45]

Christ taught Joseph Smith these witnesses "are [the] two prophets to be raised up to the Jewish nation in the last days, at the time of the restoration, and to prophesy to the Jews after they are gathered and have built the city of Jerusalem in the land of their fathers."[46] They will withstand Jerusalem's enemies with the power of the word of the Lord. As Enoch, Melchizedek, Abraham, and Moses before them, they will command the elements and forces of the earth to defend and shelter Jerusalem, wielding fire out of their mouths, turning the waters to blood, and smiting the earth with plagues. They will thus defend Jerusalem for three and a half years as they prophesy and testify of Christ and His pending return.[47]

Finally, after they have "finished their testimony," the "beast that ascendeth out of the bottomless pit"—Satan himself—will "overcome them, and kill them." The prophets' bodies will lie in the streets of Jerusalem for three and a half days while the wicked and defiant nations of the earth rejoice and refuse to bury them.[48] However, on the third day, in fulfillment of ancient prophecies of victory and release, the Lord himself will redeem His people.

To the horror of their enemies, these two martyred prophets—though broken and lifeless—like Christ will rise, and stand triumphant in resurrection's splendor as the Spirit of life from God enters into them and shakes the earth. The enemies of Zion, the wicked who had been celebrating their sinful spoils, will be struck with dread.[49]

In the stillness of this moment of brilliant power, a "great voice from heaven" will declare in chilling majesty, "Come up hither." These two sons will "ascend up to heaven in a cloud" while their enemies tremble below.[50] The surviving Israelites who sheltered in fear next to the wailing wall, after the death of the prophets will look to the Heavens, as Christ descends in power, clothed in a robe of red.[51] Christ will "set his foot upon this mount, and it shall cleave in twain, and the earth shall tremble, and reel to and fro, and the heavens also shall shake."[52]

The whole earth will quake at the very touch of the Messiah's foot on the Mount of Olives and divide Jerusalem from east to west. His presence will split the mountain in two, and create a "very great valley" as "half of the mountain . . . removes [to] the north, and half [to] the south."[53] Just like Abram's dividing the animals asunder to make a path for him to be restored as Abraham, or Moses dividing the Red Sea divided to liberate Israel from Egypt, Christ's splitting of the earth will create a path of restoration and awakening for Israel. The divide will be a valley of release for the fearful yet still unbelieving Jews. It will break open the last standing gate in the Solomon's ancient temple wall called the "Golden Gate," "Gate of Mercy," or "Gate of Repentance." This gate (with visible squares and circles intersecting to form its doors), is the very one Christ rode through on Palm Sunday before suffering His Atonement and being crucified by the Jewish nation, the same gate that years later was walled up by invading Ottoman Turks, fearful of the Messiah and the Jewish tradition of His triumphant return through the gates.[54] In fulfillment of those prophecies, Christ as that victorious Messiah will divide the ancient gate in two, or like Abraham dividing the covenant animals in two, or Moses dividing the Red Sea to free Israel.

In the wake of this disaster, the wicked will "see their folly" and the "nations of the earth shall mourn" the appearance of Christ, as He radiates triumphant in the air.[56] The Jews will run toward their Savior through the "Mercy Gate" split open by Christ on the East Wall of Jerusalem. The Israelite remnant that had been fearing their final

Image 20 *Gate of Mercy—East Wall of the Jerusalem Temple Mount*[56]

destruction will give "glory to the God of heaven."[57] In that moment when the Jews will feel redeemed and restored, finally visited by the long-awaited Messiah, the prophesied Deliverer, Redeemer, Messiah, and Lord. But then in pained confusion, they will look upon their Messiah's hands and ask, "What are these wounds in thine hands and in thy feet?"[58]

He will declare to them "These wounds are the wounds with which I was wounded in the house of my friends. I am He who was lifted up. I am Jesus that was crucified. I am the Son of God."[59] They will awaken to a gaping divide between their own paths versus what Christ had been offering them. Painfully aware of the terrible gap, pierced by the truth like the animals torn asunder by Abram as he was restored to Abraham, they will weep and their hearts will break.[60] At long last awakened by Christ's everlasting love and grace they will finally accept Him and join their hearts with the Saints until "Satan shall be bound" having "no place in the hearts of the children of men."[61]

And we shall sing! Together, using the creative power of our words, we will sing a new song that declares with joy "The Lord hath brought down Zion *from above*" and "the Lord hath brought up Zion *from beneath*."[62] Those righteous pieces of the earth that listened to ministering angels and prophets to purify their hearts will be *lifted up* to the same level as Enoch's heavenly city so they can "see eye to eye"[63] as Christ reigns in the midst of His people. In this elevated state, the earth will be "filled with the knowledge of the Lord."[64]

Christ's promises to his disciples from the Mount of Olives, and those to Joseph Smith, will be fulfilled. Together, we will build a New Jerusalem in America and restore the Ancient Jerusalem.[65] From the new temple in Jerusalem, water will issue and heal the waters of the Dead Sea.[66] Christ will wipe away all tears, and all enmity between men, beasts, and of the flesh shall cease, all walls having been removed in the presence of Christ's love, until the lions and lambs live in harmony and peace.[67]

Christ's will reign in each of His *two* Jerusalems.[68] Just as He unifies our hearts and minds, He will serve as the governmental head as King of kings and the religious heart as Lord of lords. Those who live there will be like Enoch of old, their individuality fortified in the unity of "one heart and one mind."[69] The remaining who refuse to live higher laws of love will then say to themselves, "Let us not go up to battle against Zion, for the inhabitants of Zion are terrible; wherefore we cannot stand."[70]

In that day, the Lord will reveal all things, teaching those who have come to Mount Zion the principles and laws of the celestial kingdom awaiting them, and how to renew and replenish the earth and help it regain its paradisiacal glory in Christ.[71] He will be our lawmaker, our leader, our Lord and King, reigning with His Father from a blazing throne seated behind circling gates of fire.[72] Individually and together we will grow brighter and brighter until the perfect day enjoying the blossoming glory of the "great Millennium."[73]

During a thousand years of peace, the earth will enjoy *terrestrial* glory. Christ will teach us how to knit our hearts together to rise to a celestial state, perhaps in ways that transcend time, just as His Atonement did. I wonder, will He teach us to heal not only the present, but the past, just as His Atonement did? Will we become even more like Him, participating as Saviors on Mount Zion, in His godliness, as we preach of Christ and elevate all who have ever lived on the earth that are willing to receive of His mercy and light?[74] I believe the answers to these questions are more beautiful and mind opening than our hearts can yet imagine. But even this glory, as we learn to rise to a celestial state, is not the end.

A NEW HEAVEN AND A NEW EARTH

As we knit our hearts and minds together in creative oneness, no heart will empower Satan or his darkness, for almost a thousand years. But as we begin to lift the earth to its final celestial state, Satan will rage against losing his power. He will eventually be freed by corrupt hearts and regain some power for a "for a little season" to "gather together his armies" for a final purging battle, before the "end of the earth," when it shall finally rest, released from all remaining darkness and sin, forever.[75]

We know little about this epic battle except that in its wake, all darkness will be expelled, and we will inherit a *new* Heaven and a *new* earth.[76] Quickened by its creator, the earth's mountains will be made low, her valleys exalted and her rough places made smooth until the earth will be transformed into a perfect sphere, as if the mountains that pointed us to Heaven will have served their purpose, lifted to the heavenly plane they reached for above.[77]

Elevated to the celestial realm, earth will become like a burning sea of glass—a sapphire-like crystal full of fire and light, where past and present and future will be manifest for the righteous—a grand Urim and Thummim.[78] The celestially sanctified saints "will look into the earth" like looking into a mirror to "know things past, present, and to come."[79] It will burn "like the sun" finally prepared with the saints "to be brought back into the presence of the Father and the Son," bright "like the stars of the firmament, full of light and glory . . . a body of light."[80] The earth and her spirit will be sanctified, lifted to an immortal and eternal state, crowned with her children as precious jewels of light: all the matriarchs and patriarchs, Adam and Eve, Enoch and Aadanah, Abraham and Sarah, Christ and His bride—and countless more—finally at rest.[81]

PURE HEARTS THAT DANCE AND SING

Brigham Young taught that through Christ and the spirit of truth we can obtain "hearts clear as the noonday sun" that "dance, and glorify God."[82] This comes as our hearts feel and see the needs of others until they "expand as wide as eternity" like Enoch's did as he built Zion.[83] As we soften then purify our hearts and build Zion within, we can begin to hear Christ singing to us, instructing us on how to gather and build Zion without. His song of redeeming love shows us how to make manifest our premortal gifts, as if pulling down celestial lightning from above and "brining all things to our remembrance."[84]

Feeling Christ's call in our hearts is the first step to a personal restorative awakening in Christ. As we follow those feelings, we will begin to hear His redemptive song calling to us, inviting us to grab His hand to rise up from beneath the waves of fear, pain, and darkness of this life, and feel the warmth of the blossoming light of His charity.

If I were standing in front of you as you read this, I would be smiling. One of those big, full-faced smiles that says to your heart more powerfully than spoken words can, "Look up! You've got this. Stay on the path. Look unto Him. Cling to the word of God and stay on the path that leads you to Christ. You are on your way to Zion!"

Christ knows our pain and darkness. He also knows the joy and light that await us. He is calling to each of us. As we progress, we are promised we will radiate brighter and brighter, until we are filled with light as Saviors on Mount Zion and point others to Him. We all need you to remember who we are! Listen to that voice that is calling you. Trust in God. Let Him heal your pain. Shine. Be YOU.

We create our reality around us with the thoughts and intents of our hearts—for they are the creative seats of our souls. If we want to bring peace and prepare the world for Christ's Second Coming, we must soften, purify, and join our hearts in the common purpose of Zion: to grow the gardens; erect the buildings; create the art, music, theater, and songs necessary to make Heaven on earth, here and now, so that when Christ returns triumphant with Enoch through the sky, we will rise up with our shining cities in glory, joy, and song, as Zion below in unity with celestial Zion above.

We are all of us, as individuals and as communities, meant to grow brighter and brighter until the perfect day and participate in God's glory. The Lord tells us, "If your eye be single to my glory, your whole bodies shall be filled with light."[85] As we follow higher laws, we increase in purity, brightness, and elevation. We build Zion in our own hearts, then our relationships, then our communities, until Christ's love and light will fill the earth.

The amazing truth burning in the individually tailored paths of holy patriarchs and matriarchs is this: **Everything we need is around us—already created spiritually.** Our wings of light, our joy, our peace—the miracles and purpose we seek—already exist spiritually. They have been laid out before us like a ribbon of light—a ribbon we created with our Heavenly Parents before coming to earth—to guide us home. It is up to us to exercise our agency to follow our ribbons.

This is true for us and for *everyone* around us. Each of us is invited to come unto Christ, be redeemed from the Fall and partake of His heavenly gift—and create like Him.[86] We are on a mission to find and follow the ribbons of light that God has created for us spiritually and manifest them physically, until our hearts are woven together across the earth as a tapestry of burning colors, arrayed like Zion's covenant rainbow as we *radiate and rise* back home, and fill the universe with a tapestry of light.[87]

CHAPTER 8 ENDNOTES

1 Romans 13:8–12.
2 Alma 18:29.
3 Alma 18:24–32.
4 Alma 19:13.
5 Isaiah 49:22–24; *See also* 1 Ne 21:23; 2 Ne 10:9; 2 Ne 6:7.
6 C. S. Lewis, "The Weight of Glory."
7 1 Corinthians 13:12.
8 Acts 9:18; 2 Cor. 3:14–18; D&C 76:94.
9 D&C 86:9–10.
10 Matt 24:36.
11 D&C 6:36.
12 D&C 45:10.
13 D&C 45:15–17.
14 D&C 45:24.
15 D&C 45:26.
16 D&C 45:28–29.
17 D&C 45:31.
18 D&C 45:33.
19 D&C 45:27.
20 Caroline Delbert, "Earth Keeps Pulsating Every 26 Seconds. No One Knows Why. Maybe you can solve this strange seismic mystery." *Popular Mechanics*, October 30, 2020; *see also* Anna Funk, "The Earth Is Pulsating Every 26 Seconds, and Seismologists Don't Agree Why," *Discover*, October 27, 2020.
21 Dallin H. Oaks, "Preparation for the Second Coming," April 2004 general conference. Note that the "World Almanac and Book of Facts, 2004 shows twice as many Earthquakes in the decades of the 1980s and 1990s as in the two preceding decades (pp. 189–90). It also shows further sharp increases in the first several years of this century. The list of notable floods and tidal waves and the list of hurricanes, typhoons, and blizzards worldwide show similar increases in recent years (pp. 188–89)."
22 D&C 45:36–37.
23 Matthew 21:19–21.
24 Isaiah 29:13; 2 Nephi 27:25.
25 D&C 45:38–39.
26 D&C 45:68–69.
27 Jeremiah 30:18.
28 Jeremiah 23:8.
29 Jeremiah 31:6–12.
30 D&C 45:71; 2 Nephi 8:11.
31 Orson Pratt, "Resurrection of the Saints, Etc.," in *Journal of Discourses*

18:57, 64a–65a (citing Jeremiah 30:18).
32 D&C 45:47.
33 *Teachings of the Prophet Joseph Smith*, pg. 304–305, 340–341 (citing Matthew 24:36; D&C 51:20; D&C 87:8).
34 Jeremiah 30:18.
35 Isaiah 28:8.
36 Isaiah 28:7.
37 2 Nephi 8:17–19.
38 *Teachings of the Prophet Joseph Smith*, pg. 304–305.
39 Orson Pratt, "Resurrection of the Saints, Etc.," in *Journal of Discourses* 18:57, 64b (citing Ezekiel 38:8–13).
40 Ezekiel 39:9.
41 Ezek. 38:8–13; Revelation 11:3.
42 JD 18:57, Orson Pratt, Resurrection of the Saints, Etc., 64b (citing Joel 3:1–21 Zech. 14:1–2).
43 Isaiah 51:20; 2 Nephi 8:20.
44 Zechariah 4:11–14; Revelation 11:3.
45 Isaiah 51:19.
46 D&C 77:15.
47 Revelation 11:3; 5–7.
48 Revelation 11:7–11.
49 Revelation 11:13.
50 Revelation 11:12
51 Doctrine and Covenants 133:46–48.
52 D&C 45:48.
53 D&C 45:48; Zechariah 14:3–4.
54 Eliyahu Wager, *Illustrated guide to Jerusalem* (Jerusalem: The Jerusalem Publishing House: 1998), p. 32.
55 See https://en.wikipedia.org/wiki/Golden_Gate_(Jerusalem) for a concise review of the history and symbolism.
56 D&C 45:49.
57 Revelation 11:13.
58 D&C 45:51; Zechariah 13:6; Orson Pratt, "Zion," in *Journal of Discourses* 14:343, 350b.
59 D&C 45:52.
60 Genesis 15:5–10.
61 D&C 45:55; 2 Nephi 8:24.
62 D&C 89:99–102.
63 D&C 84:98.
64 D&C 84:102.
65 D&C 45:66.
66 Ezekiel 47:1–8.
67 D&C 101:26–31; 63:51; Isaiah 2:4; 11:6–9; Isaiah 2:4; Revelation 21:4.

68 Russell M. Nelson "The Future of the Church: Preparing the World for the Savior's Second Coming," April 2020 general conference; see also Orson Pratt, "Zion," in *Journal of Discourses* 14:343, 355b.

69 D&C 45:65.

70 D&C 45:70.

71 D&C 101:32–34; Article of Faith 1:10.

72 Joseph Smith, Journal, January 21, 1836.

73 D&C 50:24; D&C 43:30.

74 D&C 138:57.

75 D&C 29:22; D&C 43:31; D&C 88:11.

76 Ether 13:9; Isaiah 65:17; D&C 29:23.

77 Isaiah 40:4.

78 Exodus 24:10; 1 Corinthians 13:12; Revelation 4:6; 15:2; 21:18–21.

79 Brigham Young, "Remarks," *Deseret News*, Jul. 3, 1861, 137.

80 Brigham Young, "Sermon," *Deseret News*, Jun. 15, 1859, 114; cf D&C 130:9.

81 D&C 77:1; 130:7.

82 Brigham Young, in "Duties and Privileges, Etc.," *Journal of Discourses*, 1:112, 120b.

83 Moses 7:41.

84 John 14:6.

85 D&C 88:67.

86 Ether 12:6–9.

87 John 16:15.

SEALS OF ZION

Seal of Christ

Seal of Melchizedek

Seal of Enoch

ABOUT THE AUTHOR

Sam Castor is a compassionate, aggressive bridge builder and mountain mover, who has spent decades in the government and technology sectors as a policy executive and attorney, negotiating billions of dollars of intellectual and infrastructure transactions and changing legislative and regulatory landscapes. He has resolved hundreds of millions of dollars of litigation and business conflicts and views conflict as an opportunity to collaborate and find solutions. His professional path includes time in all branches of federal government assisting with technology policy, including time under President Obama and President Bush. As an author and speaker (including in his TED Talk), he emphasizes how critical the elements of compassion, candor, and collaboration are to our future.

Sam met his wife when they were both serving as Especially for Youth counselors in California. They have five heavenly and gifted children. Since leaving Switch in 2022, Sam now focuses on writing, music, and building communities.

Samuel has been a seminary teacher, institute teacher, and presented at countless conferences and firesides. He is an enthusiastic supporter of The Church of Jesus Christ of Latter-day Saints and believes the Kingdom of God is rich, diverse, and full of valuable disagreement that can be harnessed into creative collaboration, connection, and joy in Christ. Samuel loves testifying of how to find a personal restoration and awakening in Christ, the Lord of Lords and King of Kings—the Redeemer of Zion.